# Praise for *Regenerative Leaders|*

"This is the must read book of 2019. I couldn't put it down. The clarity, inspiration, synergy and wisdom of this book is breath-taking"

DR **LYNNE SEDGMORE** CBE,
FORMER CHIEF EXECUTIVE OF 157 GROUP, CENTRE FOR EXCELLENCE IN LEADERSHIP

"The world is changing fast and organizations are not keeping up with the pace of transformation. This book invites leaders to catalyze the necessary regeneration to not just catch up, but to lead the world into the 21$^{st}$ century."

**CHRISTIANA FIGUERES**, EXECUTIVE SECRETARY UNFCCC 2010-2016

"Giles and Laura bring their vast experience and deep wisdom to create an evolutionary blueprint for a sustainable future for business, people and the planet"

**RICHARD BARRETT**, PRESIDENT OF THE BARRETT ACADEMY FOR THE ADVANCEMENT OF HUMAN VALUES

"This book is full of wisdom and determination! A book that will inspire leaders to pave the way towards practices in harmony with our inner nature and the ecosystems we depend on. Just what we need to succeed in the 21st Century."

**TIM FLANNERY**, PALEONTOLOGIST, BEST-SELLING AUTHOR AND CONSERVATIONIST

"Storm and Hutchins confront the challenge of redesigning the world to deliver a sustainable future with vision, energy, and creativity."

**DAN ESTY**, ENVIRONMENTAL LAWYER & POLICYMAKER, AUTHOR OF BEST-SELLING GREEN TO GOLD

"A must read for anyone who wants to shape a regenerative organization."

**JEAN-CLAUDE PIERRE**, CEO SCOTT BADER

"Seeking inspiration in the natural world, the principles in *Regenerative Leadership* provide a framework for a more inspired path forward in business and life."

**RYAN GELLERT**, CEO EMEA PATAGONIA

"Hutchins' and Storm's *Regenerative Leadership* shines a bright light on one of the most critical, and least understood capacities required of anyone and any institution seeking to work regeneratively – understanding and living into the three-fold dynamics of what the book calls the DNA of regenerative leadership."

**PAMELA MANG**, CO-FOUNDER OF REGENESIS AND CO-AUTHOR OF *REGENERATIVE DEVELOPMENT AND DESIGN*.

"Hutchins and Storm demonstrate that they are clearly at the forefront of a new leadership paradigm that maps an emerging model for sustainable organization in any institution that wishes to thrive."

**KINGSLEY L. DENNIS**, AUTHOR OF *THE SACRED REVIVAL - MAGIC, MIND & MEANING IN A TECHNOLOGICAL AGE*

"This book succinctly brings together the importance business leaders have in redefining and supporting their organizations and communities to do more good."

**NIGEL STANSFIELD**, PRESIDENT OF INTERFACE EAAA

"Hope is what Giles and Laura offer, exploring the wisdom, rules, and models for thinking, being, and doing that the natural world offers us. Business leaders will enjoy this mind-expanding journey."

**ANDREW WINSTON**,
SUSTAINABILTY STRATEGIST, AUTHOR OF THE BIG PIVOT AND CO-AUTHOR OF GREEN TO GOLD

Laura Storm and Giles Hutchins delineate how an economic and social transformation is brewing, with a new regenerative paradigm at its heart. If this is our future, we could avert the worst of the ecological crisis, and live happier more connected lives as well."

**TRISTRAM STUART**, FOUNDER FEEDBACK.ORG & TOAST ALE

Storm and Hutchins share their deep passion and expertise to show you how to ignite shared purpose and break down the silos of information and trust that are stopping you and your people from making their greatest impact on the world. Future generations will thank you!"

DR. **TAMSIN WOOLLEY-BARKER**,
PRINCIPAL AND FOUNDER, TEEM INNOVATION GROUP AND AUTHOR OF TEEMING

ISBN: 978-1-78324-119-4

Cover & Illustration Design: TrueStory

Cover images: Unsplash

Published by Wordzworth
*www.wordzworth.com*

More info:
*www.regenerativeleadership.co*

*We have chosen print-on-demand for this book as that is the most regenerative
way of getting physical books out into the world. Traditional offset printing
usually requires large orders and any books that go unsold are destroyed.
This results in wasted paper, wasted energy, added greenhouse emissions,
pulping, and landfill overflows. Print-on-demand reduces supply chain
waste, greenhouse emissions and conserves valuable natural resources.*

**All paper for the publication of this book is sourced
from SFI and/or FSC certified mills**

# REGENERATIVE LEADERSHIP

The DNA of life-affirming
21st century organizations

**GILES HUTCHINS
& LAURA STORM**

# This is our Reason for Writing this Book

As we complete this book, Laura has a baby underway and between us we have 3 young daughters under the age of 7 – the question constantly ringing in our ears is: What world are we passing on to them? How could we do all in our power to help inspire new ways that allow them to be whole human beings on a planet where ecosystems thrive again?

We have to steer this ship in a new direction as the way it's heading is catastrophic. That's the reason for writing this book: Helping leaders navigate out of our current predicament by offering a new regenerative leadership approach where organizations flourish, ecosystems thrive and people come alive.

**This book is dedicated to our children and our children's children. Not just Lilly-Belle, Hazel, Roxie and the new baby on its way; all children of this magnificent planet of ours, and all life on Earth.**

# Table of Contents

# Introduction:
## Welcome to the Journey of a Lifetime

As we write this Introduction millions of school kids and students are protesting, striking from school every Friday, and demanding adults take action to address climate change. The School Strike for Climate movement was started by a 16-year old Swedish girl, Greta Thunberg, so concerned by the state of the planet she had to do something. So instead of going to school after the summer holiday in 2018, she sat down in front of the Parliament buildings in Stockholm. As the days went by more and more students joined her and in January 2019 she was invited to address the world leaders at the annual World Economic Forum meeting in Davos, Switzerland. Here she said in a speech addressing world leaders:

*"We are now at a time in history where everyone with any insight of the climate crisis that threatens our civilization and the entire biosphere must speak out in clear language, no matter how uncomfortable and unprofitable that may be. We must change almost everything in our current societies. The bigger your carbon footprint is, the bigger your moral duty. The bigger your platform the bigger your responsibility. Adults keep saying we owe it to the young people to give them hope. But I don't want your hope, I don't want you to be hopeful. I want you to panic, I want you to feel the fear I feel every day. And then I want you to act, I want you to act as if you would in a crisis. I want you to act as if the house was on fire, because it is."*

On March 15, 2019 the climate strikes happened in over 2000 cities across 123 countries gathering millions of people. And Greta has now been nominated for the Nobel Peace Prize.

There is no doubt. We are living in a time marked by great upheaval and change, where the breakdown of global systems has become impossible to ignore. Leaders – both political and business – are being forced to cope with rising challenges: resource scarcity; high levels of stress in the work place; unpredictable, frequent and disruptive innovations; rampant social inequality, constant competition for top talent; increasing volatility and changing stakeholder expectations; rapid digitization and globalization; mass migrations and refugee populations; fragile supply chains; mounting social tensions; political extremism; endemic violence; Brexit; Trump; and rising sovereign and consumer debt levels the world over.

You get the picture.

On top of all this, biodiversity is declining globally at rates unprecedented in human history and the climate of our planet is changing faster than expected, putting additional critical pressure on all our systems.

> "The health of ecosystems on which we and all other species depend is deteriorating more rapidly than ever. We are eroding the very foundations of our economies, livelihoods, food security, health and quality of life worldwide."
>
> Sir Robert Watson, IPBES Chair

We have created production systems that are based on a linear, take-make-waste approach focused on immediacy and dehumanization. We have created financial systems based on short-term profit maximization that ignore life and debase human integrity. Our organizational systems are dominated by hyper-competition, power-and-control hierarchies, and rising stress. In our current environment, the few benefit at the expense of the many.

The old systems and structures of a post-industrial hyper-consumerist culture are slowly breaking down. The old ways cannot go on, and through this break-down, we are witnessing pioneers all over the world birthing the conditions for a new way. These pioneers believe there is a better way – to live and do business. They are reconfiguring systems and structures and instilling new business practices that actually contribute to life on Earth rather than destroying it.

It may be easier to continue doing what you've always done, and it may seem sensible amid all this uncertainty and volatility to stick with what you are comfortable with. But in the long run it eats you up inside, weakens you and undermines your organization's vitality and its stakeholder ecosystem.

The real question you have to ask yourself is: How can you help a new way to break through amid these challenging times? How can *you* act as if we indeed are in a time of crisis and help design new thriving ways?

How could you become what we call a **Regenerative Leader,** who contributes to a future where organizations flourish, ecosystems thrive and people come alive?

> "We are now entering an Age of Unreason, when the future in so many areas, is there to be shaped, by us and for us – a time when the only prediction that will hold true is that no prediction will hold true; a time therefore, for bold imaginings in private life as well as public, for thinking the unlikely and doing the unreasonable."
>
> Charles Handy, organizational culture specialist

Are you up for thinking the unlikely and embarking upon the unreasonable? Are you up for acting as an adult and realizing our collective house is on fire?

## About This Book

We – the authors, Giles Hutchins and Laura Storm – have worked in the fields of sustainability, leadership, climate policy, and executive coaching and consultancy for more than 40 years combined. We have been leaders in global organizations and have spent years gathering insights and best-practices from businesses across multiple fields and sectors.

Together we have created a DNA model of a new regenerative way of living and leading, where purpose, people, planet, and profit can thrive collectively.

We have collected pieces of the puzzle from multiple disciplines – from biology, psychology, sociology, economy, anthropology, neurology as well as methodologies such as permaculture, circular economics, biophilia, bio-mimicry, cradle to cradle, and much more.

We apply a variety of ideas and concepts drawn from theories and meth odologies relevant to systemic transformation, some of which have been available for a while now, some which are more recent arrivals, some cutting-edge. While it is important to root these concepts in research, frame-works and theory, this book is first-and-foremost written to **inspire a new leadership paradigm:** New leadership practices, new business models, new ways of collaborating and creating value. It is aimed to stimulate, guide, and support the wave of *Regenerator* pioneers who are rising-up for action in myriad ways during this metamorphic moment we're living through.

This book is born from our passion to help pave a new regenerative way with you.

In the pages ahead we share with you a comprehensive approach to developing a new kind of regenerative leadership that allows you to create life-affirming futures wherever you are and whatever you lead: a team, a start-up, a mature business, an NGO, a multinational corporation, a city region, or even a country.

We share tried and tested tools, real-world business examples, personal practices, and a peppering of **insights from nature**, and **business examples**, also sign-posts to **Dive Deeper** if you wish to explore things in greater depth.

Look for these symbols:

Insights from Nature

Business Insights

Dive Deeper

## Who is This Book for?

*Regenerative Leadership* is intended for anyone who is interested in exploring and undertaking transformational change within our systems, organizations, and communities

We invite board members, executives, line managers, intrapreneurs, change agents, practitioners, cultural creatives, politicians, media executives, designers, and entrepreneurs to rise up to what we are being called to create collectively: A new way where ecosystems thrive and people come alive. A new way where our youngsters do not have to skip school and take to the streets to fight for a living planet.

This book is designed to help provoke thought, action, and interaction in you the reader; therefore, we have included questions, insights, reflective quotes, and examples at every turn. Our hope is that you blend reading through this book with journaling, reflection time, walks in nature, conversations with colleagues, and your own pioneering plans to make our regenerative future a reality, not just for tomorrow but also for today.

We need curious, dedicated, passionate people like you and we're thrilled to have you reading this book.

Welcome to the *Regenerator* journey of a life-time.

# Breakdowns & Breakthroughs

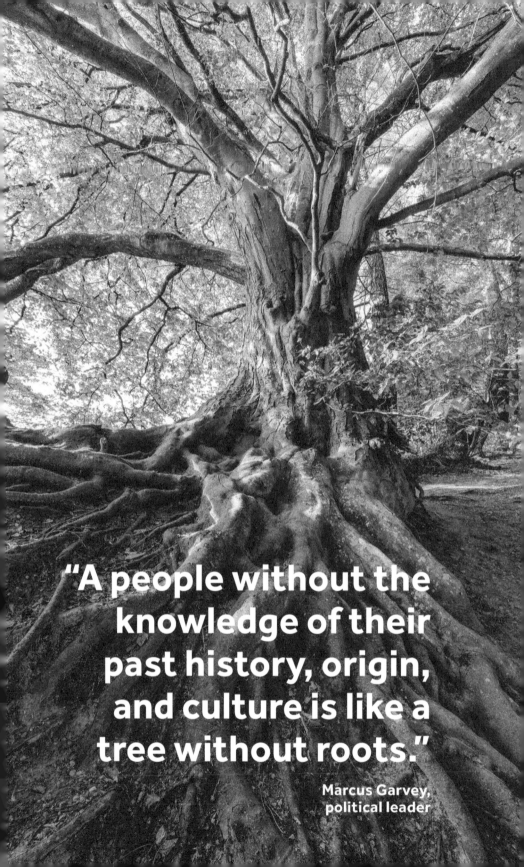

"A people without the knowledge of their past history, origin, and culture is like a tree without roots."

Marcus Garvey,
political leader

# Going Back in Time to Find the Root of Our Current Crisis

When looking around the world today, as conscious human beings we might see the erosion of ecosystems that sustain all life, the trash and plastic islands in our oceans, the declining insect populations, the shrinking of the world's forests, climate change, soil degradation and polluted rivers. Then we might also see the volatile political climate, the worldwide social inequality, the increasing levels of stress, depression and burnout, even among our young. Both our outer and inner landscapes are under great strain.

How do we change this situation? Where to start? What to prioritize first?

Before diving deeper into the state of the world, we – the authors – would like to take you on a journey back in time, in order to gain an understanding of human history culminating in today's world. We want to explore what has shaped today's society – our relationships, culture, organizations and leadership – and the underlying issues creating the inner and outer strain we witness today.

So buckle up, and get ready to go on a fascinating journey back in time.

## The Connection Between Genders and our Connection with Nature

Research shows that humans started to venture out of sub-Saharan Africa around 100,000 years ago and began to colonize various habitable places around the globe (Overy, 2006). In central Asia and Europe anthropologists have discovered archaeological evidence, dating back to around 10,000 years ago (8000 BC), that indicate *Homo sapiens* lived rather peacefully in egalitarian communities, with a close sense of community where males and females were valued equally. Research also shows little evidence of widespread aggression, social division or hierarchy, but instead plenty of time for art, dance, and communal life (Baring & Cashford, 1993).

During this epoch, humans lived in close proximity with wild, undomesticated nature and appreciated a strong sense of connection with the living Earth. Scientists studying ancient cultures and their religions have found a common thread across ancient cultures throughout the world where Sky God and Earth Goddess were worshipped. This was a masculine-feminine communion often described as a sacred marriage. A deep communion with nature and with the masculine-feminine qualities found within life was foundational to these ancient cultures (Britannica, 1998). The cultural norm in these cultures was to uphold a deep sense of reverence for all life; everything was understood to be part of a greater whole. Humans understood their purpose on Earth as not only living to survive but also being custodians of the rhythms innate within nature – custodians of the Earth.

> "For 99% of the time we've been on Earth, we were hunter and gatherers, our lives dependent on knowing the fine, small details of our world. Deep inside, we still have a longing to be reconnected with the nature that shaped our imagination, our language, our song and dance, our sense of the divine."
>
> Janine Benyus, biologist

**Dive Deeper**: Clearly it is naïve to assume that everything was a bed-of-roses during the dawn of the modern human. There certainly existed harshness and strife, yet there is detailed research that explores the equalitarian and convivial nature of our ancestors. For instance, you can look up Marija Gimbutas's work in the Journal of Indo-European Studies entitled *The Beginning of the Bronze Age in Europe and the Indo-Europeans: 3,000–2,500 BC*, and other studies are referred to in the work of Anne Baring and Jules Cashford's *The Myth of the Goddess*, Raine Eisler's *The Blade and the Chalice*, Rupert Sheldrake's *The Rebirth of Nature*, and Giles Hutchins's *The Illusion of Separation*.

## A Journey of Separation

Then a radical shift in climate and shift in society occurred from around 10,000 years ago onwards. By example, findings from a Middle Stone Age site in North Yorkshire, show that our ancestors survived a century-long drop in temperature of between 10 and 4 degrees Celsius (Nature Ecology & Evolution, 2018). This begins what anthropologist Steve Taylor refers to as the *Ego Explosion* (Taylor, 2005). Our sense of self-identity shifted from seeing ourselves as a part of nature to seeing ourselves as separate from nature. This heightening ego-awareness helped us gain a stronger sense of self and increased our self-agency and self-empowerment. It helped us survive heavy storms and harsh temperatures. And with this self-development we cultivated important aspects of our psychological, sociological and evolutionary development. This triggered the Agricultural Revolution bringing the domestication of livestock and widespread farming practices. Hunter gatherers now settled into permanent communities, growing crops, building homes and keeping animals for food and clothing.

These shifts are an important part of our adaptation and evolution to a rapid change in climate. Yet, this shift also came with a marked cultural shift: rising patriarchy, increasing stratification and division in society, the prioritization of Sky God over Earth Goddess, widespread militarization, the mechanization of weapons and tools for exploitation and domination of other humans and nature, the widespread use of currency, the advent of the written word, the right to own land, and many more cultural innovations.

This period marks a departure from being at one with nature. A *Journey of Separation* begins throughout the West, and goes through levels of incremental change in the centuries that follow: Hellenistic Greece, the Roman Empire, Medieval Europe and the Renaissance.

Throughout these cultural changes, a deep respect and connection with nature remains. Nature's wild wisdom is intimately interwoven with everyday human life right up until about 500 years ago.

## The Separation of Human from Nature; Man from Women

Around 500 years ago (the 15ᵗʰ and 16ᵗʰ century) the climate changed again quite dramatically during what has been referred to as the *Little Ice Age*. Whilst climatologists debate the exact dates of the Little Ice Age and local conditions vary significantly, it seems that Europe experienced 80 years (approximately from 1460 – 1540) of heavy storms, harsh long winters, and cooler summers. This climate change significantly impacted living conditions and the ability to grow food, as rivers and canals (key transportation networks at that time) froze over and crops failed. Famines swept across large parts of the continent leaving people starving, sick, and malnourished – epidemics spread like wildfire (Appleby, 1980). This caused social tensions people started to become scared, frustrated, and increasingly wary of the forces of nature.

During The Middle Ages there was a pervasive dogma of Christianity portraying God as separate from nature; above and beyond, *His Creation* – and The Church, made good use of the growing fears and mounting social tensions. Those who are afraid are easier to influence and control. In searching for a culprit for the tension and starvation, the Church began to frame the forces of nature as the workings of the Devil. And many women were seen as more in tune with the wisdom of nature – its healing properties, plant remedies, herbal medicines, cycles, and insights – those who practiced this connection to nature were framed as witches in close liaison with the Devil.

In 1485, Pope Innocent VIII ordered an official 'witch hunt', which lasted nearly 300 years. This was perceived as the only method to cleanse society of evil – to exterminate women who worshipped the ways of nature. Mass hysteria ensued, coinciding with the Church Reformation and the Thirty Year's War. Europe experienced a time of great upheaval, out of which emerged a heightened sense of separation from nature. The Middle Ages, with its embedded cultural norms, gave way to a new worldview: God and Man were viewed as divorced from Nature and Woman.

Protestantism, Rationalism, and Empiricism were all on the rise and the Scientific Revolution was born. Great minds – Francis Bacon, Galileo Galilei, Johannes Kepler, Thomas Hobbes, René Descartes, and many others – led the scientific and philosophic developments of the age, which helped solidify new societal views about man's relationship with nature.

Francis Bacon (1561-1626), a prominent scientist, renowned philosopher, and legal prosecutor who served as Attorney General and ultimately Lord Chancellor of England, is often referred to as the 'Father of the Scientific Method'. Francis Bacon was not only instrumental in the Scientific Revolution, but he also played a huge part in the witch trials, as a legal prosecutor. He believed that Nature *"exhibits herself more clearly under the trials and vexations of [mechanical devices] than when left to herself."* (Merchant, 1980). As historian Clifford Conner writes in A People's History of Science: *"The patriarchal imagery in Bacon's writings reflected the social position of women at the beginning of the seventeenth century. Bacon invariably portrayed Nature as a female who was hiding her secrets. He wrote of the secrets "locked in nature's bosom" or "laid up in the womb of nature", and said "she would have to be forcibly penetrated in order to make her give them up."* (Conner, 2005).

In Bacon's book *The Masculine Birth of Time* he speaks of how nature must be made the slave of man (Bacon, 1603). Whilst we ought not single out Bacon, as he was one person in a collective shift supported by many, his views do provide a rich example of the heightening disconnection of human from nature and man from women that formed throughout the Scientific Revolution. For instance, in his work *Novum Organum*, he speaks of exploiting and interrogating nature through reductive experiments, by *"the hand of man she is forced out of her natural state, and squeezed and moulded"*, so mankind is able *"to penetrate further"* beyond *"the outer courts of nature"* and *"find a way at length into her inner chambers"*. He continues: *"Nature being known, it may be master'd, managed and used in the services of human life"* as *"the object of knowledge is the control of nature. Nature in itself has no purpose"* (Bacon, 1620).

Today, we may find his words disturbing, but this thinking was part of a widespread sea-change in our collective worldview across the West. This thinking shaped the societies we have today, along with the cultural assumptions that nature is a resource to be exploited solely for human betterment.

From the Scientific Revolution onwards, nature was commodified into forestry, fishery, agriculture, and mining. Meanwhile, women (as they were said to embody and ritualize nature) were positioned as unruly and wild, therefore lacking in rational-analytic capability and in need of control and domination. During the witch trials starting in 1485 and lasting almost 3 centuries, millions of women were tortured and interrogated and hundreds of thousands were killed and burned in front of children, neighbors, and friends to set an example that being in tune with nature was no different from working with the Devil.

This widening separation and near complete severance of connection to our natural environment and our feminine essence caused us to turn our back on hundreds of thousands of years of deep integration with nature's ways and equality between the genders. Within a matter of decades, both women and nature came to be seen as wild and devilish, in need of control. This was the beginning of the prioritization of masculine traits over feminine traits.

Every human being exhibits both masculine and feminine traits, yet over recent centuries, masculine qualities have been perceived by society as superior to feminine. The table here lists some of the qualities identified as typically masculine or feminine.

| MASCULINE TRAITS | FEMININE TRAITS |
| --- | --- |
| focus on own needs | compassion toward others |
| competitive | collaborative |
| assertive | receptive |
| protective | nurturing |
| goal-oriented | relationship-oriented |
| rational thinking | intuitive feeling |
| independence | interdependence |
| mono-task | multi-task |
| bias for action | bias for flow |

Rational-analytic reductionism was the hallmark of the Scientific Revolution. The French philosopher and mathematician Rene Descartes, another one of the prime movers of the Scientific Revolution, felt compelled to reject the notion of nature as living, sentient, interconnected, and imbued with wisdom. Separating nature from mind (or spirit) was the necessary pre-condition for mechanistic reductionism – the drilling down into parts, ignoring interrelations or systemic sentience. In 1630 Descartes wrote to the Catholic theologian Marin Mersenne, *"God sets up mathematical laws in nature, as a king sets up laws in his kingdom"* thereby excluding any form of consciousness and sentience from nature (Berman, 1981). Nature became a mere outer-form of matter, perceived as nothing more than a collection of building blocks that collided and coalesced through deterministic push-pull forces.

The philosophers Thomas Hobbes and Isaac Newton also contributed to reductionism. Notably, Hobbes's basic assumption was that humanity and nature consist of atomized, competitive units embroiled in a *"war of all against all"* (Leviathan, 1651) a flawed assumption that is still with us today, one that influences Neo-Darwinism, where the whole process of evolution is seen as a process of selfish domination. Still to this day when we talk about how nature works, many automatically refer to the harsh struggle for survival in a dog-eat-dog world of ruthless competition.

*Survival of the fittest* no longer portrays Darwin's original intention of *fitting in to our niche*, instead it's come to signify the domination of others through power and control justifying war, imperialism, and selfish behavior because supposedly *it is in our nature*.

This is how many interpret the world around us. Even today's nature documentaries highlight the competitive aspects and down-play the collaborative dynamics at work. This skewed perspective influences how we behave and relate in business, in politics, and in society at large. Competition is one, but there are many dynamics at play in nature. Life thrives in myriad ways, largely through networking, partnerships, and collaboration. Ruthless dog-eat-dog competition is actually *not* the norm. However, in recent centuries, we have conditioned ourselves to see life in a certain light, one which undermines our human potential to connect and coexist.

The period of the Scientific Revolution made great strides in material progress and scientific insight that we benefit greatly from today, yet this dis-connection from nature – our natural habitat – and domination of the feminine creates an imbalance in us as a collective and as individuals. A deep, deep wound, so to speak, that manifests as a psychic trauma within our species. This collective trauma and imbalance is the underlying cause of increasing fear, anxiety, egotism, individualism, and consumerism. When we don't feel complete or whole on the inside, we start searching ever more 'out there' to fix a deep wound which is 'in here'.

As the models below illustrate, this collective Journey of Separation encompasses the separation between humanity and nature, and also between feminine and masculine. The first two stages of the journey (connection and rising separation) occur in ancient times, with heightened separation occurring around 500 years ago. This third stage is still with us today, with early signs of a fourth stage emerging – one of healing, reconnection and integration.

# THE JOURNEY OF SEPARATION

## HUMAN NATURE SEPARATION

| Up to 10,000 years ago | Up to 500 years ago | Today | The Age of Regeneration |

© copyright Hutchins & Storm

## FEMININE-MASCULINE SEPARATION

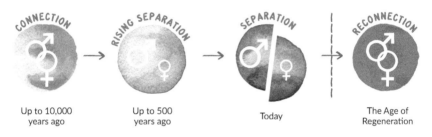

| Up to 10,000 years ago | Up to 500 years ago | Today | The Age of Regeneration |

© copyright Hutchins & Storm

 *Dive Deeper:* This relationship between rising patriarchy, the subjugation of women and feminine qualities and the dis-connection of humans from nature is explored through a wide body of research. There are many books covering this rich and deep area of interest. Some of the titles worth reading are: *Silent Spring* by Rachel Carson, *Eco-Feminism* by Maria Mies and Vandana Shiva, *The Death of Nature* by Carolyn Merchant, *The Myth of the Goddess* by Anne Baring and Jules Cashford, *The Blade and the Chalice* by Raine Eisler.

In order to heal this split, we must focus on reconnection and re-integration. Social ecologist Gregory Bateson foresaw how the separating of mind from matter – spirit from nature – creates all sorts of problems. For Bateson, this separation is an error of the most fundamental degree. This error, Bateson saw woven into Western habits of thought at deep and partly unconscious levels, undermining our capacity to flourish sustainably on Earth. He felt that it is what pits humanity against nature and provides for our prevalent worldview of survival through competition, in what he viewed as *"an ecology of bad ideas"* breeding parasitic humans, purely self-centered and destructive of their host environment. He noted that if you, *"see the world around you as mindless and therefore not entitled to moral or ethical consideration, the environment will be yours to exploit…If this is your estimate of your relation to nature and you have an advanced technology, your likelihood of survival will be that of a snowball in hell. You will die either of the toxic by-products of your own hate, or, simply, of over-population and over-grazing"* (Bateson, 2000).

Today's prevalent worldview separates mind from nature and therefore views it as an array of senseless resources to exploit with no ethical consideration except in terms of the value it has to us humans. With this mindset, our likelihood of surviving as a race is, as Bateson said, *"that of a snowball in hell."*


## The Separation of the Inner from the Outer

Central to the Scientific Revolution's reductionism is the focus on the parts rather than the whole. This method of breaking everything down into isolated bits to be analyzed in an objectified and isolated way has its benefits. It helps us reduce complexity and simplify, which makes the overwhelming reality of the world we live in easier to access. Reductive analysis has played an important part in our Western evolution, bringing great strides in many areas of our lives and enabling material advancements in technology, food production, transportation, and medicine. Yet, this reductive perspective leaves little room for understanding or tuning in to the wider inter-relational dynamics inherent to ourselves, our relationships, and all living systems.

In the centuries following the Scientific Revolution, life has come to be perceived as machine-like, a clockwork series of push-pull causalities comprised of independent objects operating in a mechanistic predictable way. These natural laws and universal principles, it was assumed, could only be fully understood in reductive analytic ways. After having analyzed the objectified parts and projected fixed rationale onto the complex dynamics of our existence, only then can we understand everything about human nature, life, and the universe.

Descartes conceived of the universe as a gigantic machine. He was keen on developing a comprehensive natural philosophy, a new vision of the natural world, all explainable through mathematical explanations. Clearly, the view that everything throughout the universe could be explained, measured, and defined had a powerful allure.

This analytic, hyper-competitive, threat-tinted lens through which we learned to view the world reduced our innate intuitive sense, our empathic connection, and sensorial embodied experience of life. It shut out key elements necessary for our wellbeing and key pathways necessary to our whole-body intelligence. It exacerbated a sense of separation of matter from mind, nature from spirit. The great mythologist Joseph Campbell noted that this, *"separation of matter and spirit, or the dynamism of life and the realm of the spirit, of natural grace and supernatural grace, has really castrated nature. And the European mind, the European life, has been, as it were, emasculated by this separation"* (Campbell, 1988).

As a culture, we no longer felt a deep empathic connection with life but instead focused primarily on outer forms of technological innovation and material progress, while deprioritizing inner wellbeing and consciousness.

The separation of inner (mind) and outer (matter) creates a wounding duality that divorces us from the immense richness of knowledge and wisdom we can only tap into when our inner-outer ways of knowing are integrated. This Inner-outer dynamic is a fundamental area of our lives that has gone through the same Journey of Separation that the dynamics of human-nature, and masculine-feminine have.

# THE JOURNEY OF SEPARATION

## INNER-OUTER SEPARATION

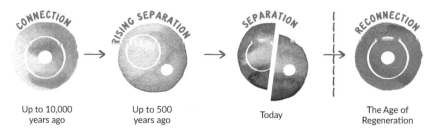

© copyright Hutchins & Storm

Even in this century, many of us don't know what it means to have a strong inner connection, or how we feel in our own body about certain situations. *Do you?* Do you know how it feels to be strongly anchored within; at peace and grounded in yourself?

Many leaders today deem bodily reactions and insights as irrational and unreasonable. Our relationship with nature's innate wisdom may often be seen as hippy-dippy and not to be taken seriously. Intuition is something that is not really understood, and viewed as questionable. Any such irrational thinking we might mock as second-rate or woo-woo. In any given situation, many of us go immediately to our brains, to analyze the situation, while disregarding any intuitive insight or gut-feeling. We react (one might say 'habitually *re-act'*) instead of taking a pause, breathing deep, and addressing a challenging situation wisely.

We have unwittingly removed ourselves from ourselves and out of our natural reality! Just look at the way we approach living. Have you ever looked to outside comfort – a new gadget, shopping spree, special food, a weekend getaway, an extreme sport experience, maybe even a date or an affair – when feeling confused or troubled inside? Have you ever put in more hours at work in an attempt to feel (temporarily) good or worthy? While we busy ourselves with outer 'doing' we are numbing our inner 'being'.

> "All of humanity's problems stem from man's inability to sit quietly in a room alone"
>
> Blaise Pascal, mathematician and philosopher

With all this in mind, let's now take a look at our brains where research shows that a heightened left-brained hemispheric way of attending has occurred in tandem with a separation from nature, a prioritization of the masculine over feminine and the outer over the inner.

## The Domination of the Left-brain Hemisphere over the Right-brain Hemisphere

Neuroscientist Iain McGilchrist has extensively explored left-brain hemi-sphere dominance in our Western culture. The left-hemisphere of the brain, according to McGilchrist's and other neuroscientists' findings, focuses on the parts of the problem by decontextualizing, narrowing down, and abstracting the problem in a closed system. This of course, helps us analyze and find a solution to the problem at hand. However, only a solution in the context of an isolated closed system, not in a living, emergent, complex system – like a business environment. By the same theory, the right-hemisphere of the brain focuses on the whole of the problem by broadening perspective, form-ing connections, and viewing the problem within an open system; we seek context, think creatively (out of the box) and develop greater understanding. It is both the knowledge of the parts (left-hemisphere) and wisdom of the whole (right-hemisphere) that we need to solve today's problems.

> "The model of the machine is the only one that the left hemisphere likes"
>
> Iain McGilchrist, neuroscientist

The qualities of the left-hemisphere have enabled us to form a civilization based on advanced technology, rationality, mechanistic sequencing, and control. This way of processing gives us a sense of power and domination over our world, which is alluring and comforting, yet it reduces down our capacity to perceive nuances, relationship dynamics, subjective feelings, and the bigger picture. That is to say, it shuts us off from the realness of life.

> "Part of the way our left hemisphere neo-cortex works in order to analyze the world and solve problems, is to break things down into their constituent parts to create boundaries. To make sense of the world we apply the analytic scissors and create cuts in the seamless web of life, but we then forget that it is our own thinking that has created the cuts and the boundaries, and we think the cuts and boundaries exist 'out-there' in the world"
>
> Peter Hawkins, leadership specialist

In his profound work *The Master and His Emissary*, McGilchrist explores this rise of left-hemispheric dominance in Western culture: *"There are obvious continuities between the Reformation and the Enlightenment. They share the same marks of left-hemisphere domination: the banishment of wonder; the triumph of the explicit, and, with it, mistrust of metaphor; alienation from the embodied world of the flesh, and a consequent cerebralisation of life and experience."* He goes on to note: *"Democracy as Jefferson saw it, with its essentially local, agrarian, communitarian, organic structure, was in harmony with the ideas of the right hemisphere. But in time it came to be swept away by the large-scale, rootless, mechanical force of capitalism, a left-hemisphere product of the Enlightenment"* (McGilchrist, 2009).

Left-hemisphere management and monitoring approaches have helped us to analyze, quantify and control to great effect. There is no denying that. Yet it has come to dominate too much of our societal and organizational design. This imbalance in our brains goes hand-in-hand with the imbalance of our human-nature relation.

## Left vs Right Brain Hemisphere Qualities

The table here lists qualities associated with the left-hemisphere and the right-hemisphere. This helps us see how left-hemisphere qualities have shaped and dominated many areas of society and business today.

| LEFT-HEMISPHERE QUALITIES | RIGHT-HEMISPHERE QUALITIES |
| --- | --- |
| you vs me | we are all one |
| linear | systemic |
| causal | relational |
| focuses in on the parts | seeks to understand the whole |
| structure and order | out-of-the-box creativity |
| polarization | seeing through tensions |

Although (scientifically speaking) you can't really talk about a 'separation' of the two brain hemispheres, the Journey of Separation does reveal a trend of rising 'domination' of left over right hemisphere – just like we have seen with the 3 other areas of human-nature, masculine-feminine and inner-outer.

These 4 areas and their collective Journey of Separation are closely coupled.

## THE JOURNEY OF SEPARATION
### LEFT-RIGHT BRAIN SEPARATION

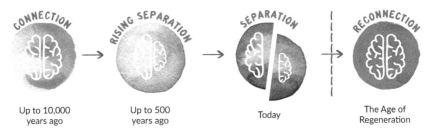

| CONNECTION | RISING SEPARATION | SEPARATION | RECONNECTION |
| --- | --- | --- | --- |
| Up to 10,000 years ago | Up to 500 years ago | Today | The Age of Regeneration |

© copyright Hutchins & Storm

Harvard-trained brain scientist, Dr. Jill Bolte Taylor, had a stroke that affected her left-hemisphere, which meant that she got to experience the world solely through the right hemisphere. Having studied the brain for decades, she was suddenly experiencing the profound differences between the two hemispheres from the inside out – through her own body. Dr. Taylor tells of how peaceful and vibrant she felt when her brain could only perceive the world through the right-hemisphere, seeing everything around her in brilliant colors and hearing only wonderful, music-like sounds. It was only when the left-hemisphere shut down that her worries simply disappeared and she would feel at one with everything. There was no separation between herself and the world. Everything was interconnected.

Yet when she slid into the left-hemisphere for a few minutes at a time, she was able to understand the severity of her situation and could use her analytic skills to call for an ambulance and explain in medical terms what was happening. Then back again she would slide into the worry-free oneness of her right-hemisphere, enabling her sense of self to connect with life.

In an interview, she explains: *"In the right brain experience, everything is connected. We are one with all that is. We require cells in the left parietal region in order to define the boundaries of where I begin and where I end. When those cells went offline, then there was no physical boundary. I was energy. I am energy. We are energy."*

When the interviewer asks her in what ways this experience changed her she responds: *"I used to focus my mind on science, in the lab, on the cells under the microscope, on theory and ideas. That whole world was what drove me. Now, I'm much more connected to the bigger picture of humanity and our relationship as human beings to the planet...my left hemisphere was driving my character before in the doing world...But now, I live it in a completely different way. My decisions are totally driven based on my intuition – if you will – about how things feel energetically for me."* (Sounds True Podcast, 2018).

Dr. Taylor has integrated her first-hand experiences into her research, which has profoundly changed her approach to studying the brain. She has become a strong advocate for a more integrated left-right hemispheric approach to life.

*Dive Deeper:* You can watch Dr. Taylor's fascinating TED talk about her experience *My Stroke of Insight*. She has also published a book by the same title.

# A New Journey of Reconnection

## *The Rise of Systems Thinking*

Over the past few decades the rise of Systems Thinking has helped us think in terms of interconnections, patterns, and processes. It recognizes the interconnected nature of business and life at large, and views the whole system as greater than the sum of its parts. Whilst mechanistic thinking helps the understanding of isolated parts, Systems Thinking fosters the understanding of complexity, change, and relationality.

A focus on understanding the parts of the system needs to be adequately balanced with a focus on understanding the inter-relationship of the parts within the wider system context. The whole-system, the whole-brain, the whole-body. Intuitively we know that life is not only made up of building blocks that can be rationalized, measured, and monitored for improved efficiency and effectiveness. It may give us comfort to believe that everything can be quantified and put into neat and tidy boxes or translated into numbers in tables that can be calculated with an excel formula, but that ain't how life really works.

Leaders of the future must embrace both – an understanding of the *parts* and how they *interplay*. Underpinning the ability for the leader to embrace both is the re-connection and re-integration of left and right-hemisphere, inner and outer, masculine and feminine, human and nature.

It is time to cross the threshold and begin a new *Journey of Reconnection* – a communion of all 4 areas.

# THE JOURNEY OF RECONNECTION

DISCONNECTION/SEPARATION                    RECONNECTION

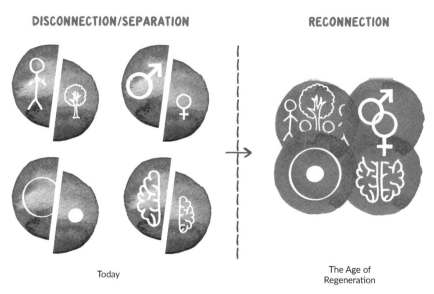

Today                                    The Age of
                                         Regeneration

© copyright Hutchins & Storm

## Outer & Inner Sustainability Must Go Together to Succeed

Despite the fact that many good things are happening – for instance, the increasing adoption of the Sustainable Development Goals (SDGs) across many sectors – the rise in sustainable business is not having the impact needed to address the inner-outer stress across our social and ecological systems in a timely way. Sustainability strategies, SDGs, CSR policies, and circular economics focus mainly on outer aspects while overlooking the deeper underlying issue – a shift from mechanistic to interconnected thinking.

Certainly, the global traction gained by initiatives such as circular economics and SDGs is very promising, yet so often these initiatives are being implemented with the same old mechanistic mindset that created the problems in the first place. The SDGs are often implemented in an old-school mechanistic way with more things to measure and control in silos. We end up doing 'outer' stuff differently while still being dis-connected, stressed and out of kilter with life itself. Hence, the change these initiatives help mobilize is incremental rather than transformative.

> "We cannot solve our problems with the same thinking we used when we created them."
>
> Albert Einstein, physicist

We have both – Laura and Giles – worked in the field of sustainability for decades and been lured in to addressing sustainability as either a technology we have to scale, a policy framework we must lobby for, or a financial and operational mechanism to implement. These particular approaches are what we call *outer sustainability*. Outer sustainability is, no doubt, an important part of the sustainability transition; however, if that is all we focus on, we will create further imbalance. We must also address *inner sustainability*, which is sustainability that fosters creativity and play, wellbeing and whole-body intelligence, applies nature's wisdom, thinks in interconnected systems, and takes into account an individual's sense of purpose within the whole. As the model below illustrates, it all goes together as part of a transition toward sustainable regenerative cultures.

## OUTER AND INNER SUSTAINABILITY

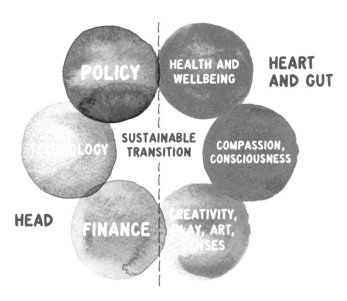

© copyright Hutchins & Storm

You may think: *Do we have the time to care about how we feel inside when we are in the midst of a crisis? Isn't the most important thing right now to scale the right technologies and get the right kind of policies and processes implemented?*

Well, yes, certainly there is a need for urgency. However, if we rush in with solutions that apply yesterday's logic and continue operating in the same old unbalanced ways, we waste time and resources and just get more of the same.

The UNFCCC COP Climate Change process is a great example of how we won't get the results we need with purely an outer focus. Laura was Director of the Copenhagen Climate Council and was heavily involved in the process leading up to the COP15 in 2009 – the big UN climate summit that, at the time, many thought would provide a legally binding world treaty on climate change (a successor to the Kyoto Protocol). In the final months leading up to the December 2009 COP15, negotiations crumbled, things fell apart, and there was a huge battle of egos behind the scene. This led to the Danish lead negotiator, who had spent years building trust amongst his counterparts, being fired. The Danish hosts then tried to bulldoze through an agreement without taking the time to listen to and respect all the different perspectives from both developed and developing countries. The negotiations broke down. Heads of States fled the scene, and international press called it *"the greatest failure of global politics ever"* (Vidal, 2009). A great opportunity (along with resources and time) was wasted due to an imbalanced left-hemispheric, hyper-masculine outer-focus.

**Dive Deeper:** If you want to know all the details of the political drama that went on during the COP15 process the Danish climate policy expert Per Meilstrup wrote a behind-the-scenes book interviewing all key officials, negotiators and politicians. The book is in Danish and called *Kampen For Klimaet* (the fight for our climate) yet a detailed summary of it can be found in English: *The Runaway Summit: The Background Story of the Danish Presidency of COP15, the UN Climate Change Conference.*

Six years later, Laura was involved in the Paris COP21 which was seen as the second chance to negotiate a legally binding global climate treaty. This was an entirely different experience. The summit was led by Christiana Figueres (the Head of the UNFCCC) and Nicolas Hulot (Lead French negotiator and long time passionate environmentalist), both of whom took time to listen to all parties, specifically including spiritual leaders and faith community representatives, while ensuring that all developing nations and island communities were fairly heard. It was a heart-led process prioritizing what some may have perceived as the *soft fluffy stuff*. And it worked wonders.

Six months prior to the summit, lead negotiators, Heads of State, NGOs, faith communities and spiritual leaders were invited by the French President and Christiana Figueres for a one-day summit to share from the heart their response to the question: *Why do I care about the planet, and what legacy do I wish to leave to my children?* There were tears and genuine personal connections made between key parties. This one-day summit laid important groundwork for reaching a successful outcome six months later at the COP21 where an unprecedented global agreement was made. Instead of a process run by big egos, there was dialogue, transparency, partnership, empathy, authenticity, vulnerability, and respect.

Let the UNFCCC COP's shift from Copenhagen to Paris be an example for all types of change processes across various organizations, institutions and communities.

## Reconnection to Life

Most people today rarely see the whole-system they're engaged in as they go about their day, whether they are shopping, vacationing, or delivering upon KPIs, all of which influence a variety of systems, relations, and structures far beyond the immediacy of the activity. People have become so separated from understanding their actions as part of a greater whole, that they barely give it much thought while working or shopping. *Which growing methods, materials, transportation means, and workers have been involved in making your new trousers, for instance? Or growing the salad you snack on for lunch? Or in making your household cleaning products?*

Your cute Christmas elf does not come from Santa's warm and rustic factory at the North Pole, but is probably mass-produced with harsh chemicals, from declining resources, maybe even by unprotected child labor. *Not cute at all.* We are so often too busy to see that we are creating the ripple effects, all the time – either positive or negative ripples emanating from us and through our decisions, transactions and choices.

To summarize, the widespread problems we face today have a deep underlying cause. Having examined the evolution of *Homo sapiens* over the centuries, we can see the effects of the growing imbalance between humanity and nature, masculine and feminine, inner and outer, and left-brained and right-brained awareness.

We must acknowledge that we are all human beings longing to integrate imbalances within us and around us. We must move forward with a different consciousness than what created the problems in the first place. We must integrate the perspectives of the left and right brain hemispheres, the inner and outer aspects of our selves, masculine and feminine qualities, and the relationship of humanity and nature.

As a human race, we have forgotten how to connect with our outer nature *and* our inner nature. It is vital that we remember, or relearn, how to read the patterns, relationships, energies, insights, and intelligences innate within life. Without this reconnecting to life's logic, we will be unable to find our way to a more balanced structure or coherent business paradigm that enables our people and our planet to thrive in the years ahead.

"We are what we repeatedly do."

Aristotle,
philosopher

Photo credit: Abishek Pawar

# Are We Breaking Down or Breaking Through?

So how has the Journey of Separation shaped today's society and business? The separation between humanity and nature, masculine and feminine, inner and outer, left and right-brain hemisphere: How has this affected our worldview? How has this affected our leadership mindset, our organizational cultures, and our social and ecological systems?

These are the questions we shall now explore. This chapter will take the temperature of today's world to assess the landscape in which leaders are currently navigating.

Regenerative Leadership is not yet another leadership approach that applies the very same mechanistic logic that caused our problems in the first place in seeking solutions to these problems. No, this Regenerative Leadership approach deals with today's landscape systemically. The epic challenges we now face demand a wholly new way quite different from the level of thinking traditional leadership approaches have applied.

In this chapter we get all cards on the table so we can address these challenges in a comprehensive root and branch fashion.

# The Rising Complexity Gap in our Business Landscape

Recent global leadership studies point to rising challenges among our leaders today and a lack of appropriate leadership consciousness to deal with the complexities we now face. Leaders of today are too stuck in an outdated way of operating that is not geared to address the severity of today's situation.

A recent report for the Churchill 21st Century Statesmanship Global Leaders Programme explores a new imperative for leadership in these transformational times. Through 60 confidential, in-depth interviews conducted with the highest-level positions across business and government, an 'executive myopia' shows: short-termism; reactive aversion and systemic fear; internalized focus on cost-cutting rather than out-of-the-box thinking; cognitive overload and dissonance; and top-level reluctance blended with anxiety, frailties and fatigue. Whilst this report is UK-focused, it compliments reports that originate in other parts of the world and contributes to a rich-picture forming of a systemic *complexity gap* in leadership across the globe.

Organizational specialists, such as the London Business School's Gary Hamel and Harvard Business School's John Kotter, have been warning us for a few years now: in order to keep up with rising complexity a new way of leading and operating is now essential. For instance, IBM research in 2014 interviewed more than 1,500 CEOs in 60 countries and highlighted a need for leaders to embrace a radical 'new norm'. 79% of these leaders described their biggest challenge as *leading in complexity* yet less than 50% felt equipped to lead in these complex business environments.

In 2018, Deloitte surveyed over 14,000 CEOs across 23 industries, and found a clear *complexity gap* in leadership consciousness – leaders who didn't feel they had the skills to address the complexities they face.

Leaders of today are dealing with a level of complexity we have not witnessed before. Below is a brief summary of the dynamics that contribute to the complexity that businesses and leadership now face:

- systemic issues such as climate change, resource scarcity, disruption of ecosystem cycles

- rapid decline of biodiversity and extinction of species
- disruptive innovations
- digitization and disintermediation
- market volatility
- fast changing customer buying patterns
- high levels of stress, burnout and depression
- low levels of employee engagement
- a war on talent
- increasing transparency due to social media and changing ethical considerations
- changing political regulation
- millennials desiring new ways of working

The current leadership logic sees each of the above as separate issues, and so deals with them individually, which is a mechanistic, left-hemispheric logic that spawns from the dis-connected way of attending we explored in the previous chapter. When we see only fragments of the bigger picture, we ignore the inter-relations between them. Dealing with things in isolation creates yet more systemic problems!

Business leaders often overlook the root problem, and therefore unwittingly treat symptoms superficially, which is to say in the same way they have always done it since the Scientific Revolution. By hanging on – dare we say, clinging on – to what is known and what has been practiced for years, leaders and their organizations remain out of touch with a landscape that has changed radically.

> "Any company designed for success in the 20th century is doomed to failure in the 21st century"
>
> David S. Rose, serial entrepreneur

Until we adequately comprehend this inherent flaw in today's business logic, we will not be able to adequately move onward, close the complexity gap, and evolve our business logic into a new and better way.

Let's look at the prevalent logic inherent in today's business paradigm.

## Viewing the Organization as a Machine

The dominating logic has been one of viewing organizations as machines and objectifying their moving parts as resources, asset classes, and levers – human resource management, supply chain management, financial management – all separate silos within a machine seeking to increase efficiency and effectiveness in a hyper-competitive, masculine, dog-eat-dog world. A perspective that gives us a neat-and-tidy feeling, allowing us to believe that everything can be neatly defined and perfectly controlled. Yet, that is merely an illusion we've created as a result of the left-hemispheric, control-based reductionist logic we are drawing from and the separateness and fear that feeds it. It is not real life; it's not reality. It is well past its sell-by date and looking increasingly out-of-place in today's world.

History shows us that this old logic is what formed the backbone of Frederick Taylor's *Principles of Scientific Management* published in 1909. This Taylorist approach was hugely influential in setting the context for viewing the organization as *a machine*. Machines performed better when optimized for efficiency, and the responsibility for optimizing the organizational *machine* became the primary concern of managers. Employees were relegated to the role of efficiently performing the duties as defined by management. This logic has created the hierarchical organization structure that we know only too well today, with its silos and bureaucracy, where management seeks to improve the efficiency of the machine, while unwittingly undermining the creativity, agility, wellbeing, and empowerment of the employees.

As today's business environment becomes more volatile, uncertain, complex, and ambiguous (VUCA) than ever before, businesses designed by 19th and 20th century logic will not be able to cope nor survive – let alone thrive – amid 21st century conditions. It's fast time to transform our leadership logic.

Future success will be determined by organizations' ability to be more innovative, agile, purposeful and resilient.

> "In times of turmoil, the danger lies not in the turmoil but in facing it with yesterday's logic."
>
> Peter Drucker, business specialist

Before we examine how to transform today's leadership and organizational logic, let's first look at the business worldview that has been created by the Journey of Separation of human-nature, masculine-feminine, left-right hemisphere and outer-inner.

## A Flawed Worldview in Business

The current and prevailing view of the purpose of business is: to provide goods and services to meet the perceived needs of the customer in order to generate profit for shareholders. The more the customer consumes the better, because the more goods and services sold, the more profit gained. This is what we refer to today as *consumerism* or consumption-based growth, which has become the driving force of economic growth. Economic growth in turn drives employment, thus providing income for consumers to consume more and, ultimately, fueling more economic growth.

This consumerism, upon which we have built our financial systems, has at least two major flaws:

### 1. *Externalities and true value of resources are not incorporated*

Business is primarily focused on providing increasingly more goods and services to generate increasingly more profit. This profit is determined by an economic value (and cost), which is disconnected from the social and environmental value (and cost) incurred through sourcing, production, and consumption of goods and services. A number of these 'externalities' are not incorporated in the economic value and cost (an organization's balance sheet does not include a wide range of social and environmental costs and benefits). That is to say that the social and environmental value (the benefits and costs to all stakeholders) of a good or service is not included in the measurement of economic value. The consumer's price paid does not reflect the true, complete value of the product. Nor do the producer's costs incurred reflect the true, complete cost of production.

## 2. Falsely created needs and desires decrease human wellbeing

Business strives to satisfy the needs of the customer. In so doing, the clever business mind seeks to encourage the desires of the customer so that their needs best align with the products and services of that business. This would seem sensible business. Business is to invest in marketing, communications, media, and advertising to help generate a demand for the goods and services it produces. Again, sensible business. As a result, the needs of consumers (we human beings) become influenced and encouraged by the needs of the business. The business stimulates needs by using methods adapted from psychology – your life will become more complete, you will be happier, will look more beautiful, be a better wife, stronger husband, etc. if you buy this product.

As economies struggle, many leaders look to stimulate growth by increasing consumption. In fact, *let's consume our way out of our crisis*, also seems to be the preferred political route too. **Encouraging more of the same is flawed.** We have developed an economy that encourages human desires that are not always (perhaps seldom) aligned to the wellbeing of the human.

> "People hold unsound ideas and views because they have absorbed the prevailing norms without testing their logic."
>
> Alain de Botton, philosopher

## Unleashing an Ecological Mega-crisis

This flawed worldview – a society fundamentally built on exploitation of natural as well as human resources – has created many impressive technological and material advances that we all enjoy; however, it has *also* unleashed an ecological and existential mega-crisis. A crisis of our own physiological wellbeing, as well as the wellbeing of the natural ecosystems we depend on for our survival.

Let's look at some of the key challenges our industrialized civilization has caused our ecosystems:

## Climate Change

As one of the top climate scientists in the world, NASA's Dr. James Hansen, put it, *"Climate change – human-made global warming – is happening. It is already having noticeable impacts...If we stay on with business as usual, the southern U.S. will become almost uninhabitable."* (Romm, 2011).

Massive global warming commenced when the Scientific and Industrial Revolution started to suck out fossil fuels – like oil, natural gas, and coal – that had been stored underground for millions of years (Hartmann, 2004). Fossil fuel is *really* old plant material that had captured carbon millions of years ago – what took a million years to capture we're now using in a year (Fischer, 2012). Our natural ecosystems can't keep up with the massive increase in Green House Gas (GHG) emissions being pumped in to the atmosphere. Hence, it causes the planet to warm significantly. According to the annual NOAA study, *"arctic air temperatures for the past five years have exceeded all previous records"* (Arctic Report Card, 2018).

Some – especially in the northern hemisphere – have enjoyed the warmer summers without seeing the changing weather as particularly worrying. Yet these weather changes greatly impact the vitality of natural ecosystems across the world.

But what will climate change mean in reality?

According to IPCC (2014) scientists, anthropogenic climate change (climate change caused by humans) will lead to:

- extreme high temperatures – intense droughts, wildfires and heatwaves
- sea levels will rise 1-4 feet by 2100 and sea temperature increases significantly
- ocean acidification which alters water chemistry affecting the life cycles of many marine organisms with all the knock-on effects this entails
- heavier rainfall, hurricanes, storms and floods
- melting of snow and ice like ice caps, glaciers and permafrost that could release catastrophic levels of methane gasses creating run-away climate change

These extreme weather events will affect human society by:

- increasing hunger and water crises, particularly in less developed countries
- making large parts of the southern hemisphere increasingly inhospitable causing massive numbers of climate refugees and potentially even wars fought due to the friction this will cause
- impacting crops, plants and fruit trees
- rising air temperatures and heat waves which will have health effects and increase viruses and pathogens
- increasing biodiversity loss, since many species can't adapt to rapid rises in temperature
- increasing natural catastrophes causing damage to homes and communities

In September 2018, a new monumental study from the IPCC written by 830 scientists from 80 countries across the globe, stated that the planet will reach the critical threshold of 1.5 degrees Celsius (2.7 degrees Fahrenheit) above pre-industrial levels by as early as 2030. This is *considerably* earlier than originally expected. The severity of climate change will point to more extreme hurricanes, droughts, wildfires, floods, harsh winters, hot summers, and food shortages that will affect hundreds of millions of people. In 30 years' time climate change is foreseen to force 50 to 700 million people to migrate (IPBES, 2019).

According to IPCC scientists, we only have 12 years left to solve this crisis to reduce the most severe damage. In the report, it was stated that urgent and unprecedented changes are needed now to keep temperature increases between a 1.5C and 2C threshold. As one of the co-chairs, Debra Roberts, commented upon the launch of the report: *"It's a line in the sand, and what it says to our species is that this is the moment, and we must act now. This is the largest clarion bell from the science community and I hope it mobilizes people and dents the mood of complacency."* (Watts, 2018).

Did you take that in? We have only 12 years to turn this around or else we are facing a dire situation. This is a situation that cannot be solved at a political level alone – it takes all of us, not just the youngsters striking every Friday – but leaders of all walks of life to step up with courage and conviction.

In their 2018 report, that was commissioned by national governments after the COP21 agreement in Paris, IPCC maps out 4 pathways to achieve 1.5C entailing different combinations of land use and technologies. Essential to all 4 pathways are reforestation and shifts towards electric transportation and greater adoption of carbon capture technologies (IPCC, 2018). Global GHG emissions would need to fall by 45% by 2030 in order to keep the warming around 1.5C. The report also highlights the significant costs of inaction now and the impact this has on future generations. Lord Nicholas Stern has been saying this for years. For instance, in his 2006 report, he warned about the severity of inaction today and the mounting burden on future generations. In an interview with the UK newspaper, *The Guardian*, 10 years after his report, he confesses: *"With hindsight, I now realize that I underestimated the risks. I should have been much stronger in what I said in the report about the costs of inaction. I underplayed the dangers."* (McKie, 2016).

In reality, many leaders and adults today are not even aware of the severity of the situation. You would think that when hundreds of world-leading scientists stand shoulder to shoulder and with a unified voice state that this is an emergency situation that we would start mobilizing the needed focus and force, but we aren't. Many who are aware are either all-too-consumed by today's busyness or are seeking to address the challenge with a new invention, technology, or policy. Yet to truly mobilize people and create the support, awareness and understanding it's not just technology or policy innovation we need but a radical change of leadership consciousness.

## Threat of Mass Extinction

The climate change warnings are dire, yet equally terrifying but far less talked about is the rapid decline of life on Earth. The increase in climate change alongside massive deforestation, use of pesticides and the widespread decrease of natural habitats are making our planet an increasingly hostile place for many species. According to the World Resource Institute we have already destroyed more than 80% of the Earth's natural forests, and are continuing to do so at the alarming rate of 20,000 hectares a day. A new 3-year UN-backed landmark study by the Intergovernmental Science-Policy

Platform on Biodiversity and Ecosystem Services (IPBES) compiled by more than 500 experts across 50 countries was published in May 2019. This report clearly states that the felling of our forests, the over-exploitation of seas and soils, and the pollution of air and water are driving the living world to a brink. The new study is the greatest attempt yet to assess the state of life on Earth and stresses how tens of thousands of species are at high risk of extinction, with human communities using nature at a rate that *far exceeds its ability to ever regenerate*, with nature's ability to contribute food and fresh water to a growing human population being compromised across every region on Earth (Huffington Post, 2019).

According to WWF's 2018 Living Planet Index, we have lost 60% of wildlife in less than 50 years, due to habitat loss, pollution, climate change, and over-exploitation. Human activity is *"pushing the planet toward a sixth mass species extinction"* (IPBES, 2019).

Unlike previous mass extinction events in the Earth's history, this one is due to the behavior of one species – us. This will have devastating consequences for all life, including humanity.

By example, a comprehensive study released in October 2017 shows that the flying insect population has decreased by 75% over the last 27 years. Insects are crucial to the biodiversity that we depend on for our survival, and 80% of plants rely on insects for pollination: *"Loss of insect diversity and abundance is expected to provoke cascading effects on food webs and to jeopardize ecosystem services"* (Hallman et al, 2017).

> "This raises the question: Will the human species be extinguished in its turn? The statistical question, perhaps the statistical likelihood, is complicated, morally, by the probability that human extinction, if it comes about soon, will prove to have been species suicide."
>
> Jack Miles, senior adviser to J Paul Getty Trust

## Massive Pollution of Soil, Air and Water

Not only are we facing drastic weather-related disasters, climate change, and a sixth mass extinction, we have also polluted the air, rivers, oceans and depleted the soil on a massive scale. Modern intensive agriculture is stripping the soil from critical nutrients like calcium, phosphorous, iron, proteins, and vitamins (Journal of the American College of Nutrition, 2004). Polluting water streams and ground water with chemicals means these toxins get in to our drinking water and in to our blood streams and body tissues (Wahl, 2016). It's simply a mess of epic proportions, all created by us.

And then there's our oceans being filled-up with plastic and debris. Every year more than 8 million tons of plastic waste flows into the world's oceans. This plastic is floating around creating huge plastic islands the size of Texas and France floating in our oceans disrupting all marine ecosystems. By 2050 there will be more plastic in our oceans than marine life (Ellen McArthur Foundation, 2017).

And it doesn't just stay in our oceans – plastic now pollutes the entire web of life. Scientists have found that 90% of all sea birds have plastic in their stomachs, and fishermen find plastic inside fish and seafood (Wilcox et al., 2015). Fibers from synthetic clothes, such as polyester and acrylic, make their way into our freshwater streams. Micro-plastic is now found in everything from beer to drinking water, from seafood to human stool, which means it's also in our bloodstreams, lymphatic systems, and livers (Vienna Medical University, 2018).

All of these: Forest fires, ocean acidification, diminishing species, hurricanes, plastic islands, collapse of the bee population, severe climate change, micro-plastics in food and water, mass extinction: **It's all on us.**

We have created systems and procedures that create havoc across the entire web of life on Earth. As Sir David Attenborough has stated: *"humans have become a plague on Earth"*. The materialistic culture, industrialization and mechanistic mindset of the last few centuries is destroying life in front of our very eyes, yet often we are too blind to see what we are doing.

WE *CANNOT* LIVE ON THIS PLANET WITHOUT THRIVING ECOSYSTEMS. THERE CANNOT BE A HEALTHY, HAPPY, PROSPEROUS FUTURE FOR *ANY* LIVING SPECIES WITH POLLUTED OCEANS AND RIVERS, DEPLETED SOIL AND DEVASTATED FORESTS.

YET WE CONTINUE
OUR LIFESTYLES,
BUSINESS PRACTICES,
AND POLITICAL
PROGRAMMES
AS IF WE COULD.

# An Inner Crisis & Inner Stress

It's not just in our societies, economies, and ecosystems we witness immense pressure and stress, our minds and bodies are out of kilter too. We have never been as *stressed out* as we are today. Stress has been labeled the *"global health epidemic of the 21st century"* by the World Health Organization and in 2018 global levels of unhappiness reached their highest point according to the annual Gallup Global Emotions Report. This report has collected data from 154,000 adults from 145 countries, and in the foreword states: *"Collectively, the world is more stressed, worried, sad and in pain today than we've ever seen it"* (Gallup, 2018).

This stress is affecting everyone – there's just as much stress among the regular workforce as at C-level suite. A Harvard Medical School Study found that 96% of senior executives in the US feel somewhat burned out, while a third of them described their stress levels and work situation as extreme. Stress leads to all kinds of health problems like depression, obesity, anxiety, insomnia, heart attacks, respiratory and digestive issues, high blood pressure and a weakened immune system (The American Institute of Stress, 2019).

In Europe sales of anti-depressive medicine has increased every year between 2000 and 2012 (The British Journal of Psychiatry, 2015). In the United States the use of anti-depressants has increased 65% over the last 15 years (U.S. Center for Disease Control and Prevention, 2017).

All these scientific findings, survey statistics and polls send a clear signal that something is utterly wrong with how we are operating. People in a constant state of stress cannot address the severity of the challenges we are facing as a collective.

Scientific evidence shows that people in a constant state of stress are less compassionate, less collaborative, less creative, less innovative, and less wise. A brain under stress is in fight or flight mode (high-beta brainwaves), which is a useful skill we developed over thousands of years as hunter gatherers. It was critical for us humans to have the ability to tune in to the challenge at hand – a predator for example – and filter out everything else. In that high-beta state we are highly aroused, incredibly focused and alert – but only on what is immediately in front of us. It is a very resource draining and energy demanding state. Today, however, many of us spend the majority of our day in that energy-intensive high-beta state due to pressing deadlines and heavy workloads. This is taking its toll on our health and wellbeing.

When we are in a constant state of stress, we are simply not able to think systemically and address issues like climate change, loss of biodiversity, refugees, food waste, and widespread ecosystem degradation (UC Berkeley, 2017).

So, while the complexity of the situation our leaders are faced with today demands that we are more self-aware, perceptive, compassionate and sys-temically-attuned, many are burnt out, depressed and caught up in a wheel spinning faster and faster.

Stress levels are damaging the health and well-being of our children even before they're born. Studies have shown that the stress we experience impacts our children in-utero. A fetus that grows in an environment with high cortisol-levels is more likely to suffer from heart disease, obesity, diabe-tes and often struggle more in school, have ADD or short tempers (Glover, 2014).

We pass on this negative feedback cycle of stress to the next generation even before it's born.

As a society, we need to acknowledge that stress and mental illnesses are an epidemic that has to be urgently addressed, not hidden under the rug with the shame and stigma that many feel is associated with stress, depression and burn out. If we don't change the systems and structures and the way we lead and show up in the world, we just perpetuate today's mess.

## It's All Connected

The stress we see today in all systems – political, financial, social and eco-systems – interrelate and influence each other. The situation will continue to worsen year by year, month by month, unless we change the underlying logic by which we operate.

# STRESS IN ALL SYSTEMS

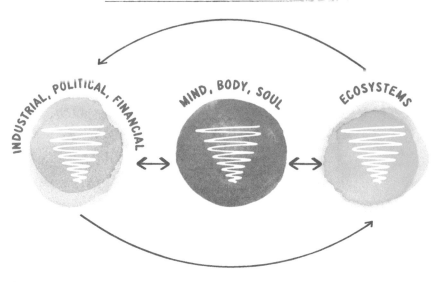

This negative feedback cycle of systemic stress will get more and more out of hand unless we put a stop to it by daring to go to the root cause and heal our interconnected crisis with a new mindset quite different from yesterday's mechanistic logic.

Let's pause for a moment, breathe deep, and gain perspective. Let's try looking at our civilization from the outside in. Imagine that we were from another planet observing our behaviors. We might sensibly ask: *What on Earth are they up to? Have they lost the plot completely?*

Humans spend the vast majority of their global ingenuity generating incomplete value for incomplete needs. In the process, they have corrupted themselves and the life-support systems upon which they depend. The warning signs are flashing in front of them, but humans plunder on – seeking even more products to sell and buy, creating even more distraction, producing even more pollution.

## Let's draw the quick sketch of what has happened

We have left our natural habitat and moved into towns and cities, full of high-rise flats and offices made of concrete and steel. We work all the time, put our elders in homes, and our kids in day-care. We eat processed factory foods depleted from vitamins and minerals and spend most of our days in front of screens. We don't feel well. In fact, we feel anxious, burned out and depressed, and our response is to numb our pain by consuming and producing stuff that pollutes us. This hectic hyper-consumerist behavior and our addictive need for fast fashion or the latest tech gadget has caused a catastrophe for all life on Earth. We have created a hostile environment for all living beings – including ourselves.

We have forgotten how to sense and respect nature within and around us. We have forgotten how to read the patterns, relationships, energies, insights, and intelligences innate within LIFE. We *Homo sapiens* have dis-connected ourselves from the logic of life and have instead designed systems and structures based on an incomplete mechanistic logic. And we are too stressed to adequately address the challenges created by our stress.

Without re-connecting to the logic of life, thinking systemically instead of in silos, we will be unable to find our way into a truly balanced, coherent business paradigm that enables both our organizations and the wider fabric of life on Earth to thrive in the years ahead.


## Leaders: Radical Change is Upon us; the Time is Now

More and more people are feeling an urge to change, to set a new course, to look for better ways.

**There is a 'push.'** Leaders in all walks of life know that something has to change, evidenced by a landscape dominated by VUCA. In wishing for our organizations to more than merely survive, but actually thrive in the volatile times ahead, we feel the urgent push into a new way of leading and operating. Much of what worked before is no longer good enough or even appropriate any more. Unceasing and rapid transformation is the 'new norm'.

ITS TIME
TO AWAKEN
A NEW WORLDVIEW
THAT SERVES LIFE.

DESIGNING A WAY
OF LIVING AND LEADING
FLOURISHING LIVES –
BASED ON PRINCIPLES
CONDUCIVE TO LIFE,
IS THE KEY MISSION
OF OUR TIMES.

Over the last handful of years, we have both (Giles & Laura) had the pleasure of engaging with a myriad of senior executives, CxOs from widely varying organizations, essentially agreeing on one thing: they are experiencing immense tension in these VUCA times. One aspect of this tension originates in the here-and-now. Just keeping their heads above water in these volatile times is a real challenge for our leaders. The other aspect of the tension is in the future – not some distant future, but just 3 years from now. There is an increasing recognition amongst leaders that for our organizations to do more than just survive but truly thrive, we need to radically transform the ways in which we operate and organize. To embrace this transformation, while keeping the wheels on the road and heads above water amid increasing turbulence, requires a wholly new approach to how we lead and operation – a new business logic.

One global CEO uses a metaphor of flying a plane, where the pilot has to retrofit the plane mid-flight, during increasing turbulence, all the while keeping the crew and passengers on-board happy, while in continuous communication with the ground-staff (Hawkins, 2016). This is the level of systemic interconnected change we face today.

> "Long gone are the days when a leader knew which buttons to press in their hierarchical organization so that decisions and resulting instructions are carried out smartly. The command-and-control structures have morphed into highly complex networks."
>
> Nik Gowing and Chris Langdon, leadership specialists

*There is a 'pull' too.* The pull is within us, within our inner being, our psyche. It is within the collective unconscious, compelling us to awaken beyond our self-absorbed slumber and become more purposeful, more human, more real, more relational, more connected, more compassionate, more authentic. We are wising-up to a deeper sense of place and purpose in this world beyond superficial consumerism, materialism and individualism. One only has to see the exponential rise in interest in mindfulness, wellbeing, yoga, meditation, organic produce, vegetarian and vegan diets, vision quests, nature-therapy, emotional and spiritual development to sense this shift.

Within this push and pull exists the birth of a new leadership norm, one that unlocks the intelligence of life and that thrives on agility, resilience, flexibility, and emergence. Leadership that is systemically attuned to the complex ecosystems we operate within. Leaders who are creating the conditions for organizations to become more agile, emergent, and systemically attuned.

Leaders of every generation and region are being simultaneously beckoned and cajoled into a new way, a new mind-set, a new operating model, one that is essentially life-affirming rather than singularly at odds with the social and ecological grammar of life. Alongside the blundering businesses that operate from flawed perspectives and worldviews, there are exemplary organizations emerging across all sectors that are pioneering new ways that reach beyond yesterday's logic (we explore these organizations in Part 2).

People do not want to work in bureaucratic soul-sapping organizations – they want to be in an environment that is creative, exciting, empowering, purposeful, and passionate. People want leaders who want to achieve more than just profit but also a positive difference. People want to feel a meaningful connection with the value they create during their work-day, rather than feeling like lost corporate cogs enslaved in the monolith of machine mentality. People want to reconnect with their inner nature and work in soulful organizations that enhance life.

*Read the above paragraph again in case you skimmed through it quickly. Take it to heart, digest it:* **People deeply crave a new way.**

There is now evidence of a shift afoot, a shift beyond yesterday's logic into a new regenerative paradigm.

It's utterly exciting yet urgently needed.

It is all unfolding rapidly, so brace yourself, as we dive straight into this next-stage business logic.

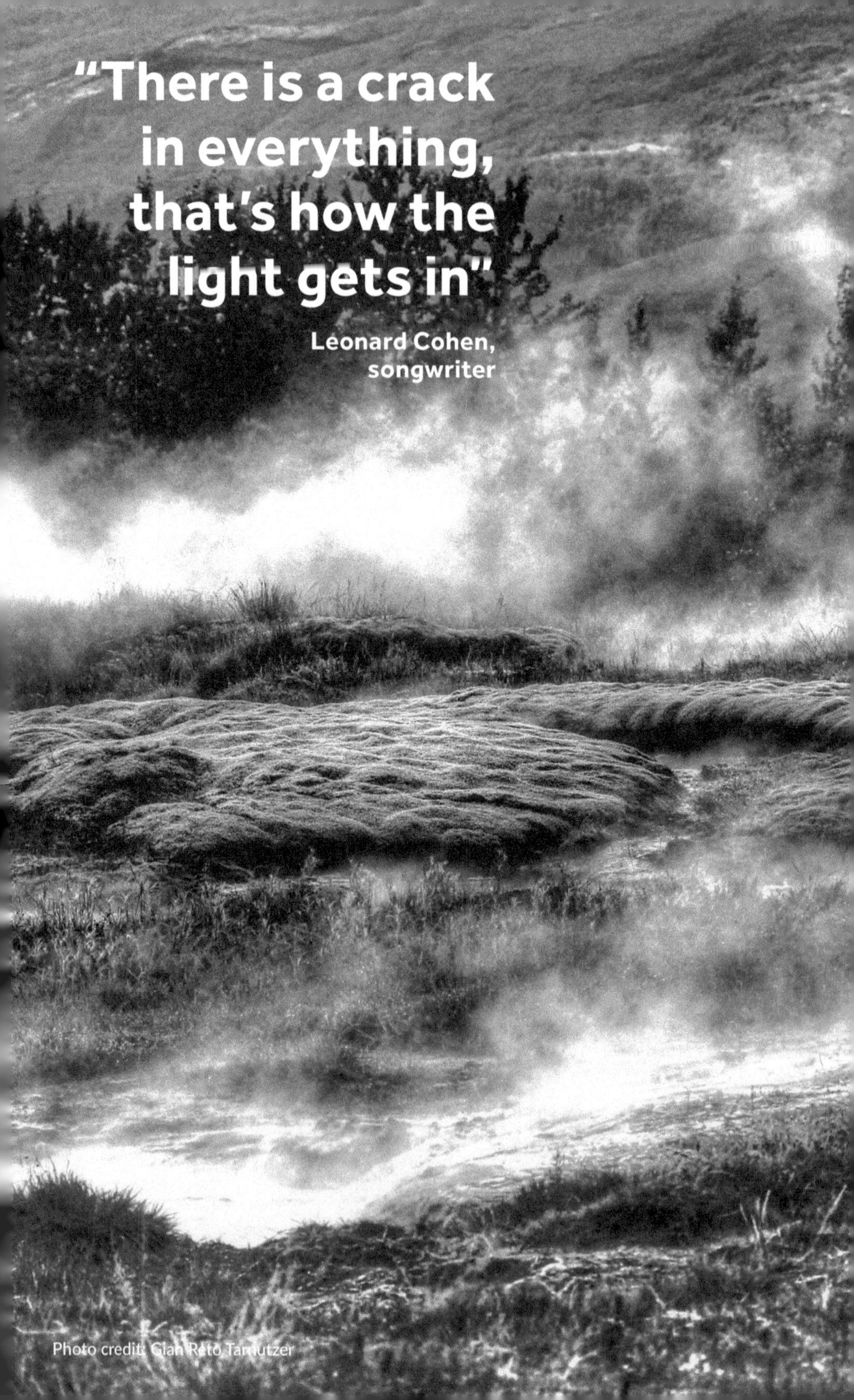
"There is a crack in everything, that's how the light gets in"
Leonard Cohen, songwriter

Photo credit: Gian Reto Tarnutzer

# The Dawn of a New Leadership Era

There is no doubt: We are living through a supreme moment of change. A moment between the old and the new, a transitional stage where simultaneous breakdown and breakthrough ruptures our status-quo worldview. Leaders are called to urgently address the systemic interconnected challenges we addressed in the previous chapter: The immense stress, fear and friction that has crept in to every corner of our society. If we so choose, we can allow this to compel us beyond the still dominant (yet dying) worldview of separateness, control, and hyper-competition.

It is a challenging, yet exciting, time to be in business. To be a leader. To be in the driving seat amid these transformational times. Many people residing in corridors of power around the world realize that our prolific and dangerous problems – which are 'wicked and systemic' in nature – can no longer be addressed with an outdated, mechanistic mindset. It is time to redesign a new way that renders the old way obsolete.

In this chapter, we explore the signs of a new leadership consciousness emerging amid this new dawn. A way that enables our leaders to be a force for good, catalyzing and spawning new systems and structures that create more value than they take. Rather than merely reducing our negative impact on life, doing less bad, we can seize the opportunity to constructively contribute to life's evolution. This is what being *regenerative* is about. This is the evolutionary imperative now upon us.

# Signs that Times they are A-Changin

We – the authors – have witnessed a rapid uplift amongst leaders interested in systemic change, conscious leadership and sustainable business. There is a growing take-up of developmental, agile, organizational approaches across all sectors of business, and more and more leaders are recognizing the importance of addressing *both* the inner (purpose, culture, wellbeing) and the outer (sustainability, stakeholders, value proposition) dimensions in business, urban development, and politics. And then there's the push and the pull that many leaders are experiencing, described in the previous chapter. These are signs of the dawning of a new era – the *next-stage* of leadership and organizational consciousness emerging today.

Let's briefly look at some of these signs.

In January 2018, the world's largest strategy consultancy McKinsey & Co launched a report – *The 5 Trademarks of Agile Organizations* – which stressed the importance of the necessary paradigm shift we are discussing here: moving away from the mindset of organizations as machines and toward organizations as living systems. This is music to our ears, as is the work and words of leadership specialist, and author of *The Age of Agile*, Steve Denning who notes that in a handful of years a paradigm shift in management will unfold. In what he calls the *"post-bureaucratic paradigm"*, he researches how next-stage organizations far outperform traditional hierarchic control-based organizations stating that "a*gile management is now seen as a key enabler of fast growth and enduring profitability."* (Denning, 2018).

Recent research by the investment manager Jay Bragdon explores how organizations embracing living-systems methods and life-affirming cultures consistently outperform their mechanistic counterparts. When researching these companies, he notes, *"Instead of modelling themselves on the assumed efficiency of machines – a thought process that emerged during the industrial age – these firms model themselves on living systems. Firms with open, ethical, inclusive traditions – where employees have a voice and a stake in what happens – have a distinct advantage over traditionally managed companies where most decisions are made at the top."* (Bragdon, 2016).

Also testament to this shift happening, is the widespread take-up and popularity across the globe by leaders and practitioners of former McKinsey consultant Frederick Laloux's *Reinventing Organizations*. His book explores examples of next-stage living organizations. Many thousands of leaders and practitioners around the globe have positively engaged with this work since the book was published in 2014. We will get back to his work in Part 2 as it offers a nice framework for showing the stages of development our leadership and organizational consciousness has gone through.

In just the last couple of years, The Massachusetts Institute of Technology (MIT) launched the Presencing Institutes' leadership training on transforming capitalism through awareness-based systemic leadership. This Institute engages around a hundred thousand leaders and practitioners across the globe. Core to this awareness-based systemic leadership approach is the psychological shift of *letting-go* – of cynicism, judgement and fear – while *opening-up* to the field, and deeply listening to the future that wants to emerge (a process referred to as *Theory U* developed by Professor Otto Scharmer). There is no way we would ever have been taught this framework at a leading business school 20 years ago. Now the MIT Sloan School of Management is dedicated to this work, with other business schools following suit. Leading business schools the world over are starting to put conscious leadership, agility and sustainability front-and-center of their educational mission to serve today's leaders.

There is also the best-selling work of Raj Sisodia and John Mackey on *Conscious Capitalism*, which has spawned a global movement with Conscious Capitalism chapters forming across the world. There is London Business School professor Gary Hamel's work on *Humanocracy* and busting bureaucracy. There is the work of leadership specialists such as Carol Sanford, John Kotter, Robert Kegan, Lisa Lahey, Richard Barrett, Michelle Holliday and many others, all contributing to this emerging new era of business leadership activating the next-stage of our evolution, one that seeks life-affirming futures. We provide you with the titles of their work in the bibliography at the back of this book.

These are all signs of a new era in business breaking through. Another sign is the exponential rise in B-Corps – businesses that agree to meet high standards of social and environmental performance, public transparency, and legal accountability. These organizations are moving away from a narrow focus on serving only shareholders to serving all stakeholders including society and the environment. Since the certification was first established in 2007, the number of B-Corps has grown from a handful to over 2,500 around the globe, and the number is rising by the day. And it's not just small organizations looking to make change – French consumer products giant Danone has now certified 30% of its brands and businesses as B-corps, and Unilever has an increasing number of B-Corp businesses within its corporation (Ben and Jerry's, Seventh Generation and Pukka Herbs, for instance).

Corporate Social Responsibility (CSR), sustainability and circular economics are no longer side-line topics relating to volunteering, measuring metrics or philanthropy. They are now recognized as core to the strategic imperative of organizational viability. Sustainability professionals are moving from cubicles in the basement to the C-suite, accompanied by large, dedicated, and often virtual teams that reach throughout the organization. The business priority of sustainability will only increase as social and environmental issues increase.

> "To prosper over time, every company must not only deliver financial performance, but also show how it makes a positive contribution to society. Companies must benefit all of their stakeholders, including shareholders, employees, customers, and the communities in which they operate."
>
> Larry Fink, CEO of BlackRock, world's largest business investor

Over the last 5 years we have seen a marked shift in the investor community from viewing sustainability, conscious leadership, ethics and corporate social responsibility as a distraction to core business performance to realizing it is essential for survival in these VUCA times. Larry Fink, CEO of the world's largest investor Black Rock, tells all business leaders that within the next 5 years, every investor will be considering Environmental and Social

Governance (ESG) criteria for every business they invest in. He sees ESG as key to understanding the future viability of any organization. Mark Carney, Governor of the Bank of England, recently stated that 70% of UK banks now view climate change as a core financial risk to their investments. In support of this, is the recently set-up Embankment Project for Inclusive Capitalism where investors with $30trn of assets under management are developing methods to ensure the long-term value-metrics of the businesses they invest in include a wide range of social and environmental issues.

> "...for those portfolio managers who happen to be human, we have a much more important job. We are racing to protect not just our portfolios, not just our grandchildren, but our species. So get to it."
>
> Jeremy Grantham, investor

Climate change and the state of our environment were also high priority for the world-leaders that gathered at Davos 2019 for the World Economic Forum Annual Summit, not because these leaders see it as a nice-to-have but because they know urgent action on this is required now.

While the future is uncertain, there is a clear, upward trend emerging toward sustainable, conscious business. In fact, it's more than just a trend. We see a new kind of organization emerging. An organization which is able to rapidly sense and respond to the ever-changing business climate by constantly engaging, co-creating, and innovating with its ecosystem of employees, customers, suppliers, resources, investors, society and environment.

This new kind of organization is the *organization-as-living-system* and is a move away from perceiving the organization as a rigid, reductive, mechanistic hierarchy – see the illustration on the next page. These organizations will be tomorrow's success stories, while those that hold on to yesterday's logic will become yesterday's news. It's simple. It's evolutionary. Adapt or die.

# MACHINE TO LIVING-SYSTEM

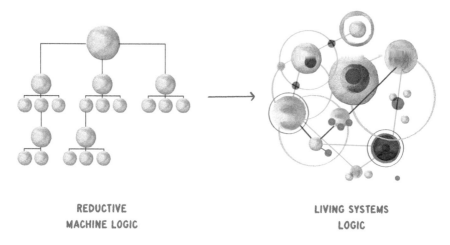

REDUCTIVE
MACHINE LOGIC

LIVING SYSTEMS
LOGIC

© copyright Hutchins & Storm – inspired by Biomimicry for Creative Innovation

We can talk about the people and the organizations making this paradigm shift and get enthused about the new direction we can see the world moving in, but the question remains: *What does this shift look like in practice?* It looks like a fundamental shift in leadership consciousness. The DNA of this new type of leadership is what we will unpack in the chapters ahead, but for now, in brief, let's begin to view any organization as made up of messy human relationships. Business is not neat-and-tidy, nor can it be effectively managed in mechanistic ways, because each organization, each business, is a vibrant living-system.

However, our ability to see the organization-as-living-system depends greatly on our ability to shift from yesterday's mechanistic logic to the logic of a new way – what we call the *Logic of Life*.

This metamorphosis in consciousness within our organizations demands a new leadership consciousness: *Regenerative Leadership Consciousness*.

THE ORGANIZATIONS
MODELED ON LIVING-
SYSTEMS IS A MOVE
AWAY FROM THINKING
OF THE ORGANIZATION
AS A RIGID, REDUCTIVE,
MECHANISTIC HIERARCHY.
LIVING-SYSTEMS
ARE AGILE, VIBRANT,
RESILIENT, RESPONSIVE,
INNOVATIVE, DIVERSE
AND REGENERATIVE.

# The Metamorphosis
# of Global Business

*The metaphor of a metamorphosis is a powerful one for the times we are in, and we like the beautiful metamorphosis of the caterpillar to the butterfly for obvious reasons. In the early stages of the caterpillar's metamorphosis to a butterfly, the caterpillar undergoes a 'breakdown' phase where the structures of old begin to dissolve. Amid this breakdown, 'imaginal cells' start to form clusters called 'imaginal groupings'. These imaginal cells are always present within the caterpillar (always present within our human systems) yet it is only amid the conditions of breakdown that they form these groupings.*

*Today we witness these breakdown conditions. To begin with, during this breakdown phase the caterpillar is caught-up in the logic of yesterday, and uses vital energy (antibodies and such like) to fight these imaginal groupings, sensing them as a threat to the status quo.*

*With time, and the persistence of these imaginal groupings, a tipping point or threshold starts to be crossed within the caterpillar (and within the consciousness of our own organizational systems).*

*The imaginal groupings are seen for what they are, prototyping the future, and with that vital energy is applied to nourish them rather than undermine them, and quite quickly the metamorphic process unfolds.*

*Ditto for our human systems; the persistence of new ways of being-and-doing is essential if the metamorphic process is to unfold in our organizations during these times of breakdown/breakthrough.*

# Regenerative Leadership Consciousness

As organizations shift from mechanistic approaches to living-systems, leaders will need to shift from the consciousness of separateness to that of interconnectedness. This shift asks us to look through the lens of adult developmental psychology applied to leadership. As the illustration below reminds us, our goal is to make the shift from the stage of *separation* to the stage of *reconnection*.

## THE JOURNEY OF RECONNECTION

DISCONNECTION/SEPARATION                    RECONNECTION

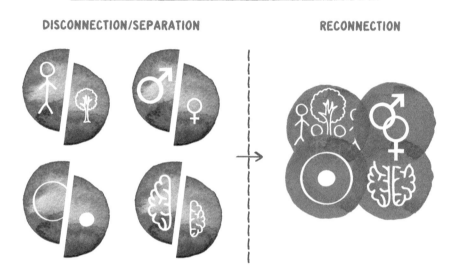

© copyright Hutchins & Storm

We can turn to psychologist Clare Graves work on human consciousness evolution (which underpins the work of Spiral Dynamics and also inputs into Ken Wilber's Integral Psychology). Graves' research revealed a step-change shift from Tier 1 Consciousness to Tier 2 Consciousness at both the personal (leader) and collective (organization) levels.

 *Dive Deeper:* If you are interested in the detailed research studies this exploration into leadership consciousness draw from, it is worth looking up Jean Gebster's structures of human consciousness culminating in

Integral Consciousness, Abraham Maslow's theory of psychological health culminating in self-actualization, Clare Graves' work on human consciousness evolution which underpins the work of Spiral Dynamics, Ken Wilber's Integral Theory, Jane Loevinger's and Susanne Cook-Greuter's work on self identity, Bill Torbert's and Barret Brown's post-conventional action-logics leadership research, and Bob Kegan's work on constructive-developmental levels of consciousness.

For the purposes of this book, we see a direct parallel between Graves' Tier 2 Consciousness and what we call *Regenerative Leadership Consciousness* – the level of consciousness now required by our leaders to enable our living organizations to thrive in the uncertain times ahead. Frederick Laloux's well-received work on Teal organizations also draws upon Graves' Tier 2 Consciousness. Laloux's Teal equates to the first level of Graves' Tier 2 – see the image below which shows the most relevant part of the Spiral Dynamics model for our exploration of this shift into *Regenerative Leadership Consciousness*.

# SPIRAL DYNAMICS

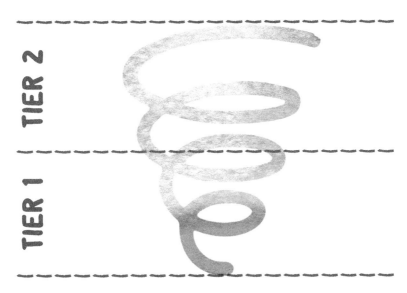

© copyright Hutchins & Storm – inspired by Clare Graves

As a model, Spiral Dynamics illustrates and articulates different levels of human consciousness. Let's hone in on the Tier 1 levels of Orange and Green, and the Tier 2 level of Teal and explain these in greater depth.

## Orange Level of Consciousness

The Orange Level represents the enterprising corporate consciousness prevalent across today's business thinking. At this level of consciousness, the main orientation is toward producing a good life and playing to win. Orange-thinking draws upon a mechanistic logic and prioritizes reductive analysis and sees mechanical cause-effect levels and power-and-control based hierarchies as the answer to organizational management. It's great at creating technology-led innovation to meet our needs, achieving material success, and engineering progress.

The organizational metaphor of Orange is *organization-as-machine*. The core values of this level are: success, autonomy, self-interest, learning through experience, meritocracy, professional development, and the power of science and technology-led innovation. The ideology of capitalist-consumerism is the product of Orange-thinking, and Orange leadership consciousness is concerned with hitting the numbers, capitalizing new markets, beating the competition, and management by objectives and financial incentives. Orange leadership does not concern itself with sustainability or ethics *unless* it is mandatory or directly impacts the bottom-line.

## Green Level of Consciousness

Green is a level up from Orange, an evolution of consciousness. The Green Level represents those who have become aware of how the Orange Level's singular striving for material progress has created imbalances, selfish greed, social inequality, and environmental degradation. Green-thinking seeks to liberate humanity from greed and selfishness by promoting a sense of community and restoring a sense of human equality.

The Green level of leadership consciousness focuses on an empowering human-centric culture to achieve extraordinary employee motivation for delivering stakeholder value. Green leadership likes consensus and recognizes the importance of emotional intelligence (EQ) and empathy in leadership. At this level of consciousness, sustainability, corporate responsibility, ethics, values-charters, sense of community and purpose, all rise up the leadership agenda. Yet, these aspects often tend to be managed and controlled by a mechanistic, silo'ed, consensus-driven approach and can get caught in the mire of rules and bureaucracy. Meetings upon meetings can stifle the vitality of the organization.

The organizational metaphor for Green is *organization-as-family*. The core values of this level are: community, equality, harmony and sensitivity for others and the environment. The Social Democratic and Liberal ideology is a product of Green-thinking and there is a lot of good work being done out of this Green leadership consciousness. Green is a healthy step up from Orange. It helps prepare us for the next stage: Tier 2 Consciousness.

Stepping up a level of consciousness from Green is a big shift – the shift from Tier 1 into Tier 2. Graves went as far as calling it *"a momentous leap for humankind"* (Beck, 2018). It is not something that can be rushed or forced, yet we can help create the conditions conducive for the shift to happen.

## Tier 2 Level of Consciousness

Unlike Orange and Green, Tier 2 consciousness is rooted in a systemic awareness of the interdependence of all the systems the organization interrelates with. The organization is perceived as a living, learning, adaptive system. Tier 2-thinking asks each individual to take self-responsibility for being part of this adaptive system, realizing that we are immersed within a 'pattern that connects'. Our inner-outer relations in everyday life are part-and-parcel of this 'pattern that connects' – how we show-up and interact with one part of the system sends ripples throughout the entire system.

"Our normal way of thinking cheats us. It leads us to think of wholes as made up of many parts, the way a car is made up of wheels, a chassis, and a train. In this way of thinking, the whole is assembled from the parts and depends upon them to work effectively. If a part is broken, it must be repaired or replaced. This is a very logical way of thinking about machines. But living systems are different…The whole exists through continually manifesting in the parts, and the parts exist as embodiments of the whole…As long as our thinking is governed by habit – notably by industrial, 'machine age' concepts such as control, predictability, standardization, and 'faster is better' – we will continue to re-create institutions as they have been, despite their increasing disharmony with the larger world. In short, the basic problem with [organizations] is that they have not yet become aware of themselves as living."

Peter Senge, Otto Scharmer, Joseph Jarworski, Betty Sue Flowers, leadership specialists

The Tier 2 organizational metaphor is *organization-as-living-system*. As leaders, we recognize that the organizational living-system is deeply immersed in myriad of ecosystem relationships within the organization and beyond, both locally and globally. Employees, customers, suppliers, investors, partners, communities, society, and the ecological systems – nothing is separate, everything is interconnected. The organization is constantly in dialogue with *all* of its stakeholders, just as a living organism within its ecosystem is constantly sensing, adapting and evolving.

Sustainability is integral to how the business realizes its mission, as there is an inherent understanding that all of life on Earth is interconnected and interdependent. Rather than silo'ed P&L responsibility and line-management, we find a desire for a more fluid and emergent way of working. It's about a coaching culture of learning, feedback and adaptation. Leadership is distributed. Meetings and decision-making protocols encourage a rich quality of interaction where people share in authentic and respectful ways while giving open and honest feedback, learning and growing as individuals and a collective. The organizational structure is much flatter; there is less parent-child behavior within the culture and more self-management – everyone is a leader, everyday a learning journey. Mission-driven purposefulness, self-responsibility and integrative wholeness are the essence here.

The core values of Tier 2 Consciousness are: inner rightness, self-learning, a life-affirming sense of purpose, self-and-systemic awareness, self-responsibility for cultivating the conditions for our true nature to unfold, and a sense of connectedness with all life.

Tier 2 leadership consciousness recognizes that people are no longer there to be manipulated for the gain of the leader, organization or shareholders. Instead every inter-relation becomes an opportunity to seek deeper authenticity and wholeness through sensing and responding with compassion, courage and vulnerability. This enables us to integrate imbalances inherent within the separateness of mechanistic-thinking (Tier 1). It's a psychological shift within ourselves and our organizations. This Tier 2-thinking equates to *Regenerative Leadership Consciousness*. The step-change from Tier 1 (Mechanistic Consciousness) to Tier 2 (Regenerative Leadership Consciousness) is not just a transition from one level of leadership consciousness to the next; it is a complete metamorphosis, an epochal change in worldview.

## The Metamorphosis into Regenerative Leadership Consciousness

This shift from Tier 1 to Tier 2 is not straight forward. Just like the metamorphosis of the caterpillar to the butterfly, the breaking-down of old ways forms a necessary ingredient in the breakthrough of a new paradigm. "*It is not merely a transition to a new level of existence, but the start of a new movement in the symphony of human identity*", notes Graves (Beck, 2018).

This metamorphic shift in consciousness requires leaders to work on themselves, to let go of old ways while opening up to what in our hearts we know is possible.

"We have to prepare for the next jump, or alternatively, face a potentially brutal and painful regression. The frustrations, confusions and the general discontent following the election of Trump as President in the US, Brexit in the EU, the fast-growing nationalism and polarization in many countries, protectionism, popularism, racism and the like are symptoms of a political/emotional energy build-up that ultimately could lead to an explosion… At the same time, however, these symptoms can be seen as small signs and indicators of exactly that level of dissonance that will precede a surge from the fading Green Meme to emerging Tier 2 Meme. This is an invitation to humanity to step-up, lead and prepare for take-off."

Teddy Hebo Larsen, co-author *Spiral Dynamics in Action*

The philosopher Ken Wilber famously said that each higher level of consciousness *transcends and includes* the levels before it. This is an important point. As we reach into Regenerative Leadership Consciousness, we are still able to draw upon and utilize the thinking of Orange and Green, as we have learned useful approaches and methods in these earlier stages. It's not about leaving it all behind but rather evolving to the next stage. The challenge and opportunity for Regenerative Leaders is to integrate Orange, Green and Tier 2-thinking amid every day pressures, while being aware of our own ingrained patterns of reactivity.

There are aspects of Orange-thinking that we need to know how to include, and also how to transcend. Orange-thinking hits the numbers, manages deadlines and budgets, drives efficiency in production, and keeps tight compliance procedures. All of which is necessary to the running of a business; however, the challenge arises when Orange-thinking dominates to such an extent that it undermines the organization's capacity to thrive as a whole. Likewise, Green-thinking is fundamental to developing a culture of respect, diversity, and inclusion. It is Green-thinking that helps us sense-in to the values and perspectives of our stakeholders and to form values-based partnerships that can generate significant business value. Yet, we also need to be able to transcend rules-based bureaucracy inherent in Green-thinking when self-management, creativity and agility are needed.

This image below shows the three levels of consciousness at the organizational level.

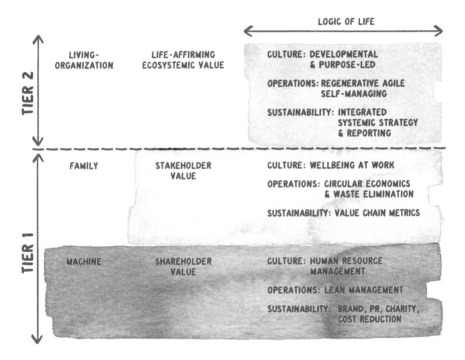

© copyright Hutchins & Storm

**Orange** is the base level – we need to draw upon this thinking. It provides efficient processes for organizational culture (human resource management) and operations (lean process improvement). Yet on its own, it provides for a mechanistic organization that lacks any deeper purpose beyond hitting the numbers. Sustainability tends to be limited to cost-reduction, compliance or brand and marketing initiatives.

**Green** is a step-up from this, and the culture is not limited to managing and controlling human resources, but more about empowering people while encouraging wellbeing in the workplace. The operational and sustainability mindset is more aware of the entire stakeholder ecosystem.

When we move into **Tier 2** the organizational culture, operations and sustainability approaches are more self-organizing, agile and fluid dependent upon the local needs and changing context. Leadership is distributed across all levels, and everyone is responsible for enlivening the culture, the operations and the sustainability of the organization.

While Tier 2 Regenerative Leadership Consciousness is crucial to the coming sea-change, leaders cannot expect every person in the organization to be operating at Tier 2 consciousness. Hence, we need to be able to notice when people, teams, and the overall organization is drawing from more of an Orange, Green, or Tier 2 mindset. *Where* is the organization's center of gravity, and *how* is this affecting the whole? In certain instances, it may be sensible for the team to be more in Orange mode, other times in Green mode, as long as the organization-as-living-system is supported by an overarching Regenerative Leadership Consciousness. Then, the leadership and the organization can transcend and include all three levels.

## Regenerative Business as the Next Step in our Evolutionary Journey

This next-stage Regenerative Leadership Consciousness consists of three terms you will become familiar with throughout this book: **Systems Thinking; Systemic Awareness; and Ecosystemic Awareness.**

*Systems Thinking* refers to the shift from mechanistic thinking to a way of thinking that perceives the inter-relation of the parts within the whole system and understands that all systems are nested within other systems. This shift also represents the shift from overly dominant left-brain processing to a more integrated left-right brain awareness, where we see the parts along with the relationships between the parts that contribute to the organization-as-living-system.

Systems Thinking is a shift in thinking that takes place at the head level. It relates to what MIT leadership specialist Otto Scharmer refers to as *open mind*. We open up our mind to see things differently, to see the inter-relations, the patterns and dynamics at the systems level.

*Systemic Awareness* refers to a shift in our relationship with the system. In Systems Thinking we are looking at the system from outside the system looking in. For instance, an organization may map out all the inter-relations and draw-up a systems map. With Systemic Awareness we take a step further as we take the map of people and processes and account for the dynamics, the seen and unseen tacit flows of knowledge, feedback and relational energy that are constantly fluctuating throughout the system. You might even call this the baggage that people in the organization bring into meetings, conversations and relationships.

Systemic Awareness embodies the way we listen or attend to others, the judgements or cultural bias we filter through, and how these factors contribute to the way we participate in the system. The history of the organization, any trauma it may be carrying, and also the cultural and historic systems it's inter-relating with all form part of the rich systemic picture we become more aware of. We transcend the level of observation to the level of immersion – a shift at the heart and body level. It relates to what Otto Scharmer refers to as *open heart* in his Theory U framework, where we open up our mind and also our heart and body to more fully sense into the emergent dynamics unfolding within and all around us.

*Ecosystemic Awareness* is reached when we open ourselves up to the full spectrum of all the nested systems we are part of – the human and more-than-human. We innately sense the interconnectedness of all life, and open up to a field of awareness that pervades reality, what we call the *Living Systems Field* (which we will explore in Part 2). In this opening-up to the field of interconnectedness, we integrate the human and nature dynamic we explored in Chapter 1, where we become attuned with nature, not separate from it. This shift from Systemic Awareness to Ecosystemic Awareness is a full-bodied and existential shift at the psychological and spiritual level of our awareness and relates to what Otto Scharmer refers to as *open will*. We open up our mind, heart and our will to be in service of this deeper field inherent in life. This further re-orientates our sense of self, place, and purpose in the world.

The three-step shift in consciousness of Systems Thinking (open mind), Systemic Awareness (open heart), and Ecosystemic Awareness (open will) is a very subtle shift within us, a shift in how we perceive and relate to ourselves, each other and the world around us. We integrate the inner-outer, masculine-feminine, left-right brain hemisphere and human-nature dynamics that came out of balance during our Journey of Separation. See the model below illustrating the re-integration of these 4 areas in relation to Systems Thinking, Systemic Awareness and Ecosystemic Awareness.

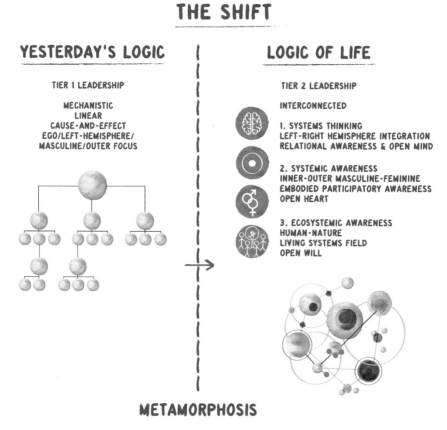

# THE SHIFT

## YESTERDAY'S LOGIC

TIER 1 LEADERSHIP

MECHANISTIC
LINEAR
CAUSE-AND-EFFECT
EGO/LEFT-HEMISPHERE/
MASCULINE/OUTER FOCUS

## LOGIC OF LIFE

TIER 2 LEADERSHIP

INTERCONNECTED

1. SYSTEMS THINKING
LEFT-RIGHT HEMISPHERE INTEGRATION
RELATIONAL AWARENESS & OPEN MIND

2. SYSTEMIC AWARENESS
INNER-OUTER MASCULINE-FEMININE
EMBODIED PARTICIPATORY AWARENESS
OPEN HEART

3. ECOSYSTEMIC AWARENESS
HUMAN-NATURE
LIVING SYSTEMS FIELD
OPEN WILL

## METAMORPHOSIS

It is a subtle yet powerful shift in consciousness, and the more we bring this Regenerative Leadership Consciousness into our ways of leading and living, the more we become Regenerative Leaders. We begin to live life beyond the illusion of separation; our leadership seeks to serve life, and our organizations contribute to life-affirming futures.

> "This is the true joy of life, the being used for a purpose recognized by yourself as a mighty one, the being a force of nature instead of a feverish selfish little clod of ailments and grievances complaining that the world will not devote itself to making you happy."
>
> George Bernard Shaw, writer

What excites us both in the midst of the turmoil our world is in, is that so much positive potential is brewing. This emergent next-stage of flourishing living organizations is what we call *Regenerative Business*, which aims to do more than reduce businesses' negative impact on life, but to create and grow businesses that contribute to the regenerative potential of all life.

*Regenerative Business* calls for *Regenerative Leaders*, those who cultivate organizations, city-developments, government policy, and entrepreneurial investments that move society toward life-affirming futures. Living organizations, communities and institutions can then thrive in a volatile world by benefiting all stakeholders, while attracting and retaining people fueled by a deep passion and purpose to serve life.

When we told Nigel Stansfield, President of Interface EAAA (one of the world's largest and most sustainable carpet manufacturers) that we were writing this book on regenerative leadership, his response was:

*"For too long many leaders have taken, competed and ignored our ecosystem focusing their business on simply making a profit. With wider societal awareness of the impact of climate change business leaders are now realizing that profit does not have to be at the expense of the environment. By creating real, long-term benefit and security for customers, employees, investors and the environment, alongside the communities and societies businesses serve we are seeing the emergence of Regenerative Leaders. This crop of leaders are taking back our planet and fronting organizations where purpose drives strategy and value. It is these Regenerative Leaders that will be financially successful and will make the greatest contribution to the planet, helping us to secure a climate fit for life for future generations."*

# Laura and Giles's Definition of Regenerative Business

*The word 'regenerative' means creating the conditions conducive for life to continuously renew itself, to transcend in to new forms, and to flourish amid ever-changing life-conditions. This primary principle underpins life-affirming leadership and organizational development, where our organizations help rather than hinder the logic of life. This goes beyond traditional CSR initiatives and sustainability as it is not primarily aimed at reducing negative impacts created by the current mind-set; rather, it is a move in to an entirely new mind-set, a 'new way' of being-and-doing in business and beyond.*

*With this regenerative logic: externalities become opportunities for additional value creation; waste of one output becomes food for another; stakeholders become partners to engage with through authentic communications and reciprocating relations; linear-thinking is replaced with systemic-thinking and circular economics; resources are not simply managed and controlled for short-term gain but perceived holistically in the wider context of the inter-relational matrix of life; rather than exploitation through manipulation we open-up into 'right relationship' with all life. Differing needs, perspectives, conflicting views and emotional dissonance are not avoided but given the space for something to be revealed through the tension into right relation. This is all about learning to become more human, while also focusing on the day-to-day reality of a profitable vibrant business.*

Regenerative Business enriches life. It enriches ourselves, our customers, and the wider stakeholder ecosystem. To materially benefit our customers while damaging the fabric of life, is a hallmark of the old logic we are moving away from. Such short-termism is no longer a viable business proposition for organizations wishing to thrive in the years ahead. This is a radical change in the perception of business and its work ethic – from it being a means to an end, a vehicle for paying the bills and acquiring power, control and material wealth to dedicating our time, resources, and creativity to initiatives that serve life. Regenerative Business transforms our role and purpose, from an essentially acquisitive 'what's-in-it-for-me' approach to a mind-set of collaboration, co-creativity, and contribution. Regenerative Leaders bring vitality and wellbeing to all our living systems for ourselves, our local neighbors, our global citizens, our children, and our more-than-human kinship. In-so-doing, we wake up to what it really means to be fully human.

> "If we truly live into the fact that we are life, that we are nature, and as such are bound by kinship and interdependence to the community of life that human and planetary health depend upon, we will come to regard the creation of a globally regenerative civilization expressed in exquisite locally adapted diversity as the creative challenge of our times."
>
> Daniel Christian Wahl, regenerative design practitioner

It requires great courage to relinquish the methods and modes of the old amid increasing volatility and uncertainty. For some, the first instinct in times of pressure is a tighter grip. *Does that sound familiar?* That when the going gets tough we stick to our comfort zone and our old ways of operating because, really, we're afraid. Afraid of being seen as insecure, unsure, not in control. Yet now, as leaders, we are called to let go and open up to a new authentic way. This new regenerative paradigm is not a pipedream. It's not utopia. It's about becoming more creative, more authentic, more purposeful, more compassionate, more in tune with life within us and all around us. It's simply becoming more human. And it's quietly going mainstream.

The pages ahead share insights, tools, business examples and a complete DNA model of Regenerative Leadership, which enables this metamorphosis to unfold in any – *in your* – organization. Part 2 draws upon a whole host of interesting developments underway, such as the rising interest in regenerative design, net positive operations, regenerative culture, and developmental organizations.

With the DNA model, you will have the capacities you need as a Regenerative Leader, and once you read on to Part 3, you will be ready to apply the tools and techniques in practice.

> "If you want to build a ship, don't gather people together to collect wood and don't assign them tasks and work, but rather, teach them to long for the immensity of the sea."
>
> Antoine De Saint Expurery, writer

*This* is what this book is about – it's about creating a deep connection with our own power of purpose and more clearly seeing how we can cultivate the conditions for organizations to be mission-driven regenerative systems of value creation.

THERE IS A DEEP
LONGING WITHIN
HUMANITY TO BECOME
WHO WE TRULY ARE:
LIFE-STEWARDS,
CARE-TAKERS AND
CO-CREATORS.

WELCOME ABOARD
AS WE SENSE INTO
THE IMMENSITY OF
THE *LOGIC OF LIFE*.

# INTERLUDE

# Our Story of Evolution Meditation

Before diving into Part 2 – where we explore the logic of life applied to leadership – we want to offer a different way for you to connect with your sense of place and purpose as a human-being here on planet Earth. This is a guided meditation inspired by ecotherapist Andy McGeeney; it's a story of our evolution. Relax into this meditation, and please take time to reflect afterwards. It provides a nice Interlude between Part 1 and Part 2 of this book, and we – Laura and Giles – often share this meditation on our Regenerative Leadership retreats and seminars.

*Before we begin take a deep breath, close your eyes and feel the connection and support from the ground beneath you.*

*Let us go back in time to an event that happened a long time ago. 14.7 billion years ago the Big Bang happened and all the universe was exploding energy.*

*We were there at the beginning – the energy that makes up everything here today was there in the Big Bang.*

*Energy attracted energy and formed atoms spinning through space and time, working at the speed of light over millennia, creating billions of galaxies. There was light and heat in unimaginable abundance – just as there is today. One of those galaxies was our Milky Way and halfway along one of its spiral arms, 5 billion years ago, an eddy of energy balled into becoming our sun – the main source of energy for us today. As other stars exploded they sent great swirls of gas towards our sun.*

*You were there too – remember?*

*The gravitational laws of attraction pulled atoms of stardust together and around the sun the planets coalesced. One of those planets, where it was not too hot and not too cold, became our home, Planet Earth.*

*To help our human minds grasp the cosmic times we're dealing with since the beginning of Planet Earth – that is to say 4.6 billion years ago – let us imagine Earth as a 46 year-old woman. Let's call her Gaia. We will now use her life, which is cosmically ours as well – to trace the story of Earth.*

*She was born as a fiery mass of molten metallic body. Comets curved into the solar system and provided elemental water for what became Gaia – The Blue Planet. Together with sunlight, water is the basis of life on Earth.*

*Fairly early in Gaia's life, deep in her ocean volcanic vents, the first molecules and complex compounds were forming. In time they grouped to form the first cells with strands of DNA. Every single plant and animal can trace its ancestry back to that these initial cells, which means that ultimately we are all related. Some cells were able to photosynthesize light and became algae. The byproduct was oxygen. Over many millennia a blanket of ozone was formed which protected life on Earth from the sun's harmful UV rays.*

*By Gaia's 8th birthday, bacteria had learnt to thrive in the oceans and atmosphere. These were the ancestors of the bacteria we all have in our gut, which help us digest our food every time we eat. All life shares this common lineage.*

*In the salty oceans of Gaia, evolution continued to bring forth new life forms: Corals, crabs, jellyfish, worms and eventually fish with backbones. We have in our bodies today the inheritance of our ancestors as they bred and evolved.*

*Do you remember developing a spine? Our backbone, nervous system, heart and gut come from our fishy ancestors. Can you recall wriggling through the sea? Can you still wriggle and flex your backbone?*

*The salt from the sea still flows in our tears and sweat. As embryos, we look like little fish with gills and a tail.*

*Can you recall using your fins to haul up onto the beach for the first time?*

*Gaia waited till she was 42 years old – 4 years ago in her life – before creating life on land. Fungi and plants began to move onto land and turn rock minerals into soil. Insects followed soon after. Reptiles evolved to seal their eggs in a water tight shell and grow a skin so they could live on land. Some developed into dinosaurs – only 2 years ago – and around the same time the first mammals and birds came into being.*

*Life evolves as survivors live to be old enough to produce the next generation. All the rest fall by the wayside and do not pass on their characteristics. We and all the living life forms today are descendants of those that did survive and succeed in life.*

*Only 3 months ago in Gaia's life we became great apes and began to use tools and think ahead, continually developing our intelligence and social skills. We are more closely related to chimpanzees than horses are to donkeys.*

*3 weeks ago we split off from the other primates as the climate changed and the forests of Africa began to shrink.*

*Our species arrived 2 days ago. Living in groups of up to 250 people we hunt and gather amid changing seasons – constantly sensing in to the rhythms and cycles of nature. We are in tune with the web of life, and play our part within this web. We use fire, make music and art. We develop the power of speech to form bonds, tell stories and pass on what we have learned to the next generation.*

*For most of our time as Homo sapiens we have lived as hunter-gatherers completely in sync with nature. We worshipped nature and Her ways. We were so finely tuned in with nature we knew the medicinal effects of plants and could communicate with animals. Our psychology and physiology developed over 200,000 years to live in harmony with nature. We were sensitive to how living systems worked, and were able to work with this logic of life.*

*What does it feel like to have a deep empathic connection with nature while being surrounded by a community you were born into?*

*An hour ago, we started to farm the land and introduced the concept of private ownership. We started to gather into large urban conurbations, and started to separate ourselves from nature – seeing it as something outside of us. When weather patterns changed and crops were damaged, we cursed nature, and even started to fear nature as the work of the Devil. And because women were seen as more in tune with nature at the time they too were seen as working with the Devil which started hundreds of years of witch hunts killing and torturing millions of women. The Scientific Revolution at the time was focused on the control of nature turning it into a commodity of forestry, fishery, agriculture and mining.*

*And with that mind-set of dominating and exploiting nature and women we have for the past 60 seconds gone through the Industrial Revolution. In these 60 seconds we have created nation states, mega-cities, governments, school systems, factories, corporations and a multitude of machines, cars and planes. The digital revolution, the concept of the internet, social media, AI and bitcoin has all just appeared this very second.*

*The majority of humanity now lives quite divorced from nature in towns and cities. We now use far more natural resources than Gaia can regenerate. We have become a destructive species out of sync with the web of life that sustain us.*

*Life on Earth is immense and rich but the systems that sustain us can no longer keep up with the way we Homo sapiens are choosing to behave.*

*Many of us feel a deep inner knowing that we cannot carry on this way. We may experience a feeling that something is wrong yet may not be able to put it into words. More and more of us are realizing that we need to radically change course if we wish to become one of the successful species that gets to continue to live on this planet.*

*Either we use our unique intelligence as a force for good – where we reconnect with our own inner nature and the natural systems we are a part of – or else we contribute to collective suicide by destroying the life-support systems upon which we depend.*

*Is our role as a collective to cultivate a more thriving way of life? How can we become a regenerative species and not a destructive one? What is **your** role in this greater puzzle?*

*What difference do you want to make in this time we live in – this split second of Gaia's life?*

***Please pause and reflect on our shared story and your role in our collective evolutionary journey.***

# PART 2

# The DNA of Regenerative Leadership

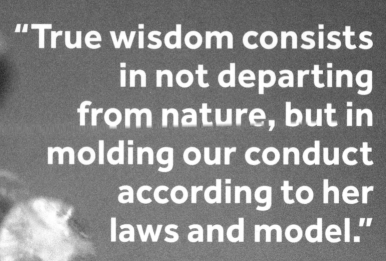

"True wisdom consists in not departing from nature, but in molding our conduct according to her laws and model."

**Seneca, philosopher**

# A New Regenerative Model Based on The Logic of Life

Many leaders often look a bit puzzled when we proclaim that the new leadership paradigm has to be based on the Logic of Life and rooted in the wisdom of nature. They question what we mean by *rooted in the wisdom of nature*.

After all, what could humans possibly learn from the forests, the ants, the fungi, or the changing seasons? Is the *wisdom of nature* just more fluffy hippy-dippy stuff, or is it grounded in real insight, evidence, examples, science, and research? How does it apply to organizations like mine?

This is what Part 2 of this book is all about – showing you how to apply nature's wisdom to organizations of any complexity, backed by science and real-life business cases. In the pages ahead, we will explore insights, examples and research from living-systems, including human developmental psychology as we humans are quite a unique species. While there is immense insight we can glean from understanding living-systems in the natural world around us, living-systems logic is not limited to biomimicry or bio-inspired insights (whether it be from the ant colony, termite mound, mycelium networks under foot, or swarm behavior of bees, for instance).

Regenerative Leadership draw upon the multi-disciplinary fields of complexity theory, cybernetics, developmental psychology, systems theory, holistic science, and more. For sure, we take learning from nature's ways of communicating, evolving and collaborating that have been honed over billions of years of evolution, and we combine this with recent findings about energy flows in complex adaptive systems, detailed studies on adult developmental growth within organizations, feedback loops within systems dynamics, and more. All of this contributes to a rich picture of how we view the organization-as-living-system that thrives through messy human relationships nested within systems upon systems of life.

There is so much we can learn from living-systems about how to equip ourselves and our organizations for the volatile times ahead, while bridging the *complexity gap* we explored in Part 1.

> "Termites and other social insects differ from us in many ways, but, like us, they are part of superorganisms, and they remain an excellent guide to understanding the forces that shape our societies."
>
> Tim Flannery, scientist

## The Elements of the Regenerative Leadership DNA

Here in Part 2, you will see how the DNA Model of Regenerative Leadership is all that any leader needs in order to unlock the Logic of Life to surmount everyday challenges and embrace potential opportunities while stepping-in to next-stage leadership.

We aim to provide the necessary depth of knowledge for the Regenerative Leader to feel equipped to lead and succeed within this new business paradigm.

As evidenced by the state of our world addressed in Part 1, what is demanded of leaders from all walks of life in this epochal hour of our existence is a transition to the Age of Regeneration. We have now reached a point in time where we *must* carve out a new way of living on this planet so that we can inhabit it for many years to come.

Business is such a powerful creative force on this planet; a force that is able to contribute either constructively or destructively to the future vitality of life on Earth. The new norm now upon us demands a new leadership paradigm, a new business worldview where profits are not at the expense of people and planet but aligned with the Logic of Life.

This DNA model of Regenerative Leadership embraces both the inner and outer technologies, tools, and consciousness that are required for the new regenerative business paradigm to unfold. It's a unifying framework that integrates vast bodies of research, different domains, and specialist methodologies – connecting the dots instead of creating yet another silo-approach.

We have been beta-testing our DNA model of Regenerative Leadership in our coaching and consulting work with leaders from myriad organizations (from small social enterprises through to massive corporations). We have showcased it at international conferences, seminars and workshops. And we have introduced it into our many conversations with practitioners and seasoned specialists working in this emergent field of living-systems applied to leadership. It is clear: There's a readiness for a holistic model that equally addresses the inner and outer aspects of how to lead and thrive in this next stage of human civilization.

On the next page is an illustration of the entire DNA model so we can sense its entirety before moving on to exploring its details.

The whole DNA model – the two interweaving dynamics and three components of Living Systems Design, Culture and Being – is set within the larger, real-life context of the *Logic of Life*, which is found consistent throughout all life on Earth. It's the core principles of how life on Earth operates.

In the pages ahead, we shall explore the Logic of Life principles in detail, but first let's get a brief overview of the two dynamics and then the three components of the DNA model (these will all be covered in greater detail in subsequent chapters).

# THE REGENERATIVE LEADERSHIP DNA

LOGIC OF LIFE

**6.DANCE**
**5.SILENCE**
**4.ABUNDANCE**
**3.PATIENCE**
**2.COHERENCE**
**1.PRESENCE**

LIVING SYSTEMS BEING

**6.ECOSYSTEMIC TRANSFORMATION & DIALOGUE**
**5.SELF-ORGANIZING & LOCALLY-ATTUNING**
**4.DIVERSITY & INCLUSION**
**3.DEVELOPMENTAL & RESPECTFUL**
**2.MISSION & MOVEMENT**
**1.SURVIVAL & THRIVAL**

LIVING SYSTEMS CULTURE

LEADERSHIP DYNAMICS

LIFE DYNAMICS

**5.ECOSYSTEMIC DESIGN THINKING**
**4.BIOPHILIC DESIGN**
**3.REGENERATIVE MATERIALS**
**2.CLEVER SHAPES & FORMS**
**1.WASTE EQUALS FOOD**

LIVING SYSTEM DESIGN

*Life Dynamics and Leadership Dynamics* – the two key dynamics of the Regenerative Leadership DNA - interweave all 3 components of the DNA model: Design, Culture and Being.

## The Life Dynamics

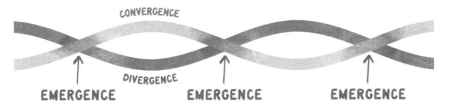

- *Divergence*: life thrives through opening up and diversifying; creativity occurs at the edge of boundaries.
- *Convergence*: life maintains balance and order by having a sense of purpose, alignment, boundary and structure.
- *Emergence:* life unfolds through the healthy tension between Divergence and Convergence; this tension impels life's Emergence.

## The Leadership Dynamics

- *Self Awareness:* leadership thrives through individuals' gaining perspective on their thoughts, habits, behaviors and blind-spots; we are able to reach beyond self-imposed limitations and open up more readily to life through self-mastery.

- *Systemic Awareness*: leadership thrives through an understanding of networks, flows and relationships within systems; we are able to sense how best to influence the organizational system toward life-affirming futures.

- *Regenerative Leadership Consciousness:* leadership thrives through cultivating both Self Awareness and Systemic Awareness; we are able to serve life attuned to nature's wisdom.

Then we have **3 DNA components**: LIVINGS SYSTEMS DESIGN, CULTURE AND BEING.

## *Living Systems Design*

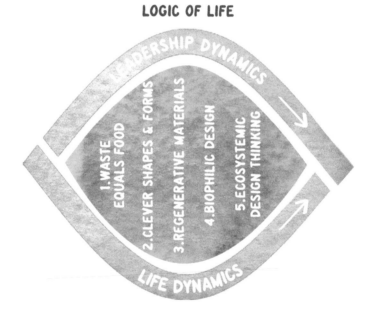

© copyright Hutchins & Storm

**Living Systems Design** explores nature-inspired design methods such as biomimicry, circular economics, cradle to cradle, permaculture, and biophilic design. Our focus will be on how leaders, engineers, architects, designers, and innovators can draw upon the wisdom of nature while designing new products, services, processes, structures, and places.

## Living Systems Culture

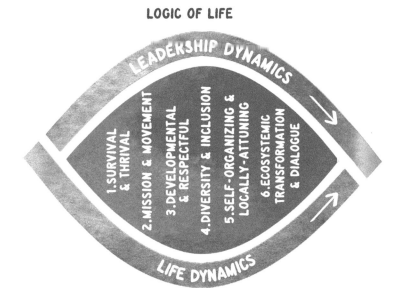

**Living Systems Culture** explores living-systems-thinking applied to organizations and communities and incorporates pioneering schools of thought relevant to exploring the organization-as-living-system, such as: Systems Thinking, Holism, Complexity Theory, Complex Adaptive Systems Theory, Adult Developmental Psychology and Integral Psychology, Deliberately Developmental Organizations, Evolutionary/Teal Organizations, Theory U, Conscious Capitalism, Systemic Leadership and Conscious Leadership.

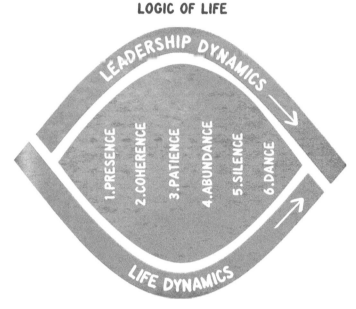

LOGIC OF LIFE

LEADERSHIP DYNAMICS

1.PRESENCE 2.COHERENCE 3.PATIENCE 4.ABUNDANCE 5.SILENCE 6.DANCE

LIFE DYNAMICS

LIVING SYSTEMS BEING

**Living Systems Being** explores our physiological, emotional and psychological nature and the qualities and practices we need as leaders to adapt, develop and flourish amid fast-paced business climes while tending towards harmony with nature within and around us. This draws on research from psychology, biophilia, neurology, quantum physics, ancient wisdom traditions, and other schools of thought.

Now we have covered the dynamics and components of the DNA model at a high-level, let's take a step back and see the model as if it were a musical instrument. Think of the underlying *Logic of Life* as the guitar, sax, or piano – you choose which instrument you prefer. We shall explore the ins and outs of the 'instrument' – the principles of the Logic of Life – very soon. Then, there are the two dynamics, *Life Dynamics* and *Leadership Dynamics* which are like the notes the Regenerative Leader uses to create the rhythm of the music so that we may dance to the music of life. Then, there are the three components, *Living Systems Design*, *Living Systems Culture*, and *Living Systems Being*, which are like the strings or keys inherent in the music of life.

Two questions have guided our work on this framework for next-stage Regenerative Leadership:

- *How can we be truly life-affirming in our collective way of doing business?*
- *How do we reclaim nature within us and around us in our modern-day urbanized lives?*

We shall respond to these questions throughout Part 2 of this book. We begin by studying and considering the *Logic of Life* for it is the very foundation on which to build life-affirming businesses and futures for all.

## Learning from the Wisdom of Nature

As mentioned in our evolutionary-story meditation in the Interlude, *Homo sapiens* have only been around for a few comparative seconds of our planet's entire life. 99% of this short time humans have lived on Earth, we have lived in deep connection with nature. For millennia, people worshipped nature, living in tune with its rhythms, seasons, dynamics, and appreciating its healing properties.

Yet, it only took humans the past few generations to rupture Earth's ecosystems wreaking havoc on the very life-support systems upon which we depend. Clearly, this is wholly unwise, some might say utterly insane. However, it is a by-product of the rising separateness that we addressed in Part 1 – the prioritizations of human over nature, masculine over feminine, outer over inner, and left hemisphere over right.

Despite the material betterments gained by our Journey of Separation, we now face the great costs of a world in urgent need of rebalance and reconnection.

In order for our new business paradigm to address this out-of-kilter situation, we must return to nature's wisdom, to the intelligence found in living-systems, to the *Logic of Life*. Nature is full of a rich, interrelating, self-organizing, and emergent intelligence: Let's put this to good use!

Award-winning scientist James Lovelock developed the Gaia Theory, which states that the entire planet we live on is a complex self-regulating web of interconnecting systems, all of which contribute to a whole that displays the ability to adapt and evolve through continuous change. Through this complex interconnectedness of all life, the Earth as a system regulates itself, continuously cultivating conditions conducive for life to flourish.

Earth has emerged, evolved and created fascinating creatures, systems, designs, and dynamics for sustaining life. Zoom in on the dynamics, the partnerships, the innovations and the principles at play in our ecosystems, and nature's systems become both mind-blowing and awe-inspiring.

Nature has a profound effect on our species. Simply by being in nature – or even looking at images of nature – our nervous system regenerates, hormone-secretion changes, brain-wave frequencies alter, our mood lifts, as does our capacity for creativity and empathy (more on this in Chapter 6).

The next evolutionary step for human-kind is to connect what we have learned and adapted during the Scientific, Industrial and Technological Revolutions with what we can learn from nature's wisdom. That is to say, integrate mechanistic analysis and advanced technological innovations with nature's insights and ecosystemic awareness. To incorporate the latter, we must renew how we engage with ourselves, each other, and the world around us. We must reclaim our own inner nature (our sense of self) and the connection to our outer nature (the natural habitat around us). We must reclaim our humanity and restructure our ways of living, our societies, and our organizations to be based on the *Logic of Life*.

Making this connection involves a healing process – a recognition of the inner and outer wounds we have inflicted on ourselves, on others, and on the world, and a reconciliation with the suppressed parts of our humanity at individual and collective levels. Thankfully, there is evidence that this healing process has already begun.

At the same time as we look around to see the polar ice caps melting, the plastics floating everywhere, and the politicians battling, we can also see this necessary healing process unfolding across the world:

- School children all over Europe going on school strikes and marches, demanding action from world leaders on climate issues
- The Extinction Rebellion 'XR' movement gathering millions across the world in nonviolent resistance to avert climate breakdown, halt biodiversity loss, and minimize the risk of human extinction and ecological collapse
- Pope Francis's Encyclical on Climate Change and his request for urgent climate action and a global transition to clean energy
- The official apology to indigenous people in Australia and America
- Near global support of and involvement in the Sustainable Development Goals
- The COP21 Paris global agreement on Climate Change
- The divestment movement (divesting from oil, coal, gas) gaining momentum across the mainstream investment community
- Rising interest in nature connection, eco-psychology, shamanism, rites of passage, 'forest bathing', biophilia, 'wild wisdom', glamping, etc.
- The rise of ancient practices to regain a strong inner connection, balance and wellbeing – like yoga, meditation, Tai Chi, etc.

These are the signs of a reconnection; a journey back to nature and to ourselves. In this regard, it is useful to study the ways of ancient cultures where humans once lived in communion with nature. This indigenous wisdom can help build bridges between our modern-day world and our old ways of being in tune with the natural world.

> "Virtually all native cultures that have survived without fouling their nests have acknowledged that nature knows best, and have had the humility to ask the bears and wolves and ravens and redwoods for guidance."
>
> Janine Benyus, biologist

## Reintegrate Indigenous Wisdom

From evolutionary psychology, we know that much of our physiological, psychological and neurological systems were formed hundreds of thousands of years ago, at a time when humans were living in tune with their natural habitat. Small groups – tribes of no more than 150 to 250 people – roamed the land as hunter gatherers. They were highly sensitized to the cycles of the year and the different ecosystems through which they traversed. These hunter gatherers saw themselves as part of the world that surrounded them, not as separate.

> "Our ancient ancestors existed in a state of full nature immersion. They had an in-built intimacy with their environment, with every part of it. It was essential for their moment to moment survival, being able to read the signs whether of poisonous plants, presence of predators or extreme weather looming."
>
> Rachel Corby, rewilding specialist

These ancient cultures worshipped different gods and goddesses that represented different aspects of nature like the ocean, forest, fire, earth, sensuality, fertility.

According to researcher Andre Van Lysebeth, the worship of the Goddess and God was an inherent part of all ancient belief systems, and speaks to an age-old deep connection with nature within and around us (Van Lysebeth, 1995). Core to these ancient belief systems is a continual attunement with the rhythms and cycles of nature. These rhythms are both physical and metaphysical. There was a deep understanding that the 'Mind of Nature' underpins and infuses all matter (Bateson, 2000). By honouring and connecting with the Goddess (Earth) and God (Universe/Sky), we tap into our deeper essence, our true nature (aka, Self or soul) which itself is immersed within and part of this 'Mind of Nature'.

These cultures did not consider a separation between the inner and outer realms of nature and aligned life with both the tangible and intangible worlds

– matter and mind, physical and metaphysical, physiological and psychological worlds integrated as one.

For millennia humans remained open to nature in a way that was lost during the Journey of Separation.

Anthropologist Michael Harner has studied different indigenous cultures and found that over millennia there has been a remarkable consistency of thoughts, beliefs, and practices among cultures, regardless of the geographic location across the world. No matter the region or continent, living in harmony with nature and revering its wisdom was the same. Harner coined the phrase *Core Shamanism* to describe the inherent commonalities of these ancient practices found throughout the world. These shamanic practices, which were central to living in a functional, sustainable and cooperative way, are what instilled connection, empathy and reverence for all life throughout these ancient cultures (Harner, 1990).

Core Shamanism provides us with a set of simple principles that can help reconnect humans to nature and offer an insight that should be part of the foundation of a new regenerative paradigm.

*Basic principles of Core Shamanism*

1.  Everything is made of energy (spirit).
2.  This energy/spirit is alive and conscious.
3.  So, everything is alive and conscious.
4.  Everything is part of a living, interconnected web of energy, which we humans are part of.
5.  By opening up to this interconnected web of energy, we gain a deep, heart-felt empathy with, and reverence for, all things.
6.  This helps us live in harmony and 'right relationship', with each other as people and the environment, and engage in 'right action'.
7.  Human beings have the (seemingly unique) ability to 'unplug' themselves from the web.
8.  This unplugs us from this sense of empathy, and 'right relationship' and we no longer act with 'right action'.
9.  This makes us ill individually, as organizations, and as societies (physically, mentally, emotionally and spiritually), and leads to us harming others and the environment. In unplugging and separating off we lose something profound.
10. Healthy human beings (and so, healthy human organizations and societies) feel part of nature, not separate from it; not above it, not better than it.

The principles of Core Shamanism illustrate that everything is made of energy and everything is interconnected, a notion that was banished from our worldview with the rise of the Scientific Revolution. In place of inter-connection with the natural world, humans began to focus on bits and bytes divorced from their natural habitat, and before long the reductive analytic and left-hemispheric way of processing had tuned us out of a participatory way of engaging with life itself.

Matter had come to be seen as divorced from mind and the physical was divided from the metaphysical. By the 17th Century humans and nature were perceived as separate, connected only through mechanistic, cause-effect relationships, and what scientists were not able to measure or quantify through reductive experiments simply did not exist.

Not until the turn of the 20th century did this neat and tidy mechanistic view of the world get ruptured by a new group of scientists – the likes of Einstein, Bohr, Plank, Nernst, Schrödinger, Bohm – each of whom made discoveries to prove the existence of an all-pervasive field. Today, many refer to this field as the Quantum Field or Zero-Point Energy Field. In this book, we refer to this field as the *Living Systems Field*, as it pervades all of life.

*Dive Deeper:* If you are interested in exploring the science around the Quantum Field and how this relates to the new emerging worldview, three books worth reading are Giles's *The Illusion of Separation*, Ervin Lazlo's *What is Reality* and Jude Currivan's *The Cosmic Hologram*.

The acknowledgement of the Living Systems Field is a key to humanity's return journey amid the Age of Regeneration, whereupon we begin to realize the innate interconnectedness of life once again. The ancient knowing of our shamanic heritage is now being revisited and renewed in our contemporary language of ecosystemic awareness, which draws upon an inner-outer attunement and an opening-up to the scientific discoveries of a Living Systems Field. Adult Developmental Psychology recognizes this return as the shift from Tier 1 to Tier 2 Consciousness, where at a higher level of consciousness we are capable of cultivating empathy with and reverence for the interconnectedness of all life.

Let us be very clear here. By no means do we suggest going back to how things were before we separated ourselves from nature. On the contrary, we can use our magnificent inventions and scientific revelations to guide us on this return journey amid the Age of Regeneration.

We make no argument here to start from scratch or go back into the woods and live in huts as hunter gatherers. No, not at all. What we are asking of Regenerative Leaders is to *reclaim* a way of living that draws on ancient understanding and nature's wisdom, and integrate this with our modern scientific findings and technological inventions.

The pages ahead distill this natural wisdom in a way that makes sense for business leaders while building on the work of the thinkers and teachers that have come before us. Understanding how life works is incredibly important when we embark on a journey of creating organizational cultures that add more vitality to their internal and external networks than they take.

Regenerative Leaders must seek to understand how we can mimic life's natural patterns, dynamics and principles. Only then are we able to translate them into an organizational setting. That is how we apply the *Logic of Life*.

## The work of pioneers we have drawn insights from

To help us gain an integrated understanding of life, we have drawn upon a number of well respected and well researched frameworks, principles and scientific studies. There are simply too many sources to mention here, yet some core ones worth mentioning are:

- The work of scientists, environmentalists and pioneers like James Lovelock, Tim Flannery, Rachel Carson, David Attenborough.

- The work of the well-respected systems-theorist Fritjof Capra, who has written several best-selling highly acclaimed books on the web of life, living-systems and eco-literacy.

- The work of the holistic scientist Alan Savory, founder of The Savory Institute, who originated a detailed Holistic Management methodology that explores the 4 ecosystem processes found within life.

- The work of the biologists, Janine Benyus and Dayna Baumeister, co-founders of the Biomimicry Institute, who have developed a set of Life's Principles to inspire designers and engineers.

- The work of regenerative practitioners like Michelle Holliday, Daniel Christian Wahl, Pamela Mang and Ben Haggard.

- Complexity Theory, Complex Adaptive Systems Theory, in-particular the work of organizational specialist Ralph Stacey, and also sociologist and urban scientist Jane Jacobs' work on energy-flow networks, in her book *The Nature of Economies*, supplemented by Sally Goerner, Dan Fiscus and Brian Faith's paper on Energy Network Science for system vitality.

- The Permaculture Design Principles that apply living-systems insights to place, product and culture design.

- The work of the pioneering and influential educationalist, statesman and natural scientist, Johann Wolfgang von Goethe, who recognized principles at work in organic nature.

- The anthropologist Michael Harner's Core Shamanism principles.

- The multi-award winning scientist Edward O Wilson's work on human-being's natural affinity for and connection with life, known as *biophilia*.

- The life-time work of the environmentalist and Way of Nature teacher John P Milton who has been a student and teacher of some of the world's oldest spiritual traditions including shamanism, nondual Advaita Vedanta, Buddhism, Taoism, Tantra and Zen.

# The Principles of the Logic of Life

So what are the principles behind the Logic of Life? What does it mean? In the following pages, we will explore the 7 principles of the Logic of Life to allow you to connect with them and see them at play in both nature and next-stage leadership.

## The Logic of Life's 7 principles

1. **Life-Affirming:** This is the over-arching principle. Life creates conditions conducive to life. The Regenerative Leader seeks only life-affirming activities and outcomes, being watchful for anything that could be toxic, life-denying, degenerative.

2. **Ever-changing & Responsive:** Change is an inevitable aspect of life we can embrace for the opportunity and leverage it offers us for learning, adaptation, resilience and evolution.

3. **Relational & Collaborative:** Everything in life consists of inter-relating, interconnected systems nested within each other. Understanding these interconnections frees our perception from seeing and thinking in silos and instead into systems.

4. **Synergistic & Diverse:** Vital to life is the presence of diversity and the working through of tensions into synergy.

5. **Cyclical & Rhythmical:** The emergent nature of life contains rhythms of cycles and seasons, that ebb and flow. The more we understand the pulses of how life flows, the more we can tap into nature's wisdom.

6. **Flows of Energy & Matter:** There are innate ecosystem processes that life depends upon, and as such everything flows in a cyclic interconnected way. Designing and operating with this understanding of energy flows enables us to recycle, reuse and renew in ways that do not undermine life's ecosystems.

7. **Living Systems Field:** Both shamanic and scientific evidence points to an all-pervasive field, a ground-of-all-being that informs all form. We have been brought up in an age where the understanding of this field is largely absent from how we see the world. As we step-change into Regenerative Leadership Consciousness, we sense the interconnectedness of all life and recognize this field of interconnection.

Let's now explore each of these Logic of Life principles in a bit more detail:

## 1. Life-Affirming

*Life creates conditions conducive to life.* Yes, the over-arching principle for all life on this planet is *that* simple. Pause for a moment. Reflect on what that unassuming sentence means to you: *Life creates conditions conducive to life.*

It was award-winning biologist Janine Benyus, who was able to capture in one sentence the notion that all life facilitates more life. Life, itself, is naturally life-affirming. This is the reason diverse species have been able to evolve through billions of years, at times enduring harsh and life-threatening conditions. When an apple falls from its tree, it does not create toxic waste, but sustenance for other organisms, the food for microbes and bacteria, birds, and worms, and within its core are seeds for new life. One apple rotting adds diversity and vitality to its surrounding environment. From the death of one part of the system emerges the nutrition for new life. Life simultaneously feeds on and contributes to itself, which goes beyond maintaining a status quo. Every cycle, every species, every creature, every person, every moment is different from what came before and what will come after.

To see this life-affirming principle in action, we can look to the ecosystem of a forest, which recycles nutrients and provides the conditions for its species to survive, thrive and evolve. Even parasites and viruses play their part in the interrelating emergent system. The forest is constantly breaking down the old and transforming it into new growth, while dealing with changing seasons, weather disruptions, or system-shocks (like a wild-fire); all contributing to the complex dynamics of the forest's continuous adaptation and evolution.

A continuous dis-equilibrium always exists in nature, as perfect balance would bring stasis, which would halt the energy of life and its evolution. To see the greater picture – the Logic of Life – is to see that within nature's imbalance every part finds its place within the whole, every species can adapt to its niche, and the overall system lends itself to a coherence within the creative chaos of constant change. Nature continually seeks harmony and allows rich diversity to contribute to unity.

Now, with this understanding of nature's ability and necessity to be life-affirming, let us observe the effects of modern-day agricultural practices. Take for example a land practice that clear-cuts woodland to grow monoculture crops, ploughing the soil every year and planting large-scale mono-crops (for instance, expansive wheat fields with no trees or hedges for miles). In order to combat weeds, insects and fungi, the farmer regularly applies pesticides and herbicides. And to increase the crop yield, the farmer applies artificial fertilizers. In maximizing crop yield, the diverse conditions for life to thrive are no longer in play. The artificial fertilizers, pesticides and herbicides create all sorts of imbalances not only reducing the regenerative capacity of the field, but also polluting the wider ecosystem with toxins. The capacity of the ecosystem to support the evolution of life is eroded. Rather than cultivating conditions conducive for life, we unwittingly undermine and erode life's regenerative capacity.

> "How can we live here gracefully over the long haul? How can we do what life has learned to do? **Which is to create conditions conducive to life.** Now in order to do this, the design challenge of our century I think, we need a way to remind ourselves of those geniuses, and to somehow meet them again."
>
> Janine Benyus, biologist

Instead of the widespread practices that erode the nature of life – such as mono-culture farming practices – we can create a society that is life-affirming. We do have a choice in what kind of community we cultivate and how it interrelates with its surrounding ecosystems. For instance, communities that are powered by renewable energy – solar, wind, hydro – are more regenerative by comparison than communities powered by fossil fuels. Drilling, pumping, and strip mining – burning underground energy-stores that pollute the surrounding air, land, and water – disrupts the natural carbon and water cycles. The use of non-renewable energy resources is myopic and life-denying. Today, the amount of fossil fuels humanity uses in one year took one million years to build up underground (Wahl, 2016).

Read that sentence again and take it in – *one million* years of energy reserves we exhaust in only one year.

The way our society chooses to feed and power our lives is degenerative. We can say the same for the materials we use to make our clothes, medicines, appliances, furniture, detergents, cosmetics, cars, laptops, phones, plastic sandwich wrappers – *everything*. Much of what we manufacture contains chemicals derived from fossil fuels and other resources from nature that have been mined and harvested in toxic and unsustainable ways. This is how polyester ends up in our fresh water supply, our food, and ultimately in our bloodstream.

When we depart from nature's wisdom, we humans run amok and wreak havoc. Not only does the concept *life-affirming* apply to nature, humanity, and ecosystems, but it applies to organizations – we explore this once we get into the components of the DNA model. For now, let's explore the next Logic of Life principle.

## 2.   Ever-Changing & Responsive

*Change is inherent within life.* Change occurs all the time, everywhere, and we can either be afraid and resistant to change by trying to control it or we can embrace it as a source of creativity and innovation, and ride change like a wave.

To embrace the ever-changing nature of life is to experience one of life's true joys: No two moments are ever the same. No two days or sunrises or snowflakes are ever the same. As the Greek philosopher Heraclitus stated, *we can never step into the same river twice*. Life is a river of continuous change; a song of ever-changing melodies and symphonies.

In this VUCA age, the ways in which organizational conditions change will only become more complex, more volatile, and more *in-your-face-all-the-time*, and we have the option to react with increasing fear and create more stress as we attempt to control the uncontrollable or instead embrace the challenge of change and allow the breakdowns of old systems to yield the breakthrough of the new.

> "It is not the strongest species that survive, nor the most intelligent, but the ones most able to adapt to change."
>
> Charles Darwin, biologist

Darwin's survival of the fittest is not, in fact, the survival of the most aggressive, competitive or dominating, but instead the survival of the species who are best able to adapt to change. By 'fittest' species he didn't mean the strongest but the one most able to *fit-in* to changing conditions by being the most agile and responsive; the same goes for our organizations.

Let us look at this principle in a species that has been alive on this planet for over 100 million years, one that far out-numbers humans: The ants. The success of ants boils down to their ability to adapt to their surroundings and work collaboratively together as an organization. Today, there are 14,000 different species of ant, each of which have adapted to different climates and can thrive in deserts, rainforests, wetlands, even cities by continually attuning to their environment. They have developed skills, such as using pheromones that provide feedback to the colony if a predator or an opportunity is on the horizon to mobilize others, move fast, and address the changing conditions. It is these self-organizing principles that make colonies of ants incredibly resilient, as they do not sit around waiting for the queen (or boss) to make a decision that then must be disseminated through the ranks. When it comes to ants, all individuals are responsible for sensing into their environment, assessing the situation, and communicating to others around them all in an effort to keep the whole colony protected.

> "Ants create strength from weakness by pooling their individually limited capacities into a collective decision-making system that bears an uncanny resemblance to our own democratic process."
>
> Tim Flannery, scientist

Akin to ants, our own leadership and organizational ability to adapt to change relies heavily on the sensing and responding capacity of our leaders and teams. The mechanistic way of structuring organizations around hierarchies of bureaucracy and control decreases organizational agility and creates cultures that reduce the individual's and the collective's capacity to see new potential and to cope with threats quickly and effectively.

This marriage of mechanistic stability and a fear of change is what has led to the soul-sapping stress-filled working environments we find prevalent in business today, and it is exactly this fear-based mindset that locks our organizations into a culture where true innovation is limited and evolution is undermined.

> "Change in nature happens everywhere, all the time, in a self-organizing urge that comes from every cell and every organism, with no need for central command and control to get orders or pull levels."
>
> Frederic Laloux, organizational specialist

Traditional assumptions about *change management* are what need to be challenged and transformed into a living-systems approach where business leaders enhance the personal and organizational readiness for change by cultivating a culture of feedback, learning, sensing and responding. Regenerative Leaders are tasked to establish teams of individuals who are able to tune in to these ever-changing conditions and make informed decisions quickly.

Regenerative Leadership is about unlocking the brilliance of our people by seeing change as an inevitable part of life. Change is what catalyses creativity, and brings fresh energy which we can tap into with the right mindset of playfulness, openness and curiosity.

## 3. Relational & Interconnected

*Life thrives through relationships.* No man is an island. Yet, the machine-mentality has encouraged a hardening of boundaries in order to atomize, control, protect and maximize our means of life, which has led us to a siloed mentality of separation. However, Regenerative Leadership encourages a permeating of boundaries in order to foster collaboration, shared value, and co-innovation, all the while maintaining respect for security, safety, local customs, and differing cultural values and ownership approaches.

> "Nature does not show us any isolated building-blocks, but rather appears as a complex web of relationships between the various parts of a unified whole."
>
> Fritjof Capra, systems scientist

Let's take nature's example of the awe-inspiring mycelium underground. Mycelium (fungi) works in partnership with the roots of trees, helping transport vital minerals and nutrients throughout a field or a forest. The mycelium also connects trees to communicate, sharing important messages about predator viruses approaching the forest (Wholleben, 2015). Scientists have now identified that trees are sharing nutrients with all sorts of different plant species and that this relational interconnectedness – facilitated by the mycelium – enables the forest as a whole and the individual trees to best adapt to change. *Facilitation ecology* is a growing area of interest for scientists studying how ecosystems adapt to change. It seems that life adapts and evolves best when there is rich relationality and interconnection (Wilson, 2014). We will explore partnerships in greater depth in Chapter 6 addressing what we call *living systems partnerships*.

> "Life on Earth has proceeded through ever more intricate arrangements of cooperation and co-evolution. Partnership – the tendency to associate, establish links, live inside one another, and cooperate – is one of the hallmarks of life."
>
> Fritjof Capra, systems scientist

The slogan of old was, *"It's all about the numbers"*. However, this old school of thought is now giving way to a recognition that actually, *"It's all about the relationships"*. Co-innovation partnerships (two or more organizations openly collaborating on a range of activities) and open-source innovation approaches (where organizational boundaries become far more permeable, with ideas openly exchanged, and collaborative prototyping activities embracing many different parties) along with co-creation hubs, open inno-vation platforms and face-to-face gatherings, are becoming the *new norm*. Organizations thrive on partnerships – just like nature.

*"It's all about the relationships"* is now challenging the ownership and con-trol mechanisms of our old ways. Today, we see Story Cafes, World Cafes, Open Space Technology, Hackathons, Swarms, Agile Sprints and other forms of collaboration sessions, each of which aim to bring together, include, engage, and empower people in ways that encourage listening, ideating and co-evolving in self-organizing ways that transcend traditional hierarchical decision-making processes.

This relationality is the life-blood of adaptive, resilient, regenerative busi-ness, and the more we increase the relationality within our teams and across the organizational silos and stakeholder ecosystems, the more we allow the organization to embrace the Logic of Life. Hence, like nature, the more resilient and agile the organization becomes.

## 4.   Synergistic & Diverse

*Diversity breathes new life.* As we have just explored, everything in life inter-relates in varying degrees, and the more we celebrate this relationality the better. In fact, every time systems collide, something new emerges out of the inter-relation.

Systems scientist Fritjof Capra notes *"The essential properties of an organism, or living system, are properties of the whole, which none of the parts have. They arise from the interactions and relationships between the parts."* (Capra, 1997). In mangroves, for instance, the sea's ecosystems collide with the land's eco-systems. The resultant is rich biodiversity.

As human development increasingly encroaches on mangroves, we are realizing the immense importance of mangroves for sustaining life and pro-viding regenerative capacities for both land and sea ecosystems. Also in our human societies and communities sociologists know only too well how a rich diversity of cultural backgrounds and perspectives yields creative vibrant communities. Difference provides creativity.

Our organizational systems are made up of relational tensions of difference, which unleash new perspectives, innovations, and creative energy that allow the living-system to adapt and evolve. Social psychologist Henri Mazel first coined the term *social synergy* when he recognized the importance of synergistic relations in human organizational systems. Synergy is where two or more inputs come together and form something greater than the constituent parts – the whole is greater than the sum of its parts. *Social Synergy* is where two or more people come together with different ideas and perspectives, and through the different inputs emerges something greater than the sum of the parts.

Although diversity and synergy create the tension that is the driving force of organizations, both are often overlooked in the worldview that see organizations as machines rather than living, relational systems. Unfortunately, many organizations often avoid hiring team members or employees different from the norm out of fear of difference.

> "Our uniqueness, our own special abilities that set us apart from each other as individuals, occur so that with such diversity manifest we should thrive; our differences allowing a flexibility, mutability, so that the beauty of life on this planet survives no matter what. And yet we have turned it upon ourselves. The most basic and essential truth of the universe has been lost along its way. And so, we experience our individuality, our uniqueness, as a separation from each other, and the rest of nature … We are lonely people scared of each other, of any difference, and rather than celebrating the abundance of diversity we fight wars because of it."
>
> Rachel Corby, rewilding expert

We tend to view synergy as two or more complimentary and cooperative relationships coming together to strengthen the greater whole. While this is often the case, there is plenty of evidence in nature and in human-nature of differing relations – those that seemingly oppose each other – colliding or coming together in order to release new opportunities, new systems, new life. In the case of humans, the strength of our living-system dynamics depends on how open, curious, and compassionate we are in holding such tensions, whether they be derived from opinion, race, gender, background, upbringing or perspective.

Human relationships carry inevitable tensions. Business can be messy. However, in Regenerative Businesses relational tensions are no longer nec-essary to mitigate, nor are they problems to avoid or shy away from, but the very things that enliven organizational systems and enrich productivity.

This is what the architect György Doczi refers to as *dinergy*, his own word created by combining the Greek *dia* (meaning across, through, opposing) and energy. Synergy and dinergy both involve a confluence of relations; however, dinergy further emphasizes that opposition is involved, and it is the integration of difference that provides richness, new insights, and new ways of operating.

As Regenerative Leaders we must seek to encourage people to bring more of their whole-selves to work – bring their differences and uniqueness to the table. We can work through our differences in ways that enable us to move further together, rather than one seeking to dominate and control the other, or one seeking to avoid tension by submissive behaviour. Tension speaks directly to the root of one of life's paradoxes explaining why at every turn we find opposing tensions – the yin and yang of life. The creative commu-nion between these seemingly opposing forces is what induces wholeness, growth, and breathes life.

This calls for leaders to open up perceptual horizons, to embrace diverse perspectives, and be more than okay surrounded and informed by views different than their own. Let us see that relational tensions are what create synergistic energy, which impels growth and innovation. No tension in a system signifies no aliveness, no learning, no evolution.

## 5.  Cyclical & Seasonal

*The seasons of life are at the very heart of nature's wisdom.* We see this everywhere we turn – the ebb and the flow of tides, the cycles of the moon, the sun, the seasons, death and rebirth, and rest and regeneration.

Emergence in life contains a cyclic rhythm. Emergence continuously unfolds through pulses and phases of development that can be likened to the four seasons.

**Spring** is the phase of new shoots bursting forth, animals leaving their hibernation and seeking new partnerships – a period of rapid innovation, growth spurts and development. **Summer** is the phase when growth rates stabilize as plants and animals attune to their surroundings – a period of incremental development through increasing efficiencies and effectiveness. **Autumn** is the phase of harvesting the fruits fertilized in spring and grown over summer – a period of capitalizing on the market-position yet aware of change in the air, a realization of the need to let-go of the current proposition, just like the trees dropping their leaves, preparing for a significant phase shift as life conditions change. **Winter** is the phase of letting-go; a breaking down of old ways to make space for reflection and renewal – a period marked by slowing-down, taking stock, and perhaps hibernation during which reorganization, reinvention, rebirth and renewal occurs.

These season-cycles are present everywhere in life. In our organizations, we witness the life of a product, seeing it through phases of continuous adaptation, learning, renewal and reconfiguration. We pioneer the new product or service, launch it into the marketplace, fuel its growth, and gain market position. Significant disruptions may affect the product's viability, such as new technologies, new entrants competing in radically new ways, or radical shocks to market conditions, and so the business enters a period of releasing and reallocating resources in order to reorganize, re-envision and sense new possibilities for innovation and investment.

The same cycle is apparent in creative ideation and innovation. There is the rush of excitement that arrives with a new idea, which then moves into prototyping and testing in order to bring the idea to fruition using high levels of energy to sustain its execution, followed by the inevitable need for a recuperation and incubation period to recharge the creative chambers to function again.

Take a moment now to sense in to the model below representing the season-cycle in a figure-of-eight rhythm. This model is what we call the *Rhythm of Life*. In our retreats and seminars we always dive into this rhythm asking the participants to check-in with where they are in their lives – spring, summer, autumn, winter – and to become conscious of the honouring of each phase at different times in our work-lives.

# RHYTHM OF LIFE

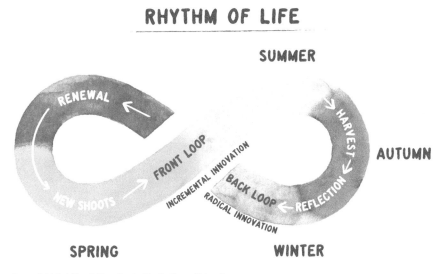

The cycles of creativity, growth, release and renewal can occur over long periods of time – a year, a seven-year cycle or a life-time – or over shorter time periods – a few weeks, a single day, or even a couple of hours of down-time.

 *Dive Deeper:* In their book *Panarchy* systems scientists Lance H. Gunderson and C.S. Holling explore how living-system ecological development phases form a continual looping round through a figure-of-eight cycle known as the 'adaptive cycle', and what we refer to here as the *Rhythm of Life*. Also in their book *What We Learned In The Rainforest*, former CEO of Mitsubishi, Tachi Kiuchi, and former President of Future 500, Bill Shireman explore in detail the application of these ecological phases or 'seasons' in business.

In nature, and in business, each of us experiences these rhythmic phases in our lives – the unfolding, growing, letting-go, reflection and renewal – as continual phases of breakdown and breakthrough. Each cycle can open us up to a deeper connection within ourselves and with our surroundings. It can feel like a mini-death to live through a divorce, a burnout, an illness, getting fired, or losing a loved one, but there is much wisdom to gain from these dark nights of the soul if we dare be with these phases of life and not rush on to the next spring without adequate reflection and renewal. These cycles of death and rebirth within our psychology are vital for the emergence of our authentic selves. The more conscious we learn to become of our own rhythms and cycles of psychological growth and renewal, the more effective, compassionate and authentic we can become as leaders.

## 6.  Flows of Energy & Matter

*Life depends on flow.* There are ecosystem flows at the biological, psychological, socio-economic, and ecological levels – referred to here as 'bio-psycho-socio-eco' flows for short.

At the biological level, life depends upon the flows of water, minerals and nutrients. We also know that the living-system of Gaia – our world's entire biosphere – has natural limits and boundaries that these flows of energy and matter must operate within. There are macro-flows, such as the carbon, nitrogen, oxygen and water, that operate at the global system level and also micro-flows and microclimates that vary depending upon the locality.

If we dive right down into the inner workings of our own cells, for instance, we find that each cell contains its own set of complex energy flows, and each cell inter-relates through flows of energy and matter with other cells around it. Cell biologist Bruce Lipton helps explain this: *"the quantum perspective reveals that the universe is an integration of interdependent energy fields that are entangled in a meshwork of interactions. Biomedical scientists have been particularly confounded because they often do not recognize the massive complexity of the intercommunication among the physical parts and the energy fields that make up the whole ... Cellular constituents are woven into a complex web of crosstalk, feedback, and feed-forward communication loops."* (Lipton, 2008).

What is often overlooked by the mechanistic perspective of yesterday's logic, is that our organizational and community systems also have flows running through them as well. These human systems depend upon the biological ecosystem flows that exist in nature in conjunction with the vitality of the flow of information, the flow of resources, the flow of relational and psychological energy, and the flow of purpose and meaning.

Recent research explores the behavior of complex adaptive systems and their network flows to show that an ecosystemic perspective of these bio-psycho-socio-eco flows is important in understanding how our organizations adapt and evolve in today's VUCA environment. The more we can study and understand the nodes, channels, fractal behavior and emergent unfolding of these ecosystem flows, the more we can understand and apply ecosystemic flows in the designs and structures of our organizations for optimal vitality and resilience.

 *Dive Deeper:* Christopher Alexander's work on *pattern language*, Warren Weaver's research on *organizational complexity*, Ralph Stacey's research on organizations as *complex responsive processes of human relating*, Steve Johnson's work on *emergence*, Jane Jacobs's work on *energy-flow networks* enriched by Sally Goerner, Dan Fiscus and Brian Faith's research on *Energy Network Science*, and so much more, contribute to a rich body of research exploring system vitality at the level of economies, cities, communities and organizations.

From this ecosystemic perspective, organizations are, indeed, energy-flow networks, and it is by understanding the nature of these flows that we can discern how best to stimulate energy or dampen feedback, as and when required, for optimal organizational resilience. As Regenerative Leaders, we learn to become conscious of the hidden, intangible patterns and inter-relations that make up our organizations.

Jane Jacobs's work on *The Nature of Economics* explores how the systemic vitality of an organization, community, or city can be enhanced by increasing the diversity of system circuits that recycle, reuse, and pass energy around the system before being discharged by the system. This helps us become aware of both the energy leakages within the organizational system and the opportunities for recycling this energy more effectively. Such mapping of ecosystem flows across our organizations provides us a topology of network flows, which we refer to as *Ecosystemic Mapping*, a tool we will explore in Part 3.

Regenerative development and design specialists Pamela Mang and Ben Haggard highlight the importance of identifying the flows of energy and resource materials that enable life, *"The significance of pattern, whether in a landscape, organization, or body, is that it can provide designers with a framework for understanding what is sourcing life in a particular place."* The 'nodes' are where flows of energy, resources and information intersect and conglomerate. Mang and Haggard give the example of a beaver dam as a node in a network, *"a convergence point, where the habitats for beavers, other mammals, birds, amphibians, fish, bugs, and plants overlap. This increases the quantity, quality, and diversity of the exchanges that are possible."* (Mang & Haggard, 2016).

Carol Sanford's work on *Regenerative Business* highlights the importance of sensing into these organizational flow dynamics in order to reveal the living-system's essence and to further find ways to develop and express its potential by learning how best to intervene at these systemic nodes – or acupuncture points – where relatively small actions can affect large whole-system change (Sanford, 2017).

Whereas ecologists study the ecosystem flows at the biological level, we need people within our organizations that can study the bio-psycho-socio-eco flows that our living organizations and communities depend upon. This requires a retooling of ourselves, from being overly reliant on linear business plans and mechanistic strategies to welcoming-in systemic tools such as Ecosystemic Mapping and Ecosystemic Facilitation.

## 7.   The Living Systems Field

*Life is an interconnected whole.* Yet, we are the products of the Journey of Separation and come from a generation that has been raised in a society that neither understands nor acknowledges the presence of a Living Systems Field that underpins, infuses, and connects everything.

> "Aboriginal cultures do not make the usual distinctions among rocks, air, and humans; all are imbued with spirit, the invisible energy. This is the world of quantum physics, in which matter and energy are completely entangled ... a world in which the whole planet is considered to be one living, breathing organism, which needs to be protected from human greed, ignorance and poor planning."
>
> Bruce Lipton, cell biologist

Even though a multitude of brilliant 20th century scientific minds, from Einstein to Schrodinger, knew about the presence of this all-pervasive energetic field, today it is still a culturally unpalatable reality for the majority of the population. However, as more and more scientific evidence mounts – corroborating what many of us often intuit – we are beginning to see more and more business leaders openly acknowledging the presence of this energetic field. This increasing awareness of a Living Systems Field coincides with the shift in consciousness sweeping across today's society, one that we are able to witness as individuals move from Tier 1 Consciousness to Tier 2 Regenerative Leadership Consciousness.

More and more people of all ages are becoming more comfortable with what philosophers, mystics, and shamans throughout the ages have long understood and what pioneering scientists are now showing in their research. With today's sophisticated scientific instruments, we can now peer straight into the atoms and sub-atomic particles within our own cells where we do not find the hard, massy, impenetrable objects of Newtonian physics. We find quark strings and vibrations of light, each humming away to their own unique tune. These sub-atomic particles, which exist within every atom within every cell, exist in the all-pervasive field, the field that pervades your entire body, the entire room you are sitting in now, the entire planet, the entire solar system, and universe.

A nature metaphor may be useful here. Take the waves on the ocean. Each wave has its own form. No two waves are ever the same. And yet the wave is never separate from the ocean. This is the same for the energetic vibrations within our cells. Everything is immersed within this oceanic field, never separate from it. It is only our mechanistic minds that create this sense of separation. All matter in the universe is connected by waves of energy, and the Living Systems Field is the underlying ground energy for all energy fields that inform all matter.

In fact, there are now many scientists that believe this underlying field contains a dimension of consciousness that informs all energy fields found throughout all physical form. The scientist Stephen Schwartz notes that *"the spacetime Yang of the physical energy dimension and the nonlocal [field] Yin of the dimension of consciousness and information are intrinsically interconnected and related."* (Laszlo, 2016). Our physical dimension, that which we can sense and touch, is pervaded by a dimension of consciousness we cannot see or touch, yet one that we can tap into. In fact, we are always in the field, and it is simply a case of becoming conscious of our participation within it.

According to the award-winning scientist Dr Ervin Laszlo, this primordial ground holds all memory and thought in the universe, creating an interconnected, irreducible whole that we all form a part of. Our mind, rather than being the originator of consciousness, is actually a sensing-and-responding organ that allows us to pick up on the right frequencies emanating all around and within us. The brain, the heart, and the gut are the neurological centres we have within us that help us make sense of the consciousness inherent within the Living Systems Field.

Psychologist Carl Jung referred to this field as the *collective unconscious*. He found that each of us, by means of the process of *individuation*, can learn to become more conscious of our own unconscious shadows and also the wider unconscious aspects influencing cultural life. This process of individuation is what supports the shift from Tier 1 to Regenerative Leadership Consciousness and is what enables us to become more conscious of the field and our sense of place and purpose within this interconnected world (we revisit *individuation* in Chapter 5).

Our lives, our relations, our thoughts and feelings are all immersed and participating within this field of consciousness that is evolving all the time while we participate within it. We can either ignore it, as we have largely done since the Scientific Revolution, or we can start to become conscious of it once again, like the ancients were, and like many next-stage conscious leaders are today.

Recall Michael Harner's Core Shamanic Principles, which are based on the fact that everything is energy, and everything is connected. Well, pioneering scientists, with their increasingly sophisticated instruments and experiments, are also realizing that everything is energy, and everything is connected.

To summarise, the Logic of Life is as rich as it is deep. As we shift our leadership consciousness from mechanistic Tier 1 to ecosystemic Tier 2 Regenerative Leadership Consciousness, we open-up our minds, hearts and wills to be in service of life. This comprehension of the Logic of Life enables us to sense and respond to the ever-changing inter-relational ebbs and flows, complexities and synergies inherent in the organization-as-living-system. From this Regenerative Leadership Consciousness, we can enable the health and vitality of the living organization to be optimized, while providing places of work, products and services that enhance instead of undermine life.

The Logic of Life is the foundation upon which the DNA model is rooted. Now we shall explore the two dynamics that thread through the entire DNA model: The Leadership and Life Dynamics.

"Your vision will become clear only when you can look into your own heart. Who looks outside, dreams; who looks inside, awakes"

Carl Jung, psychologist

Photo credit: Abishek Pawar

# The Two Dynamics in Regenerative Leadership

In this chapter, we will explore the two key dynamics that weave through the entire DNA model and its three components.

You may recall the music analogy mentioned earlier – the underlying Logic of Life infusing the entire DNA model, and the two dynamics – *Life Dynamics* and *Leadership Dynamics* – that weave through the model like the notes the Regenerative Leader uses to create the right rhythm and beat for next-stage organizations to thrive. *Life Dynamics* relate to collective tensions we find throughout all living-systems, including our teams and organizations. *Leadership Dynamics* relate to the individual capacities we each need to cultivate as leaders in order to tune in, adapt, and evolve amid transformative and challenging times. Let's explore each in turn, starting with the *Life Dynamics* of living-systems applied to organizations.

## Life Dynamics

*Life Dynamics* embody the rhythmic tension of *Divergence* and *Convergence* that creates *Emergence*.

*Divergence* is opening up, diversifying, and exploring. *Convergence* is bringing together, aligning, and consolidating. Together they create a tension that creates the right rhythm and vibrancy for life's emergent evolution to unfold. Philosopher Alfred North Whitehead referred to *Emergence* as *nature's creative advance*. It is the way of life – the way life adapts and unfolds to the ever-changing terrain.

The Life Dynamics of *divergence-convergence-emergence* lie at the heart of how living-systems behave. In the model below you can see how the dynamics of convergence and divergence alchemize to create emergence.

## LIFE DYNAMICS

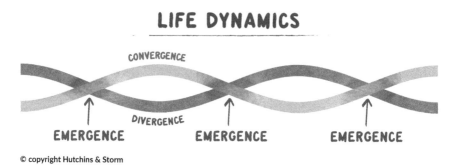

© copyright Hutchins & Storm

Let's dive deeper in to this exciting aspect of nature's wisdom, by unpacking what we actually mean by divergence, convergence and emergence when applied to our organizational living-systems.

### Divergence: Opening Up, Exploring, Experimenting, Connecting

As we know from the Logic of Life, living systems thrive by means of diversity and diversification which enable the living-system to open up, create, adapt, relate, and evolve. Life itself banks on diversity and cross-pollination. Rather than the monocultural, corporate mentality we see practiced in many areas of society, we need to think outside the box and invite in unconventional mindsets, work across departments, and bring in different perspectives. The best ideas are not born in silos or by avoiding feedback and input from a broad spectre of stakeholders; the best ideas are created by going beyond borders and getting curious about other approaches, cultures and procedures.

Diversity and diversification has brought innovation throughout human history. By example, The Silk Road – the interconnected set of trade routes through Europe, China, and Africa, dating back to prehistoric times – became increasingly important to traders during the 14th century. Goods such as silks, perfumes, spices, jewelry and pottery were traded on route but the trades were not limited to material goods. The Silk Road was just as well-known for being a cultural exchange, as it allowed the cross-pollination of ideas and perspectives from far-flung cultures, religions and artistic styles that inspired European painters, designers, artists, architects, chefs and musicians (Puchner, 2012).

Cultural cross-pollination is also what brought Howard Schultz, the owner of a few coffee shops in Seattle, massive success. After a visit to Italy in 1983 he saw that the American coffee-culture was lacking something: Ambience and good quality coffee. With that inspiration, he changed the concept of his cafes and the Starbucks chain took off.

In relation to the Regenerative Leader, divergence is seen as welcoming diversity in terms of age, creed, culture, gender and differing perspectives across the working environment. Leaders can stimulate divergence by working across boundaries both within the organization (holding space for people from different silos across the business to share perspectives) and beyond the organization (holding space for external stakeholder groups to share perspectives).

*Business Insight: IKEA – a global furniture manufacturer and distributor.* IKEA successfully embarked on a 'Future Search' workshop to design a new global approach to product design, manufacturing and distribution. What usually would have taken months of complex systems design and rounds of sign-off and agreement, IKEA managed to do in 3 days. 58 stakeholders, decision makers and executives from around the world worked together in a convivial creative atmosphere, sharing perspectives across silos and stakeholder groups. The outcome of this 3 day workshop far exceeded what would have normally taken months, as people gained an embodied experience of the whole system enabling them to relate and empathize with other stakeholders more effectively. It led to better working relations post-workshop and helped the success of implementing the strategy.

In Regenerative Businesses divergence is encouraged by way of distributing decision-making, which ensures that key decisions are not made by the few but spread throughout the organization. Decentralized decision-making empowers responsiveness to change at the local level, encouraging people to tune in to local changes without having to rely on control-based hierarchies. Divergence enlivens the organization. We free up our roles, positions, and decision-making protocols from outdated and burdensome mechanistic managerial procedures which more often than not stagnate creative energy.

Organization specialists Henri Lipmanowicz and Keith McCandless point out that today's operational convention of agenda-inspired meetings, managed discussions, status reports, and weekly presentations is often designed to control and direct rather than to include, inspire and engage. Yet, by introducing tiny shifts in the way people hold meetings, host workshops, and engage in conversations, an organization can transform decision-making and in turn unleash the latent creative potential of its people. The outcome will be better decisions, more innovation, and improved sociality, whereupon each member of the organization will feel more connected, empowered, responsible, and liberated.

*Dive Deeper:* Henri Lipmanowicz and Keith McCandless have come up with a menu of 33 well defined yet simple structures that are designed to allow the inclusion of everyone across all levels of the organization and stakeholder community. They refer to these simple structures as *Liberating Structures* in their book of the same title.

## Convergence: Bringing Together, Consolidating, Grounding

Alongside the opening-up, exploring, experimenting and connecting, we must also align different perspectives and consolidate our findings. Without alignment and focus, an organization can become too chaotic and fail to deliver its strategic intent as it gets pulled this way and that. Traditionally, organizational alignment and focus has been achieved through power-based hierarchies of control and bureaucracy, coupled with neatly defined 3-year business plans and fixed quarterly targets. This desire for control and certainty is rooted in yesterday's logic, and we believe it heavily saps the organization from unleashing its creative potential, ingenuity and aliveness.

Still, we do need focus. We need it to bring all of the inspiration and input together in a cohesive, collective understanding in favor of the strategic direction and mission of the organization.

*Purpose* becomes the critical driver in providing the kind of focus that brings divergent perspectives together and inspires agile teams working across boundaries to bring coherence across the vibrant living system. To be clear, what we mean by purpose here is not the re-jigging of mission statements, a shiny new values-charter posted on the wall, or the engagement of an expensive external consultancy to come up with new slideware cleverly defining the mission and values. No, we need to cultivate what we call a *resonant sense of purpose*, from the inside out, which can only occur when a number of people in an organization resonate with the organizational purpose.

Recent studies indicate that as little as 10% of people are needed to create a tipping point for organizational-wide change to start happening. One such study from Social Cognitive Networks Academic Research Center (SCNARC) at Rensselaer, used computational and analytical methods to discover the tipping point where a minority belief becomes the majority opinion. *"When the number of committed opinion holders is below 10%, there is no visible progress in the spread of ideas. It would literally take the amount of time comparable to the age of the universe for this size group to reach the majority"* said SCNARC Director Boleslaw Szymanski who led the study, adding: *"Once that number grows above 10 percent, the idea spreads like flame."* (Rensselaer Polytechnic Institute, 2011).

The Arab Spring, the Climate School Strike movement, the Occupy movement, the Extinction Rebellion movement, are all examples of self-organized social movements that spread like fire once this threshold is reached.

The same is seen within teams and organizational cultures. When the number of people who resonate with the organizational purpose reaches a threshold, something extraordinary happens. The living-system experiences a shift in consciousness, and it becomes much easier for the organization to start letting go of power-based hierarchies, or, at least, begin running them in tandem with more self-organizing, divergent, and agile ways of operating.

This magnetizing power of purpose takes its root in the everyday values, beliefs, and behaviors within the organizational culture. We explore this power of purpose and values-based culture when we explore the DNA Component of Living Systems Culture in Chapter 7, but for now, it is important to understand convergence as an aligning, cohering power created through heart-felt values and purpose rather than fear-based power and control.

*Business Insight: CWB Systems – an IT services company.* A couple of decades ago, the founder Christiane Wuillamie grew the company around 100% year-on-year into a multi-million-pound enterprise. She puts this company success down to the rich values-based culture and leadership style the company nurtured over the years. Wuillamie recalls that she took the company through a culture transformation where everyone in the company, regardless of hierarchic position, went through experiential workshops to explore and experience the values that would become core to the company culture. Every stage of the employee process was linked to the values, as was managing performance. Volunteers across the company became 'culture champions'. When speaking about these champions Wuillamie notes: *"Those are the kind of people who usually have a lot of what I'd call, some irritating aspects, like overly creative, or the vocal shop steward who always complains. We channel their energy to being the leaders of our corporate culture. And when you turn those around, it's almost a magical effect"* (Gowing, Langdon, 2017). Profits soared, customer feedback improved, employees were happier and more motivated.

It is through a resonant sense of purpose and rich values-based culture that Convergence counter-balances Divergence, so that the organization finds its flow, its sweet rhythm of Emergence amid a volatile world.

*Business Insight: W. L. Gore Associates – a global manufacturing organization.* As a business, W. L. Gore has out-performed in a highly changeable and competitive landscape for decades due to its agility and flat hierarchy.

Everyone in the business is at the same level in the hierarchy regardless of tenure or expertise, and everyone operates by the same basic rules of fairness and equity, with everyone having the autonomy and self-respon-sibility to tackle issues as they come across them while ensuring they seek out the relevant expertise in finding suitable solutions. Not only is the company able to become highly profitable and adaptable in a competitive fast-moving landscape but it also regularly wins 'best employer of the year' awards and can attract and retain high quality talent wishing to work in such a purposeful environment.

Going back to the examples used when describing divergence – the Silk Road and Howard Schultz's success with Starbucks: When chefs and archi-tects brought back spices and architectural ideas they then translated this inspiration into inventions and designs that would fit in to the niche and market in which they were operating. The massive success of Chicken Tikka Masala in the UK is an example of a recipe translated to fit into its local market as the British people loved eating their meat with gravy. And for Howard: He went back and consolidated his idea into a concept that has a coherence, a convergent quality, regardless of whether you visit a Starbucks café in Seattle, Sydney or Singapore.

## Emergence: The Alchemy of Divergence and Convergence

Emergence is how life expresses itself. All living-systems have an emergent quality, and as Regenerative Leaders, we can learn to tune in to the emer-gent dynamics at play within the organizational living-system. Emergence is self-generating, and emergent systems exhibit synergistic effects. This is the nature of nature, where individual parts of an ecosystem interact to catalyze the unfolding of events and the creation of life. This emergent synergy is what feeds the aliveness and growth of the living-system.

From slime mold to ant colonies and bee swarms, from self-learning computer games to advanced web-analytics, from local community behavior to city planning, emergence is the key to how complex adaptive systems unfold. In organizations, we find a sea of unpredictable local relationships. People are conversing next to the coffee machine, down the corridor, In meeting rooms, across email, or on whatsapp, all of which are interactions that contribute to the vitality and aliveness of the organization as it adapts to its ever-changing context.

Ralph Stacey, an organizational complexity theorist, refers to this as *"complex responsive processes of human relating"* (Stacey, 2012). A whole host of human relationships form through informal and formal communications, such as organized meetings, office gossip, after-work socials, cliques, and power relations. Collective adaptation emerges from the individual members striving to adapt and enhance themselves and their relationships while also aligning to the overarching purpose, values, and intent of the whole.

In fine-tuning the tension of *divergence* (opening-up, exploring, experimenting, connecting) with *convergence* (bringing-together, cohering, consolidating) we encourage liberation from the bottom up and the freedom to self-organize and contribute to the whole in ways that serve the evolutionary potential of the living organization. We allow a *river of life* to emerge as a constant presence, a continual flow, within the living organization: the flow between the river-banks of *divergence* and *convergence* creates the river's *emergence*.

> "Those who flow as life flows know they need no other force."
>
> Lao Tzu, ancient philosopher

# THE RIVER OF LIFE

*Do you get the impact of this?* Regenerative Leaders can allow for opening-up, exploration, stakeholder-dialogues, out of the box thinking, and wildly creative employees because coherence is provided through clear values, a resonant sense of purpose, and simple ground-rules guiding everyday business behavior.

It is this alchemy of divergence-convergence-emergence that enables the organization as a whole to continuously sense, respond and evolve in a VUCA world. The role of the Regenerative Leader is to be able to play with the tensions of convergence and divergence in order to spawn the right level of emergence appropriate for the ever-changing environment the organization is operating within. In Part 3 we explore tools to enable this right blend of *divergence-convergence-emergence*.

## Leadership Dynamics

Leadership Dynamics are the counterbalance to Life Dynamics. They are about how you, as a leader, individually show-up during the day-to-day of organizational life. The Leadership Dynamics are *self-awareness* and *systemic-awareness* alchemizing to create Regenerative Leadership Consciousness.

Self-awareness and Systemic-awareness are the two essential capacities that help us reach beyond the *complexity gap*. The alchemy of self-awareness and systemic-awareness enables us to cross the threshold in leadership consciousness from mechanistic to living-systems and shift our worldview from one of separateness to one of interconnectedness. See the model below, showing this alchemy of self-awareness and systemic-awareness spawning Regenerative Leadership Consciousness.

## LEADERSHIP DYNAMICS

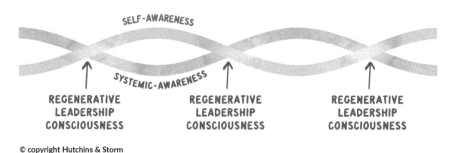

© copyright Hutchins & Storm

Let's now take each dynamic in turn, starting with self-awareness.

### *Self Awareness*

When the 75 members of the Stanford Graduate School of Business's Advisory Council were asked to recommend the most important capability for leaders to develop, their answer was nearly unanimous: Self-awareness (Elworthy, 2014).

Self-awareness is first-and-foremost about us getting to know ourselves, so that we can build confidence and keep our projections, insecurities, and shadows at bay so we don't undermine our engagement with life. It is a lack of self-awareness – which we unfortunately see in many c-level executives today – that creates friction and negative ripple effects throughout the organization. Emotional outbursts, envy, finger-pointing, back-stabbing, ego-boosting to protect an insecure ego, serve as only a few examples of typical behavior patterns in people who shy away from exploring their inner landscape.

As leadership specialist Richard Barret wisely puts it: *"To become proficient in personal mastery, you have to realize that no one or no situation can upset you. You always upset yourself. Every bout of impatience, frustration, or anger is self-generated. The situation, actions, or words of the other person are simply the triggers that bring up the conscious or subconscious fears of your ego and cause you to either project the venom of your unresolved emotional scars out into the world or sit nursing your irritation and becoming increasingly grumpy and disconnected. If you want to stop behaving in these ways, you need to own your reactions and make yourself accountable for every emotion, feeling and thought you have. Please understand this. Nobody ever upsets you. You upset yourself"* (Barrett, 2010).

Many of us experience non-stop mental chatter. Whether in a meeting or commuting to work or relaxing on the weekend, there is often a backdrop of mental noise within us, sometimes racing away, other times quietening down a bit. At times this mind-chatter is filled with worry, fear, and sadness. Other times, it's an ongoing assessment of *every* minor detail in our lives. *"Why was I not invited to that dinner? Why did he have that tone in the meeting? Why did I not say anything? What should I have said?"*

*Does this sound familiar?* The good news is that we can turn these worries into a powerful force if we learn how to train and tame our inner dialogue and to improve its quality so that our constant thoughts serve a more life-affirming way of living and leading: regenerative instead of degenerative.

Thoughts, opinions, assumptions, and worries about what has been (the past) or what might be (the future) can stir up emotions inside us which trigger anxiety, stress, and distraction. Before we know it, this mental noise has created a version of life that is not reality – not what is happening right before us. If we were able to release ourselves from this mental chatter, we could experience life in a less distracted, more present, more joyful way, and more conscious way. In fact, as soon as we gain perspective on the mental chatter and are able to observe our own thinking, we can enter a Tier 2 level of consciousness (Regenerative Leadership Consciousness). When we draw our awareness out of the reactive ego-mind and gain perspective on its ramblings, habits, annoyances and projections we become able to assess situations more calmly and wisely.

> "It takes courage … to endure the sharp pains of self-discovery rather than choose to take the dull pain of unconsciousness that would last the rest of our lives."
>
> Marianne Williamson, activist and author

Many specialists use the metaphor of being on the dance-floor, in amongst our thought-patterns gyrating around, sparking off feelings and sensations within us. We can, with self-awareness, take ourselves up to the balcony overlooking the dance-floor. We gain perspective on the mind-chatter and thought-patterns unfolding within us. We observe ourselves on the dance-floor. We notice our thoughts, we watch our reactions, our habits and judgements, our fears and feelings. We can sense feelings rising within us and can become conscious of them before we react to them. As soon as we notice the thoughts and feelings in this detached way, their power over us loosens.

## Taming and Training our Self Awareness

The greatest obstacle to this subtle shift in consciousness is our individual selves: our fears, thought patterns, triggers, issues, and acculturated busyness.

> "I think 99 times and find nothing. I stop thinking, swim in silence, and the truth comes to me."
>
> Albert Einstein, physicist

On that note, let's pause for a moment, and breathe deep. Let's bring our awareness to reading this book, sense our surroundings, sense our breathing, and our body posture. Take a couple of deep breaths. Become aware of how you feel in your body. Be present with what is.

As we sense into the present moment and our bodily sensations we are able to relax into a state of receptive awareness. We can acknowledge our changing feelings, attitudes, moods and thoughts and see them for what they are; short-lived projections and triggers that we can learn and grow from as long as we don't allow them to run the show.

The most direct route to practicing being present in a given moment is through meditation. Scientific studies now show how regular meditation boosts memory and increases focus, compassion, happiness, creativity but also improved performance (Seppälä, 2013). Meditation is becoming more widely accepted in the West and is increasingly being practiced at values-based organizations, many of which are designating special rooms for employees to make meditation a part of their work-day. During meditation, our brain-waves change frequency and our inter-hemispheric balance is regained. In Part 1 we mentioned how many of us operate from a constant high-beta (fight or flight) brain wave frequency, where we have myopic perspectives, tend toward overly controlling and defensive actions, and find it hard to think systemically. Meditation can help us shift out of high-beta and instead into alpha or theta brain waves, which are restorative and regenerative and can help us gain clarity, new ideas and energy after meditation.

The more we become aware of the mind-chatter of our ego, the more we allow space for our true nature and inner vitality. We are then able to reach beyond separateness and sense the interconnectedness. We can start to tune in to the Living Systems Field.

As the author of *Holism and Evolution*, Jan Christiaan Smuts, insightfully noted in his ground-breaking and profoundly influential work almost one hundred years ago, *"the apparently individualist Mind is in reality deeply and vitally influenced by the universal Mind ... It is rooted in and dependent on the greater whole."* (Smuts, 1926).

*Dive Deeper:* Psychologist Sigmund Freud explored the 'ego' as an important part of our psyche that enables us to operate in the interconnectedness of life with a differentiated sense of ourselves. After him, the psychologist Carl Jung explored the relationship of the ego with a deeper part of our psyche, what he called the 'Self'. Jung explored in detail how, through a process of 'individuation' throughout our lives, we learn to bring in more of this deeper Self into our everyday awareness. The Self has also been referred to as the 'soul'.

As we learn to cultivate our self-awareness, our dominant mode of perception shifts from a largely left-brain hemispheric rational-analytic ego-awareness into a more balanced left-right hemispheric awareness. We become more authentic, more in touch with our inner nature, while still calling upon the left-brained ego-mechanistic logic when required to focus-in and get the job done.

## Systemic Awareness: Sensing into the Field of Interconnected Systems

The dual aspect of the Leadership Dynamics is self-awareness alchemizing with systemic-awareness to create Regenerative Leadership Consciousness. Systemic awareness is a natural capacity we all have as human beings. Since the Scientific Revolution's prioritization of the mechanistic and rational-analytical worldview, we have been suppressing our natural systemic capacity – the very capacity we need to thrive in our current times.

Systems nested within systems are the very stuff of life. Systemic awareness is our ability to sense into the networks of systems within the living organization and throughout the wider stakeholder ecosystem, including our family and friends, local community and wider ecology of life.

> "Learn how to see. Realize everything connects with everything else"
>
> Leonardo Da Vinci, polymath

Rather than control and domination through hierarchic carrot-and-stick methods, where the leader is divorced from the operations, pulling leavers on clever dashboards (as if operating a machine), leaders become consciously aware of the vitality of the organizational living-system through systemic awareness. This does not mean that Regenerative Leaders abandon all the dashboards. Those tools have their place, but systemic awareness allows for leaders to open up their perceptual horizon to other qualitative inputs from the system, rather than being overly inured in excel sheets, big data and other quantitative means.

When leaders put systemic awareness in to practice, they are able to sense where best to unlock flow or revitalize stagnated energy. Their role becomes one of facilitating the system – as *Ecosystemic Facilitator* – one who holds the responsibility of enlivening the system, keeping the system healthy so it can adapt and evolve in its own way; allowing the individual parts to unlock their brilliance and creativity to flow more easily throughout the organization unencumbered by power-and-control based bureaucracy. The key to being an Ecosystemic Facilitator is the capacity to 'hold space' – to provide a psychologically safe container for generative dialogue to successfully happen between diverse people with divergent perspectives, while sensing into relational flows.

 *Business Insight: Pukka Herbs – an international herbal tea and supplements provider.* Pukka is a fast-growing mission-driven business with a complex supply-chain operating in a difficult market. While advising Pukka, Giles has facilitated 'Heart of Pukka' circles where key players from across the business come together for open-hearted generative dialogue. Care is taken to ensure the space is safely held, so people share their truth about what they sense from their unique perspectives about their stakeholder landscape. The participants listen-in to the system, and share perspectives through deep listening (a technique we explore in Part 3) around the circle, so that a holistic understanding of the organizational living system can be sensed by the entire group. This provides systemic insight on how the system is responding to change and how it can best be nurtured to realize its fuller potential.

It is through this deeply felt sense of the system dynamics – understanding the particular nodes, flows, stagnations, and acupuncture points of our organization – that we can learn how best to nudge the system.

In Complexity Theory, there is the notion of *strange attractors*. A system can reach a threshold, a limit to its capacity, after which it bursts and transforms into its next-stage of evolution. The field shifts, and the system starts to behave in a different way, influencing different parameters across the organization. When it comes to human behavior, this calls for a need to unlearn what we had been learning about the organization's behaviors and observe its new behaviors as the organizational field shifts.

## Regenerative Leadership Consciousness: The Alchemy of Self-and-Systemic Awareness

When we alchemize the dynamics of self and systemic awareness we step in to *Regenerative Leadership Consciousness*.

Regenerative Leadership Consciousness asks for a calm inner grounded-ness and awareness of one's own triggers, habits and shadows combined with an intuitive sense of the inter-relationality of living systems. This consciousness seeks authenticity, thinks systemically, designs for complexity, works with tensions, spawns life-affirming futures, and understands the Logic of Life.

The alchemy of self and systemic awareness creates the *Regenerative Leadership* abilities to:

- tame and train the ego;
- gain perspective on shadow-aspects, triggers and habitual behaviors;
- sense our inner knowing;
- embrace life as a learning journey;
- deal gracefully with adversity;
- seek wisdom beyond rationality – embracing the intuitive, complex, ambiguous, non-linear nature of reality;
- become comfortable with the uncomfortable;
- not simply ask a question and seek a solution but live a question and sense the synchronicities that respond to this lived question;
- strive for wholeness by cultivating the masculine and feminine aspects within us;

- deepen our relationship with life/nature, tap into the Living Systems Field, and apply living-systems insights.

As Regenerative Leaders, we are constantly tending, cultivating, catalyzing, clearing away, healing, and nurturing the channels of connectivity by facilitating rich conversations and encouraging people to open up and deepen both self-awareness and systemic-awareness. This involves us immersing ourselves in the global and local networks at play throughout the ecosystem we operate in. Whether its regular field trips, deep dive immersions with diverse stakeholders, cross-sector co-creativity, stakeholder dialogue sessions, and such like, we are enlivening the transformative energy across the systems we engage with.

This constant sensing into the system of the living-organization is what the leadership specialist Otto Scharmer points to when speaking of *"sensing into our emerging future"* (Scharmer, 2016). The future is unfolding here, in this present moment, and depends upon the quality of our self-and-systemic awareness as we attend to this moment. The more we open up to life through our cultivated self-and-systemic awareness, the more life can unfold through us. We become life-affirming leaders who are operating in harmony with our inner and outer nature.

> "He who is harmony with nature hits the mark without effort and apprehends the truth without thinking."
>
> Confucius, Chinese sage

We are no longer separate from life, but immersed within life feeling an aliveness, not in a hurried excitable way, but in a calm coherent way. The moments of flow, synchronicity, inspired creativity, heightened intuition, joy and peak experiences allow us a reawakening of what our ancient indigenous ancestors experienced as they walked the Earth, a wisdom that is within us, within everything.

Through Regenerative Leadership, we can learn to become more skilled at tapping into that wisdom. We can maintain self-reflexivity, and our sense of unique self, along with the ability to apply advanced technologies, mechanistic tools, and analytic thinking, as part-and-parcel of an integrated balanced engagement with the organization-as-living-system. We find ourselves reunited with critical elements we lost during our Journey of Separation.

Regenerative Leadership is not a return to our shamanic past, as much as it is a return toward harmony with all of life. It's a reach into our *next-stage*.

> "The greatest voyage of our lifetimes is not in the seeking of new landscapes but in the seeing with new eyes."
>
> Marcel Proust, philosopher

In his widely acclaimed Theory U model, Scharmer explores a shift in awareness from **absencing**: *Ignorance* (closing of the mind), *hate* (closing of the heart) and *fear* (closing of the will) to **presencing**: *curiosity* (open mind), *compassion* (open heart) and *courage* (open will). All the time, every day, we oscillate between states of *absencing* and *presencing*, yet as we cultivate our self-awareness entering the state of presence becomes easier. In Chapter 8 we specifically explore *presencing* as a core quality of Living Systems Being.

> "Every profound innovation is based on an inward-bound journey, a going to a deeper place where knowing comes to the surface."
>
> W. Brian Arthur, economist

## Activating our Super-Nature

As leaders we allow the integration of self-and-systemic awareness to occur by *activating our super-nature*. Activating our super-nature is about tapping in to our full potential by drawing on our whole-body intelligence, beyond the rational, analytical and mechanistic tendencies we have been trained in. It's about opening up to a greater wisdom than the left-hemisphere of our brain allows.

The famous psychologist Carl Jung was fascinated by the notion of tapping in to our whole-body intelligence and extensively studied our different ways of knowing: intuitive, rational, emotional, and somatic. Essentially, crossing the threshold from separateness (mechanistic logic) to interconnectedness (living-systems logic), involves an integration of these four natural intelligences to *activate our super nature.*

## Jung's 4 Ways of Knowing

*The intuitive way of knowing* is inner insight and intuition, and has often been related to the element *fire* and *SQ* (spiritual intelligence). This requires us to quieten and still ourselves, so we can better listen inwardly to this subtle intuition. This also requires an inner trust to go with what feels true, aligned and coherent with our deeper Self. We learn to listen to that soft inner voice that often immediately knows about the rightness of a situation which is easily over-ruled by our busy rational mind.

*The emotional way of knowing* is the ebb and flow of feelings and emotions, and has often been related to the element *water* and *EQ* (emotional intelligence). We cultivate this emotional way of knowing by allowing our feelings the non-judgmental space they need, so we may gain perspective on what is underpinning these feelings and how best to respond to them. It is a subtle yet important shift from blind emotional outburst – when we become the slave of our emotions – to informed emotional intelligence.

*The somatic and sensorial way of knowing* is the sensations we have in our body: gut pangs, hairs on the back of the neck, butterflies in our stomach, or chest perturbations. It has often been related to the element *earth* and *PQ* (physical or somatic intelligence). Our soma (our body) is full of psycho-somatic sensations that can inform how we attend to everyday interactions. Most people get a tense, unpleasant physical sensation when they are stressed. That's the body's intelligence letting us know to ease up, breathe deep, take a break, and relax. More and more scientific research is emerging about how this somatic way of knowing works alongside our emotional and intuitive ways of knowing (Claxton, 2016).

*The rational analytic way of knowing* is our thinking mind's ability to focus-in on things and analyze, and is often related to the element *air* and *IQ* (rational intelligence). This is by far the dominant intelligence we call upon in today's business environment. It is a powerful tool that helps us make sense of, delineate, focus-in and compartmentalize complexity. It is what dominates today's meetings, strategies, dashboards and decisions and in Part 1 we covered the reason for this domination. It is but one intelligence within our human repertoire, and a very useful tool for sure, yet when it dominates too much, it can suppress our other ways of knowing, creating a *complexity gap* in our leadership consciousness.

When we allow these four ways of knowing (intuitive, emotional, somatic, and rational) to cohere within us, we allow the four elements of our inner nature (fire, water, earth, and air) to integrate in their rightful way, and as we integrate these four elements, we open ourselves up to the fifth element. Ancient and modern cultures have many names for this fifth element, such as Akasha, Spirit, Source, Universal Mind, and so on – we call it the Living Systems Field.

The illustration below – activating our super-nature – shows the shift from our prevalent imbalance in to an integration of our four ways of knowing, which activates our *super-nature* – our innate human capacity to open-up to the field and tune-in to life beyond separateness.

## ACTIVATING OUR SUPER-NATURE

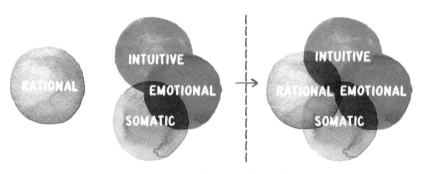

CROSSING A THRESHOLD

© copyright Hutchins & Storm – inspired by Carl Jung

This understanding of our individual mind reverberating within a deeper Mind is becoming more widely accepted as scientific studies in this area gain wider recognition. For instance, the internationally-acclaimed neuroscientist and pharmacologist Candace Pert coined the phrase 'bodymind' (Pert, 1998). Rather than thinking of our mind as encapsulated in our head, the bodymind pervades our entire body (drawing on the somatic, intuitive and emotional as well as the rational), and this bodymind continuously senses and responds to changes within us and all around us.

Scharmer explores the importance of learning to let go of the dominant ego-mind in order to open up to the 'field' within and all around us – what he calls 'Source' – as this is where wisdom resides. As we let go, we connect more deeply with our Self (or 'soul') and also with the wisdom inherent in the 'field'. Then, we can invite in this wisdom to inform us about our own emergence (Scharmer, 2016). Essentially it is about getting out of the way and letting a greater wisdom emerge – the emergence of Regenerative Leadership Consciousness that can flourish within us and through our relationships.

The importance of such findings for ourselves as leaders and our organizations as collectives of conscious people, is simply this: the more we open up to our natural intelligences (emotional, somatic, intuitive and rational) and to nature's wisdom within and around us, the more able we are to help our organizations flourish in the ever-changing business context we now face. We can draw upon both a mechanistic perspective and a living-systems perspective.

## Integration of mechanistic & living-systems logic

- Mechanistic & systemic
- Rational analytic & intuitive
- Left-brain hemispheric attention & right-brain hemispheric attention
- Head thinking & embodied knowing
- Masculine qualities & feminine qualities
- Outer objectification & inner subjectivity
- Human & nature
- Matter & mind

This integration enables the crossing of a threshold in our leadership, through the integration of the 4 areas we allowed to get out of kilter during our Journey of Separation.

# THE JOURNEY OF RECONNECTION

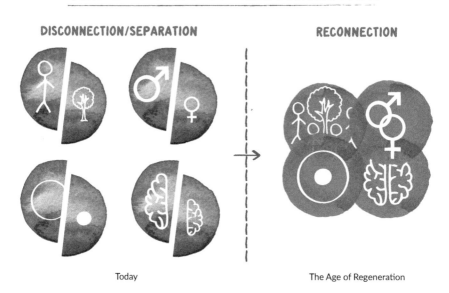

DISCONNECTION/SEPARATION                    RECONNECTION

Today                                       The Age of Regeneration

© copyright Hutchins & Storm

This threshold-crossing hits the sweet spot of left-hemispheric and right-hemispheric integration and also the integration of three powerful organs of perception within us – the head, heart, and gut. With this neuro-biological-electromagnetic coherence, we shift psychologically and physiologically. We become more human, more able to deal with life, more able to embrace the realities of the VUCA landscape rather than trying in vain to fight it with fear and control.

While this shift into being more aligned with our inner and outer life is in some regards quite simple – it requires no credit card, no PhD or complex scientific undertaking – it is not necessarily easy in today's world. The shift may come with a mid-life crisis, a radical change in one's career or life-style, or what is sometimes referred to as a dark night of the soul, which can last many months or years through which we change on the inside, shedding layers and facing inner triggers.

We undergo a metamorphosis in terms of how we embrace life and how we relate to others. We may become almost unrecognizable by people we knew before our metamorphosis, while in our caterpillar phase. And we may have to let-go of certain relationships or transform them so they no longer hold us back but nourish our next-stage of being.

## METAMORPHOSIS IN OUR MIDST

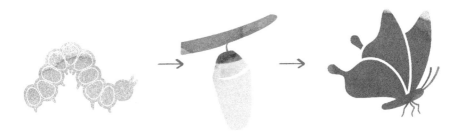

© copyright Hutchins & Storm

"How does one become a butterfly?" Pooh asked pensively.

"You must want to fly so much that you are willing to give up being a caterpillar" Piglet replied.

"You mean to die?" asked Pooh.

"Yes and no" he answered. "What looks like you will die. But you will really live on."

Photo credit: Yoal Desurmont

Both of us – Laura and Giles – have experienced these metamorphic periods of transformation in our lives. Laura suffered a minor traumatic brain injury and was confined to silence and nature for two years, from which she emerged a different person. One day she was leading an organization with 25 employees being super-busy and the next she was stripped of all of her abilities to execute, plan, act, write, and lead. All she could cope with was silence and nature. Laura had to learn to surrender completely to stillness, presence, and recovery. To the unknown. Not easy; but it has proven to be a major blessing in disguise.

Giles's metamorphosis began the day he resigned from corporate life on his 40th birthday. From travelling the globe, receiving hundreds of emails a day, in hyper-delivery mode and always on, he retreated to the oak woods of Devon for many months where he found his own way back to stillness and inner wisdom.

Our stories, although perhaps different on the outside, share similarities. On our separate journeys, we have both experienced excitement, insecurity, fear, faced inner demons, tapped into new courage, and slowly shed the layers that no longer served us. Standing strong in our own essence and navigating from true alignment to a deep inner knowing. (We have included our personal stories on the website *www.regenerativeleadership.co* if you're curious to know more about each of our journeys).

We share this, because in the leadership workshops that we facilitate, we often meet leaders who are going through these transformative periods in their lives. Sometimes leaders are metamorphosing while still engaged in their current role and responsibilities, while others take time out. There is no right way, as each of us experiences unique situations and life conditions, yet, gaining perspective on what we are working through and having an understanding of what we are opening up to (Regenerative Leadership Consciousness) can be very helpful during what can be a challenging, lonely and testing time in our lives.

In Part 3 we provide some simple yet powerful techniques that help us with this metamorphosis.

For now, let's keep the Life and Leadership Dynamics in mind as we go through each of the 3 DNA components of Regenerative Leadership: DESIGN, CULTURE, BEING.

These two dynamics (life and leadership) weave through it all. They are always present.

"There is no better designer than nature."

Alexander McQueen, artist and designer

Photo credit: Asdrubal Jose Medrano

# Living Systems Design

When we look to nature, we find it packed full of inspiration, and if we look carefully enough, we can see that nature's wisdom has come up with all kinds of innovations to meet all kinds of challenges. Nature is like a library for Regenerative Leaders, granting access to 3.8 billion years of R&D that provides inspiration, information and application for redesigning thriving societies, living organizations, and life-affirming products and services that add value to a wider ecosystem. This is the approach bio-inspired design frameworks take - such as biomimicry, circular economics, cradle-to-cradle, biophilic design and permaculture. These frameworks align with the ways of nature, and are what Regenerative Leaders need to be aware of as they influence how we engage with products, services, processes, and places.

In this chapter, diving in to the first DNA component of Living Systems Design, we wish to make these bio-design frameworks relevant and understandable to you, the leader, so you can apply these approaches to your organization.

> "The first rule of sustainability is to align with nature."
>
> Paul Hawken, environmentalist and entrepreneur

There are so many amazing books written on biomimetic design, biomimicry, circular economy, permaculture, cradle to cradle and biophilic design, we have not tried to add another one to the list, instead we draw insights from other books, guides and methodologies, while tying these nature-inspired concepts together into a framework relevant for leaders.

# LIVING SYSTEMS DESIGN

© copyright Hutchins & Storm

## The key DNA strands of Living Systems Design are

1.  Waste Equals Food: See all resources as valuable nutrients to be recycled, upcycled, reused and reintegrated into the value chain

2.  Clever Shapes & Forms: Seek inspiration in nature for time-tested shapes, forms and structures

3.  Regenerative Materials: Use regenerative materials and products in all your designs and purchases

4.  Biophilic Design: Design in ways that allow people to reconnect with nature within and around them

5.  Ecosystemic Design Thinking: Facilitate vitality and life-affirming potential throughout your network of stakeholders

We will now go through each of these 5 DNA strands in turn starting with:

## 1. Waste Equals Food

*Objective: See all resources as valuable nutrients to be recycled, upcycled, reused and reintegrated into the value chain*

In nature, the waste from one species becomes the food of another. Matter and energy morph, transform, and cycle through ecosystem relations - this is simply how life works.

Take a tree, for instance. The tree is part of a vibrant inter-relating ecosystem, systems upon systems all feeding off each other, where waste of one becomes food for another. Throughout the year the entire tree is host to millions of microorganisms, bacteria, fungi and insects, all playing their part in the vitality of the ecosystem. The tree sequesters carbon, cleans the air, produces oxygen and enriches the soil. Tree blossom enables insects to pollinate and every year we see the beauty of leaves bursting forth in spring, transforming solar energy into tree growth throughout summer. And when the season changes to autumn the leaves fall to the ground, and over the winter they are recycled and reused. No plastic bags littering the streets unable to biodegrade, only leaf-litter that fertilizes the topsoil with rich nutrients for the next batch of production in spring. And ultimately when the tree dies the trunk and its branches, essentially made of water, minerals, and sunlight, will release nutrients for the next generation of trees and for other life-forms to live.

Everything from the tree to the soil to the seasons to the parasites are giving, receiving, and playing their part in this interweave of ecosystemic life. It's nature's wisdom at work, a wisdom that reaches far beyond what rational-analytic left-hemispheres can define with neat-and-tidy categories. Imagine if we applied these dynamics to our factories, processes, and products. Instead of 'waste' being toxic and hazardous to the health of humans and the wider ecosystem, we might learn to design like nature where everything breaks down into reusable, biodegradable waste that becomes an energy source for another.

Today, the only sensible means for humans to address their own resource scarcity, while combating increasing pollution and GHG emissions, is to apply bio-inspired design principles to products, services, systems and cities. However, we have been designing based on a linear, take-make-waste production model and encouraging growth through advertising and marketing designed to stimulate over-consumption that creates enormous amounts of toxic non-biodegradable waste. We have also established a cultural mindset where fear, scarcity, and unhappiness trigger us to buy more stuff. This is a direct departure from the Logic of Life and triggers our catastrophic, systemic problems.

Our food, our clothing, our electronics, our transportation, our way of packaging - everything - is made using linear production methods that are undermining life on Earth. Not only are products made from components that damage our environment, many have *built-in obsolescence* in which the product's design makes it unusable after a certain period so we have to throw it away and buy a new one: cell phones, computers, printers, refrigerators, are but a few examples.

William McDonough and Michael Braungart have long been pioneers of the movement known as *cradle to cradle*, which utilizes the 'waste equals food' circularity and reuse principle in product and process design. Their book *Cradle to Cradle* is a key contributor to the fields of circular economy and bio-inspired innovation: *"This cyclical, cradle-to-cradle biological system has nourished a planet of thriving, diverse abundance for millions of years. Until very recently in the Earth's history, it was the only system, and every living thing on the planet belonged to it. Growth was good. It meant more trees, more species, greater diversity, and more complex, resilient ecosystems."* (McDonough & Braungart, 2002).

The *circular economy* is a part of this movement. As defined by The Ellen MacArthur Foundation, the circular economy *entails gradually decoupling economic activity from the consumption of finite resources, and designing waste out of the system.* It is based on three principles.

- design out waste and pollution
- keep products and materials in use
- regenerate natural systems

This circular model makes a distinction between *biological nutrients*, those originating from nature, and *technical nutrients*, those material components from the man-made world. In a regenerative society, biological nutrients are able to decompose, whereas technical nutrients cannot decompose but can be recycled, reused, or upcycled in an industrial process. See the model below illustrating the constant flow of materials and nutrients in a regenerative based society.

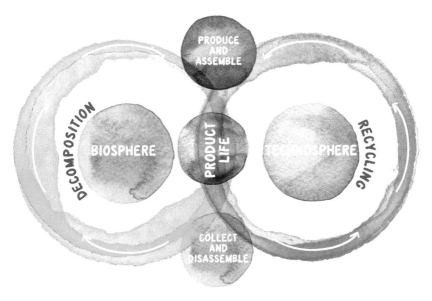

## CRADLE TO CRADLE

Source: Cradle to Cradle

This move away from linearity into circular design and production is an important part of enabling your organization to thrive in the years ahead.

*Business Insight: Interface – a global carpet manufacturer.* The company, which was founded by Ray Anderson in the seventies, knows all about changing a business mindset from the 20th century to the 21st. In the mid 1990's the company moved away from a traditional industrial take-make-waste model and geared production toward a circular economy business model. It all started with the CEO and Founder Ray Anderson having an epiphany in 1994. At that time, his company was 99% petroleum based and he had cared little about the negative impact his company was having on the environment. Then, in 1994, he read *The Ecology of Commerce* by the environmentalist Paul Hawken. It was *"a spear in the chest"*, Anderson wrote. *"I was dumbfounded by how much I did not know about the environment and about the impacts of the industrial system on the environment. A new definition of 'success' began to creep into my consciousness, and the latent sense of legacy asserted itself. I was a plunderer of the Earth, and that is not the legacy one wants to leave behind."* (Vitello, 2011). This kick-started a journey that led Interface to be global pioneers and role models on how to transform a large global production company into a regenerative business model while outperforming competitors in the process. A key guiding principle for all their operations is to ensure they run like natural ecosystems. They are currently working with The Biomimicry Institute on a 'factory as a forest' concept where their factories can sequester carbon, purify water, transform sunlight into energy and transform waste into useful inputs for other parts of the system. A factory that is truly *life-affirming* rather than toxic. They have proved that it's possible to close the loop of technological and biological components while running a profitable business in a challenging competitive market.

*Business Insight: Fetzer – an international wine producer.* All of its 100,000 acres of vineyards are certified organic and half are biodynamic (following the rhythms of nature). It was the first winery to be certified carbon-neutral in the US and pays close attention to the way its operations work in-tune with nature's regenerative ways. By example, one area of considerable energy use for Fetzer is the handling of waste water in the process of making wine. Fetzer has come up with a 'regenerative by nature' design that harnesses the digestive power of worms and microbes to remove the contaminants from the waste water and convert it into clean water used in irrigating the vineyards and rich fertilizer that is used on the land. The waste-water equals food for the worms. This chemical-free recycling system consumes far less energy while producing the very useful bi-product of fertilizer for the soil. It's a win-win-win achieved through closing the loop. 15 million tonnes of waste-water each year are returned to nature without toxicity, and rich soil health to-boot.

## 2. Clever Shapes & Forms

*Objective: Seek inspiration in nature for time-tested shapes, forms and structures*

Over billions of years nature has evolved shapes and forms that efficiently use materials and regenerate themselves by design. Dating all the way back to the medieval and ancient epochs, designers and artists, such as Da Vinci, Gaudi and Michelangelo, have been fascinated by the forms and shapes of nature. In architecture and design, nature's shapes and forms have been mimicked for centuries, which is what architects refer to as *biomorphism*. This design concept does not necessarily use bio-inspired materials and processes but allows shape and form to lend inspiration to the final design.

> "Nature is the source of all true knowledge."
>
> Leonardo Da Vinci, polymath

Many of the best shapes and forms we see in nature today are the product of billions of years of adaptation using the simple life-affirming principles of minimizing materials, designing smart, and being regenerative.

The Amazon Water Lilly uses minimal material to create huge leaves (up to 3 meters in diameter) by strengthening the underside with a network of strong ribs getting its strength from its shape not its mass. The horsetail, one of the oldest plant species on Earth, was here when the dinosaurs were, and has incredibly strong, yet hollow, stems that allow for minimal use of materials. This strength comes from two thin layers held apart by braces. The same is true for the bamboo that also grows much quicker than trees and yet still provides great durability through its shape. Nature uses hollow tubes to build efficiently – human bones, plant stems, bamboo, feather quills, and more, all inspiring product designs.

Bees build honey combs using a six-sided hexagonal structure as that uses the smallest amount of beeswax to store the biggest amount of honey, cleverly maximizing honey storage and minimizing materials. This beautiful hexagonal structure has been used throughout the ages in our designs. Architect and systems-theorist Buckminster Fuller explored nature's patterns in his famous geodesic domes, and The Eden Project in the UK utilizes the hexagon, and also the pentagon, shape in constructing its beautiful, yet strong and durable domes. The shape and structure of the maple seed enables it to propel itself away from the mother tree, therefore reducing the chance of competing for sunlight with the mother tree. NASA has mimicked this structure for planetary exploration aircraft that can be released in to the air propelling back to Earth while collecting data.

One of the world's fastest trains, the Shinkansen, travels between Tokyo and Hakata at an impressive 300km/hour. The first generation of these trains were so incredibly noisy that engineers started studying shapes in nature that could slide through air and water at impressive speed. Kingfishers, with their long, pointed beak, are shaped to catch fish at speed, while creating minimal ripples as they dive in to the water. This inspired the current train design, resulting in quiet, streamlined trains that use far less energy.

 *Nature Insight: Clever air conditioning.* Termites have mastered the art of cooling their homes. Despite living in Africa, with its hot sun and heavy winds, termite mounds, which can grow to 3 meters (10 feet) high, provide a cool and safe home to thousands of termites. It's truly one of the most fascinating building structures in the world. Scientists have found that even when temperatures on the outside vary by up to 20C the inside temperature wouldn't fluctuate more than 8C – the structure is designed to keep temperature inside relatively stable. The air simply flows through cool mud channels while the hot air flows out the top of the mound. By mimicking this design, architects and engineers can drastically improve energy efficiency in buildings. For instance, the architect Mick Pearce, designed the award-winning Eastgate Center in Harare, Zimbabwe, where the walls are porous, just like the termite mounds. When the wind blows through the tunnels on hot days, the walls suck up the heat, cooling it before entering the shopping center. By mimicking termites, energy use is significantly reduced.

 *Nature Insight: Antibacterial surfaces.* Shark skin has been mimicked by many products. For instance, professional swimwear which desires materials that reduce turbulence in water. Tiny, grooved scales cover the skin of the shark forming channels alongside the body of the shark which means there's no hard surface for the water to create turbulence and drag, and so aiding the shark to swim at impressive speed. Shark skin from the

Galapagos Shark is antibacterial, and has now been mimicked by Sharklet Technologies for a surface-film used in hospitals to lower the need for antibiotics which often create resistant superbugs. The film is applied to door knobs, beds and other areas with intense human contact to minimize the need for spraying antibiotics

There is a wealth of shapes, forms, and functions in nature that designers can take inspiration from. However, if this mimicry mindset is not truly life-affirming, if it is merely hacking shapes, forms, and structures for short-term financial gain, with little systematic benefit, then it's degenerative. Pure mimicry is not regenerative design, but instead is nothing short of exploitative, reductive, bio-hacking.

Opening up to the patterns, shapes, forms, textures in nature with curiosity to explore how nature has solved all kinds of design problems is exactly the role of the Regenerative Leader. It means you can create more efficient products and inventions as you lean on the intelligence of nature's billion years of tried and tested shapes and forms. *Biomimicry* is a design approach that mimics life while embracing a systemic-design approach, which aligns with the circular economics and cradle to cradle design standards. Biomimicry as a concept has been around for centuries, yet has only gained popularity over the last two decades. Today, biomimicry is becoming widely known and well received by not just designers but businesses seeking bio-inspired innovations.

## 3. Regenerative Materials

*Objective*: *Use regenerative materials and products in all designs and purchases*

We have what it takes to transform our material culture into a regenerative one. Nature has already created non-toxic glue, dirt repellent structures, anti-bacterial surfaces, self-healing properties, and durable lightweight materials. There are all sorts of solutions, made from water-based and non-toxic methods, manufactured without high heat, extreme pressure, or excessive energy. Yet, most of today's man-made materials tend toward the opposite end of the spectrum - needing extreme heat, intense amounts of energy, and chemical compounds that cause great harm to surrounding environments and cannot easily breakdown or be reused.

"Biologically inspired materials could revolutionize materials science. People looking at spider silk and abalone shells are looking for new ways to make materials better, cheaper, and with less toxic byproducts."

Janine Benyus, biologist

Again, we can turn to Braungart and McDonough, as they point us to the importance of cradle to cradle approaches to avoid *monstrous hybrids* - materials that are impossible to recycle due to the concoction of chemicals and components they contain. Unfortunately, these 'monsters' are everywhere in plastic, cardboard boxes, bottles, clothing and construction materials.

As a Regenerative Leader, it's important to know that alternatives exist: materials that can either decompose or recycle, or are designed for ease of disassembly. There's a rapid rise in the interest of bio-inspired materials and what is referred to as *green chemistry*, chemical engineering focused on the design of products and processes that minimize the use and generation of toxic substances. This is good news.

A NEW BIO-INNOVATION CULTURE IS ON ITS WAY. REGENERATIVE LEADERS ARE THE ONES WHO EMBRACE THIS SOONER RATHER THAN LATER TO TAP INTO THESE OPPORTUNITIES.

Photo credit: Unsplash

*Nature Insight: Self-repairing material.* Shells are often admired by designers for their form – they have phenomenal resistance to cracking through platelet structures where the flexibility in the polymer helps distribute loads over a larger area of the shell. By example, the abalone sea creature assembles an incredibly durable shell without chemicals, heat or complex equipment. Mimicking the structure of the abalone shell has offered a unique way of building complex shapes sustainably without compromising on tensile strength and material efficiency. The abalone shell even repairs itself from the inside out. When a crack develops on the outside – cells automatically multiply to fill the crack from the inside. Scientists are trying to mimic this function in beams and pipes where foam is used inside the beams to prevent air-leaks (Pawlyn, 2016).

*Nature Insight: Dirt-repellent design.* The Lotus flower is always spotlessly clean due to tiny hydrophobic (water-repelling) bumps covering the leaves and petals. When it rains the water-droplets roll off the waxy bumps picking up the dirt as they roll down the petals and leaves. Scientists are mimicking this feature in paint and surface structures by adding microscopic water-repellent bumps to the mixture which means the buildings and surfaces becomes dirt-repellent by design.

As already mentioned, *biomimicry* (which includes *bio-inspired innovation*) is a fast-growing area of interest; a systemic design approach where life-affirming ways of designing and revitalizing material sources and component reuse are embraced. It is a fascinating area sparking lots of interest in Silicon Valley and other hot spots. Singularity University, Stanford, UC Berkeley and many other universities around the world have dedicated research areas to bio-inspired material innovation and biomimicry, and we see many new incubator and accelerator programmes focusing on this too, with it gaining increasing interest from investors, designers, scientists, entrepreneurs alike.

For instance, San Francisco based Indie-Bio is a relatively new incubator programme that matches PhD material scientists with business strategists, entrepreneurs, and investors to bridge the gap of commercializing great innovations and bringing bio-innovations to market.

*Business Insight: ViaeX – a start-up material-science company.* Vivian Qu, a young Materials Science and Engineering student from UC Berkeley recently set up ViaeX to transform bio-waste into renewable nanomaterials for water purification, industrial separation, skin care, food and beverage filtration, wound healing, and more. Currently, ViaeX is developing a material portfolio that utilizes *chitosan*, an abundant bio-waste that has been shown by researchers in leading universities across the world to be a material with enormous applicability. Chitosan naturally exhibits antimicrobial activity and has an affinity for heavy metals, so ViaeX is taking advantage of these properties by processing the polymer into highly energy-efficient filtration membranes. These membranes catch bacteria, preventing them from proliferating into the biomass, and therefore significantly increasing the lifespan of the filter. By using bio-waste as a source material, ViaeX intends to change the way manufacturers approach product development. By providing filtration solutions that are both efficient and economical, they are reducing pressure on our natural resources.

*Business Insight: Interface – the multinational carpets company mentioned earlier.* Interface employees recently came up with an innovation to eliminate the toxic glues used in carpet installation. Looking to nature for a replacement, they came across the Gecko, a lizard that relies on the inter-molecular force of more than a million tiny foot hairs to stick to surfaces at any angle. This inspired a glue-free installation system that uses the inherent strength of the backing of the carpet tiles to create a dimension-ally stable 'floating floor' that hugs the floor creating stability without the use of glue. The carpet tiles eliminate the mess and toxicity of glue making it easy to replace a single dirt-stained tile instead of the entire carpet. This bio-inspired solution has lowered the carpet's environmental footprint by 90%.

There is no way around this for leaders – a new bio-innovation culture is on its way. Regenerative Leaders are the ones who embrace this sooner rather than later to tap into these opportunities.

> "We are on the brink of a materials revolution that will be on par with the Iron Age and the Industrial Revolution. We are leaping forward into a new age of materials."
>
> Mehmet Sarikaya, materials scientist

Jay Harman is a bio-inspired entrepreneur and founder of Pax Scientific, an engineering research and development firm that specializes in finding innovative nature-inspired solutions for industrial problems. According to Harman, the amount of investment in bio-inspired materials has sky-rocketed over the last 10 years, with such products already generating billions of dollars in sales. He says: *"Biomimicry lays the groundwork for future profitability and, by providing solutions that don't create new problems, it offers something that short-term, cost-saving solutions can't."* (Jay Harman, 2013).

 *Dive Deeper:* For more on biomimicry and bio-innovation insights look on-line at The Biomimicry Institute's framework and check-list for design-ers, also see Michael Pawlyn's book *Biomimicry for Architecture* and Janine Benyus's book *Biomimicry: Innovation Inspired by Nature.*

# 4. Biophilic Design

**Objective:** *Design in ways that allow people to reconnect with nature within and around them*

If we are to reduce stress in all our systems, we also need to ensure that the final products, workspaces, schools, government buildings, cities and systems are designed to enhance the wellbeing of the users. The concept of biophilic design is based on the notion that building design, city planning, and architecture can relieve stress, improve creativity, and enhance well-being by helping to reconnect and align us with nature within and around us. There is now ample scientific evidence showing measurable psychological and physiological health benefits, as well as numerous other positive effects that regular contact to nature has on our lives (Keniger 2013, Sandifer et al. 2014).

Biologist E.O.Wilson, in his ground-breaking book and winner of two Pulitzer Prizes, *Biophilia* explores our natural affinity for life in what he termed 'biophilia'. This empathic connection we have with nature is, according to Wilson, the very essence of our humanity. Connection with nature enriches us, and if we do not adequately attend to this emotional affiliation we have with nature, then we will degrade ourselves physiologically and psychologically (Wilson, 1984).

> "Humanity is a biological species, living in a biological environment, because like all species, we are exquisitely adapted in everything: from our behavior, to our genetics, to our physiology, to that particular environment in which we live. The earth is our home. Unless we preserve the rest of life, as a sacred duty, we will be endangering ourselves by destroying the home in which we evolved, and on which we completely depend."
>
> E. O. Wilson, biologist & author

More and more research shows that people gain emotional nourishment, as well as increased levels of concentration, intuition, and creativity, through a healthier engagement with nature. In 1984 Roger Ulrich carried out a groundbreaking study demonstrating that people recovering from surgery who had a bedside window overlooking nature, healed on average a day faster, needed significantly less pain medication, had fewer post-surgery complications and treated nurses nicer than patients without a window overlooking nature (Ulrich, 1984).

In 2001, there was a study undertaken in Chicago comparing public housing buildings that had little or no vegetation to buildings with high levels of greenery and the results showed that the buildings with high levels of vegetation around them had 48% fewer property crimes and 56% fewer violent crimes than otherwise identical apartments with only barren surrounding land. Even modest amounts of greenery were associated with lower crime rates. The greener the surroundings, the fewer the number of crimes that occurred (Kuo & Sullivan, 2001).

The Japanese have an age-old practice of *Shinrin-yoku* which translates as 'forest bathing'. This is the act of walking slowly and mindfully through the woods. There is now ample scientific evidence showing how this simple practice of walking in nature has physiological and psychological benefits on human health and wellbeing. Many Japanese cities have established Forest Therapy Bases to help the population lower cortisol levels, boost immune systems, and improve mental and physical wellbeing (Wang, 2015).

"Indoors, we tend to use only two senses, our eyes and our ears. Outside is where we can smell the flowers, taste the fresh air, look at the changing colours of the trees, hear the birds singing and feel the breeze on our skin. And when we open up our senses, we begin to connect to the natural world."

Dr Qing Li, forest therapy expert

# Scientific findings on the effect nature has on humans

Here are just some of the scientific findings related to nature's influence on health, well-being, productivity and creativity:

- Being in nature reduces pulse rate, blood pressure and cortisol levels (Chiba University, 2009)

- Being in nature unplugged from multi-media increases creativity by 50% (Atchley et al, 2012)

- Being in nature leads to improved cognitive functioning and mental well-being (Kaplan, 2001)

- Nature has positive effects on mental/psychological health, healing, heart-rate, concentration, levels of stress, blood pressure, behavior, and other health factors (Brown and Grant, 2005).

- Exercise outdoors in a natural environment improves mood and self-esteem and is more restorative than exercise outdoors in an urban environment (Barton and Pretty, 2010)

- Spending time in nature boosts the immune system and increases resistance to cancer (Qing Li, 2009)

- Exposure to natural daylight makes us more productive, improves concentration and short-term memory (California Energy Commission, 2003)

- Flowers and plants in the workplace increase cognitive functioning and can create a 15% rise in innovative ideas and more creative, flexible problem-solving (Ulrich, 2009)

- Connection with nature has a significant positive effect on autonomy, personal growth, and sense of purpose in life (Nisbet et al., 2011)

- People who spend 15 minutes each day in nature developed a more positive outlook than those who don't (Mayer et al., 2009)

- Workers exposed to sunlight and natural elements in the workplace report better moods, higher satisfaction with their work, and more commitment to their employer (Colarelli et al., 2016)

- When immersed in a natural environment, people report feeling more connected to others and to the world around them (Terhaar, 2009)

- Walking in nature improves memory by up to 20% (Berman et al. 2008)

- People are more considerate and generous when exposed to nature (Ryan & Weinstein, 2009)

Biophilic design can enhance our sense of connection with nature; not just through views or access to greenery but also through bringing the outdoors into our interior design. Most humans spend 90% of their time indoors (Klepeis, 2001) which mean that for us to fully thrive inside (when being outside is not an option) we must bring our natural habitat indoors and integrate it into our design. natural flow designs, the sensation and feel of natural materials, the currents of air and water flow, natural lighting levels and even natural sounds being played within the work environment. Spending just a few seconds looking at a nearby potted-plant helps ease your mind and restore your ability to focus. This has led companies like Google, Etsy and many more to redesign their office spaces with plenty of green walls and plants (Schwab, 2019). This Biophilic design makes us happier, calms our nervous system and cultivates a more coherent inner-state.

 *Dive Deeper:* For more on biophilic design, a good on-line report is *14 Patterns of Biophilic Design – Improving Health and Well-being in the Built Environment* by Terrapin Bright Green. And some good books on biophilia and biophilic design are *The Nature Fix* by Florence Willliams, *The Biophilia Effect* by Clemens Arvay, *Handbook of Biophilic City Planning and Design* by Timothy Beatley, *Nature by Design* by Stephen Kellert, *Shinrin-yoku* by Professor Yoshifumi Miyazaki.

Knowing the impact our habitat has on us, and our need for nature-connection, we must question our current designs and structures. During our Journey of Separation, the design of buildings and cities became increasingly influenced by mechanistic logic with little understanding of the impact this has on the wellbeing of ourselves.

 *Business Insight:* **Google – technology giant.** The company has, for some years now, been integrating aspects of biophilic design principles into workspace design to increase employee's health, wellbeing and productivity. Google actively works with biophilic designers to increase the variability of indoors sensory stimulation to mimic aspects of what it's like for humans to be outside, and has increased natural light, added many plants to work spaces, green walls, and carpets with natural patterns. Google asserts it has made their employees more creative, productive and increased their ability to focus (Schwab, 2019).

Cities are frequently planned with little access to nature and instead have been designed for cars and maximum occupant utility, often with an almost hostile approach to all living things – nature and humans alike. Buildings made of primarily concrete, steel and glass, donned with dull facades, dominate today's cities. And the inside of our buildings, schools and workplaces often mimic factories with little natural light or fresh air.

Whether it's our offices, schools or cities, we have veered away from nature's ways and inadvertently suppressed our inherent need for nature-connection. Thankfully, in recent years biophilic design principles are gaining traction in urban design and architecture communities worldwide. Today, it's becoming an exciting fast-growing area, continually strengthened by scientific research that supports measurable, positive impacts of biophilic design on health. By example, The Biophilic Cities Project aims to create awareness and attention around the importance of integrating our natural habitat into urban spaces. And a 2016 report from engineering firm Arup argues that buildings should be covered with greenery to help sequester carbon dioxide from the air, filtering air pollution, reduce noise and keep cities cooler (Schwab, 2019).

The Regenerative Leader is one who knows about the potential of biophilic design on improving workspaces, schools, public spaces and cities to increase happiness, satisfaction, productivity, connection, belonging and creativity.

## 5. Ecosystemic Design Thinking

*Objective: Facilitate vitality and life-affirming potential throughout your network of stakeholders*

To fully embrace regenerative design, we believe a key component often neglected by the fields of bio-inspired innovation, circular economics, cradle to cradle, and biophilic design, is the understanding of the systemic awareness needed for Living Systems Designers to understand the overarching systemic impact of their designs.

As well as scientifically observing the specific shapes, materials, forms, or models of nature, we need to see ourselves as *Ecosystemic Facilitators* that understand and tune in to the system of interrelations and web of stake-holders involved in the design, production, and application lifecycles of products, processes, and places. Embracing this systemic perspective, by taking into account the conditions and dynamics of the given place, build-ing and product in a wider context, will ensure that the design is not only functional but also life-affirming. This is where the Leadership Dynamic of systemic-awareness is applied to the design context.

It's easy to be fascinated by the antibacterial skin-structure of the Galapagos shark, or the structure of the burr that inspired Velcro, or the beak of the Kingfisher that inspired the fastest train in the world. But if we then design and build using toxic degenerative materials in a way where the occupants', consumers' and natural ecosystems' health and wellbeing is undermined by its utility, it is *not* regenerative.

The pioneering systems-thinker Fritjof Capra points out that the study of ecology is really a study and science of the relationships between all the members of Earth's home, the interconnected systems of Gaia. Wherever we see life, we also see interconnected, nested networks of materials, resources, and people – this is the nature of life. Much of today's design methods all too often rely on reductive mechanistic frames of perception, which encour-age designers to focus in on specific parts of the system, while only paying lip-service to the wider context within which their design products, services and processes operate in. This leads to unintended consequences.

We must move beyond merely 'hacking nature' for insights into actually attuning with nature's inherent interconnectedness. This ecosystemic prac-tice asks us to dive deeper into the causalities and inter-relations involved throughout the product's entire life-cycle.

Velcro and dirt-repellent paint inspired by patterns and structures in nature, yet using toxic chemicals, are obvious 'hacking nature' examples: What good do these products do, really, if they only apply cool bio-innovations yet then undermine nature through their toxicity?

A Living Systems Designer knows the importance of applying the Logic of Life in its entirety to material sourcing, production, logistics, utility and reuse - the whole life of the product, service or place. Everything your service/product touches throughout its process is part of its life-cycle, and so as ecosystemic designers we need to be aware of the systemic footprint and legacy of our products and services. It's a move from:

**Degenerative design → Regenerative design**

**Reductionist thinking → Ecosystemic awareness**

**Silos → Systems**

A critical part of ecosystemic awareness is the ability to cultivate what we call *living systems partnerships*. Partnerships exist everywhere in nature. A bee would be nothing without the flower. The forest relies upon the fascinating mycelium.

> "Around the world, animals and humans exhale carbon dioxide, which plants take in and use for their own growth. Nitrogen from wastes is transformed into protein by microorganisms, animals, and plants. Horses eat grass and produce dung, which provides both nest and nourishment for the larvae of flies."
>
> William McDonough and Michael Braungart, design specialists

Take our own human body, sitting here reading this book, where there are trillions of cells constantly relating and collaborating, sensing and responding, without us giving any orders. Partnerships, collaboration, each part sensing and responding, all contributing to a life-affirming living-system – *this is the very stuff of life*. Without partnerships life would collapse.

> "Life did not takeover the world by combat, but by networking."
>
> Lynn Margulis, biologist

There is interdependence throughout the forest, as each tree relates with, and in varying degrees is affected by, the other. There is an intelligent sensing, responding and inter-relating throughout all the interconnected systems in the forest: from birds and insects in the air to microbes and mycelium in the soil.

*Nature Insight: Mycelium networks.* Fungi specialize in interconnecting other living entities, with most land plants depending on them. Fungi are much older than plants and evolved in the sea some 700 million years before plants, and then moving to land 70 million years before plants did. Fungi extract minerals and nutrients from rocks which they then feed to plants in one of the most fundamental partnerships on the planet. This partnership allowed plants to thrive on the Earth's surface, and led to the oxygenation of our atmosphere, a crucial evolutionary step for life on Earth. Whilst the fungi gain sugars from the plants, the plants gain vital nutrients and life-supporting services from the fungi. The fungi, through their network of mycelium underground, connect stationary plants with hundreds of other plants, and share nutrients between plants, which encourages diversity within the ecosystem. These underground mycelia networks can, for instance, connect one tree of a certain species, say an oak, with another tree of a different species, say a beech, and share nutrients between them where one tree may be rich in one mineral and the other is deficit.

As we shift from reductive design-thinking to ecosystemic awareness, we shift our perspective from silos and separate bits and bytes to seeing the connections, networks, partnerships, feedback loops, and flows. This allows for a shift in consciousness, a new way of seeing the world, a way that prioritizes partnership and collaboration over competition and control, and today we are finding more and more organizations taking this ecosystemic approach to their operations and partnerships.

*Business Insight: Atlantic Leather – an Icelandic fish-skin leather provider.* In Iceland fishing is one of the main industries, and there is a lot of leftover waste in the form of fish skins. An entrepreneur saw a potential to tap into this biological nutrient instead of sending it to landfill, and today Atlantic Leather produces exotic, durable and beautiful leather made from the skin of salmon, wolfish, perch and cod, which is upcycled and then sold to luxury brands for furniture and fashion. The partnerships Atlantic Leather has formed, have transformed waste into new products, creating jobs and contributing to economic sustainability on the island of Iceland.

 *Business Insight: Toast Ale – an international craft beer company.* Toast Ale was founded by food-waste activists who were sick of seeing perfectly good bread go to waste. Every year we waste enough food to feed the entire planet. Food production is the single biggest impact humanity has had on the environment as it uses huge amounts of land, fuel, energy and pesticides. In the USA, bread is top of the list of our most wasted household food items. As much as **44% of all bread produced in the UK is wasted** but almost half of that is before it even reaches our homes. Sandwich factories discard the heel and first slice of every loaf – that's 17% of the loaf – because we don't buy sandwiches made with crusts. Toast has set up partnerships with bread factories that supplies Toast the end loafs to use in the brewing of Toast Ale. The profits from Toast Ale go to support local food waste charities it has formed partnerships with, as well as an international food-waste NGO call Feedback.

Tapping into beneficial partnerships has grown the so-called *Sharing Economy* to a billion-dollar market in a few years, and it's estimated to grow from $14 billion in 2014 to $335 billion by 2025. The sharing economy is a new industry based on sharing resources – like cars, power drills, apartments, bikes - mainly through technological applications. These platforms make it easy for people to share resources instead of buying their own. Data shows that private vehicles go unused for 95% of their life time (Yaraghi, 2017). In the US, there are 80 million power drills that are only used for 13 minutes on average throughout their lifetime (New York Times, 2013). We are wasting resources on a massive scale in part due to mechanistic design-thinking and in part due to mechanistic behaviors around product use and ownership. Rather than interconnections we have created silos of separation.

Just like the mycelium transporting nutrients and communicating underground, the internet provides a means of sharing resources and enabling communication between humans that would have never met without this technology. Car-sharing services allow us to tap into a partnership potential in the wider ecosystem – tap into hidden unused potential. This increasing tendency to share is referred to as the rise of 'collaborative consumption', and it is a reason why many organizations transform their business model into selling a service rather than a product.

Another advantage of *living systems partnerships* is the synergies and creativity that can happen when people and organizations join forces in mutual win-win relationships that actually create win-win-win synergies – unlocking benefiting not just for each party in the partnership but also for other stakeholders like the wider society and the environment).

There is a permaculture principle known as the *edge effects*, which explains how rich creativity and biodiversity is found in areas where two systems or cultures overlap. In nature, we can see this phenomenon where ocean meets land in mangrove ecologies (where land and sea interface) and reef ecologies (where coral and ocean interface) both of which are some of the most biodiverse and innovative natural ecosystems. The interface between two systems spawns richness. In organizations, we find this when we bring together different teams and stakeholder groups, from across the organization's different silos. We transcend the silos of separation, and allow creativity and innovation to spawn.

 *Dive Deeper:* Permaculture started out as a concept focused on regenerating land by offering an alternative to monocultural approaches that reduce biodiversity. It explores the principles for how to design thriving ecosystems, principles that can inspire our design-thinking in organizations too. In the book *Permaculture: Principles and Pathways Beyond Sustainability*, 12 principles of holistic permaculture design approaches are explored, and provide useful insight for the Living Systems Designer.

As a Living Systems Designer, it's your task to ensure that all stakeholders thrive, and that you have perspective on all the nested systems affected by your designs, not just what's immediately apparent. You work with the whole-system – take everything into account and think through the ripple effects each action creates. If the design is not life-affirming, then it is not worth pursuing. Or if one action is beneficial when looked upon separately but is not when the whole system is taken into account, *then you redesign*.

An example could be a state-of-the art green net-zero conference center with all the 'right' energy efficient solutions and technologies implemented, and lots of prestige around communicating how GHG emissions have been reduced, gaining international recognition. Yet, upon closer inspection, the furniture is produced using degenerative production approaches, and non-recyclable plastic cutlery is used in the cafeteria, with food coming from non-organic non-fair-trade suppliers. The building – the shell – may be celebrated as state of the art, but as a *whole living system* this 'green net-zero' conference center is not regenerative.

Living Systems Design is ultimately about designing for evolution: Every organism, every living-system, is a participant in evolution. By their very nature, they are inter-relating with other systems and participating in this creative, emergent unfolding of life. Our human systems are no different, whether referring to the human body, an organization, a local community, or a city. The Living Systems Designer is tasked to get curious, be present, and open up to the wonder of the interconnections and inter-relational capacities of the entire ecosystem – this ecosystemic awareness is unfortunately rarely taught in design or architecture schools today.

This ecosystemic awareness requires us to connect to our inner and outer nature, through what leadership specialist Otto Scharmer calls *open mind, open heart, open will* (Scharmer, 2016). As leaders and designers, we must cultivate this ecosystemic awareness so we tune into the system, sense into what could emerge in any given place or situation.

As we open up to ecosystemic awareness, we open ourselves up to the emergent ever-changing and inter-relational nature of real life. Change is an inherent part of life's evolution. A designer's role is dynamic and ever-evolving, as it constantly senses into the system and asks what is needed now, while being conscious of how best to tune-in to ever-changing local and global conditions. The Living Systems Design is ever-evolving, ever in tune with its surroundings – never static. This awareness can be expansive, playful and creative if we allow ourselves to let-go of certainty and predictability.

> "Designing for evolution requires us to treat change as a source of creativity … [it] entails working with a complex, layered, and dynamic set of relationships … By abandoning the illusion of control, designers enter a deeper practice, fostering the inherent creativity of the system in which they are working."
>
> Pamela Mang and Bill Haggard,
> regenerative development and design specialists

At one level, we are all designers, as we are all participating in living systems, and can, if we so choose, become conscious co-creators by deepening our perception of the inherent creativity and relationality of the systems we are operating within. Rather than viewing ourselves as consumers driven by our unconscious biases, sub-conscious whims, ego-urges, mechanistic managerial norms and outdated societal influences, we may begin to see ourselves as participants in this rich dance of life that is for-ever unfolding and evolving with each day, hour, moment. This shift in way of seeing ourselves comes with a humbling personal and collective responsibility, to participate in ways that enrich this dance of life rather than corrupt, exploit and undermine it.

As Mang and Haggard note, "*Designing for evolution doesn't mean **designing evolution**. Evolution is an **emergent** process – one that arises out of multiple interactions among living beings and their environment … we can create evolution-friendly conditions.'*" (Mang & Haggard, 2016).

Essentially, we are asking ourselves to enhance our capacity to sense-and-respond to life's ever-changing context in ways that **honor the integrity of life**. This is designing with the Logic of Life right at the heart of our design-thinking, all the way from design to end-of-life and new beginnings.

In Part 3 we will look at tools to integrate this Living Systems Design into your everyday leadership. Now, we turn to the next DNA Component, Living Systems Culture.

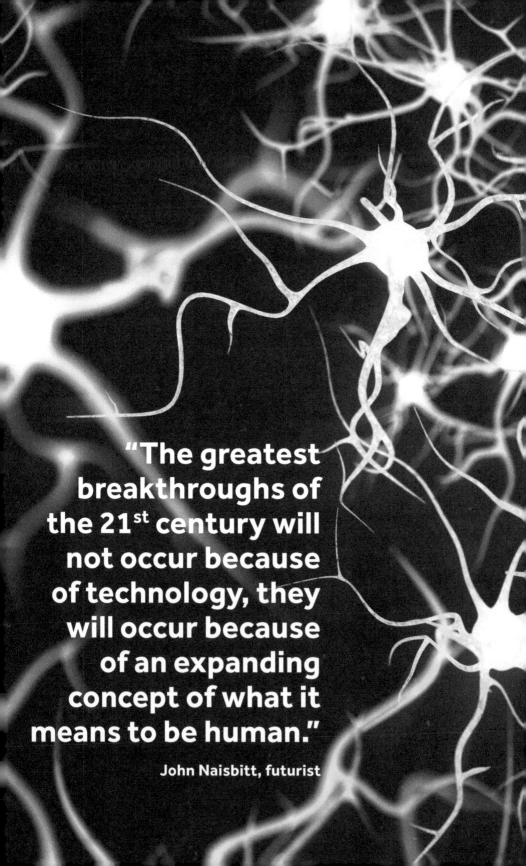

"The greatest breakthroughs of the 21$^{st}$ century will not occur because of technology, they will occur because of an expanding concept of what it means to be human."

John Naisbitt, futurist

# Living Systems Culture

Much of today's business management literature and business school programmes perceive organizations as a series of clock-work mechanistic components rather than complex systemic inter-relations. They assume that our organizations can be controlled, monitored, and reduced down into neat and tidy siloes of units and departments. They portray change and organizational transformation as something that is best managed through top-down, linear, formulaic procedures and that new initiatives are best created by a separate innovation team or by the C-suite who then cascade change down through the ranks.

This view, we believe, stifles organizations; making them unfit for dealing with a fast and ever-changing landscape. Too many organizations today, we believe, are locked in an old mindset that does more harm than good. When we zoom in on many organizations today we find rigid, mechanistic hierarchies dominated by people on the verge of burnout, with cultures ridden with fear, competition and scarcity. This only serves to limit and weaken the potential of the organization and its stakeholders.

Changing this paradigm is a big reason for us writing this book and co-creating a new approach to building healthy successful organization geared for the 21st century. We have explored the practices, cultures and leadership styles of those pioneering this new paradigm, and thankfully they are many in number. Leaders are starting to realize that the old ways are no longer fit for the world of today.

The mindset we as Regenerative Leaders must cultivate is one where we see the organization as a dynamic life-affirming living-system. The Regenerative Leader sees his/her role as an *Ecosystemic Facilitator* constantly tuning in to the entire web of the living-system while cultivating the right conditions conducive for the organization to flourish.

This is the shift Regenerative Leaders will facilitate – a shift from mechanistic structures to that of living-systems. This is a shift in our human consciousness at personal and organizational levels. As the futurist John Naisbitt notes, this expanding concept of what it means to be human will define our 21$^{st}$ century.

## LIVING-SYSTEMS LOGIC

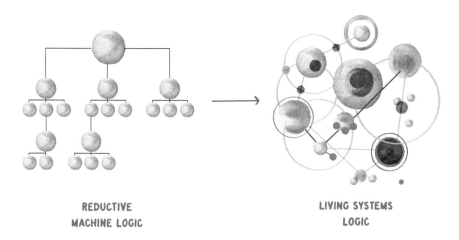

REDUCTIVE
MACHINE LOGIC

LIVING SYSTEMS
LOGIC

© copyright Hutchins & Storm - inspired by Biomimicry for Creative Innovation

Now, let's dive into the rich cultural soil of the living organization, and the key attributes that make up a Living Systems Culture. The essence here is tuning in to what makes a living-system thrive, and cultivating the leadership skills and cultural capacities now needed in 21$^{st}$ Century business.

# LIVING SYSTEMS CULTURE

The DNA Strands of Living Systems Culture are:

1. Survival & Thrival – To thrive the business has to deliver healthy financial results

2. Mission & Movement – Make sure the organization is contributing to something bigger than the organization

3. Developmental & Respectful – Hold space for yourself and others to learn, grow, and develop in respectful ways

4. Diversity & Inclusion – Valuing diverse backgrounds and perspectives as part of an inclusive values-rich culture

5. Self-Organizing & Locally-Attuning – Unlock resiliency and agility through self-organizing principles

6. Eco-systemic Facilitation & Transformation – Attentive care and understanding of the entire system in which the organization operates

# 1. Survival & Thrival

**Objective:** *To thrive the business has to deliver healthy financial results*

The essence of Regenerative Business is that it adds more value than it takes throughout its ecosystem of stakeholders (both human and non-human). This value is understood in a systemic way – the systemic value to all aspects of life, including but not limited to monetary profit.

Make no mistake, first-and-foremost the organization needs to know how to survive and thrive financially. Regenerative Business does not rely on philanthropy or grants. Yes, grants and government incentives may be a useful contributor to the overall business approach, but the core business has to be able to generate its profit through the products or services it provides. How the organization chooses to use that profit is often telling. Profit can be reinvested back into the vitality of the business to support its mission or profit can be siphoned off to far-removed shareholders and investors that may show little interest in the company's mission.

Since the 2008 financial crash, more and more organizations are seeking to purge themselves of parasitic investor relations, those that do not benefit the long-term vitality of the organization. For example, when Paul Polman was CEO of one of the world's largest and oldest corporations, he chose to re-profile Unilever's shareholder base to win over benign long-term investors: *"We spend a lot of time disengaging from shareholders who do not benefit our strategy, and attracting those who do buy into what we are doing. There will always be people driven by short-termism, greed and self-interest, but we'd rather not have them associated with our company."* (Confino, 2014).

Another high-profile example is founder of the Virgin Group, Sir Richard Branson, who notes: *"One of the more devastating theories of the 1970s was that no matter what it took to achieve it, the primary purpose of business was to maximise value for its shareholders. This principle has led to a variety of social ills where businesses discard employees (at the drop of a hat), pollute our air and waters, or create short-term gains that are unsustainable. It is important for people in business to recognise that long-term shareholder value is more likely to be created by companies that value their employees, act as good environmental stewards and think long term in general."* (Branson, 2011).

*Business Insight: Iberdrola Group – multinational electricity provider.*
Iberdrola Group is a large multinational energy provider with over 35,000 employees. In 2001, the organization set about radically changing its business strategy to decarbonize its assets, move away from oil and coal, and embrace renewables. Back in 2001, there were many raised eye-brows across the investor community. Investors mocked Iberdrola's strategic decision as 'bad for business'. Over the years that followed, the company has consistently made good on its ambitious commitments to radically decarbonize while increasing revenue growth and shareholder value. Back then it was 20th in the world, now it is world's 5th largest electricity provider, and provides energy to over 100 million customers worldwide. Its business strategy is focused on the 'war against climate change' and its commitment to 30% carbon reduction by 2020 was achieved before the deadline, and it's on track for 50% by 2030 and zero emissions by 2050. Over the next 4 years the company will invest $34bn in renewable networks. Its mission-driven sense of purpose attracts and retains talent, and its rapid reduction in polluting power-generation has put pressure on competitors to follow suit creating a virtuous cycle across the energy market. Due to it consistently meeting its short and medium-term commitments, investors are realizing that decarbonization is actually good business sense rather than bad for business.

This Regenerative Business approach offers a better way of tapping into tangible and intangible value throughout the organization (human resources, materials, processes, culture, value-chain partnerships) and generates healthy profit by flourishing inside and out. It doesn't just look at the bottom-line but at value-creation throughout its system which ultimately makes the business more resilient and agile.

The Global Living Asset Management Performance (LAMP) Index has been tracking 60 companies for over two decades, and detailed research shows that those embracing a regenerative business approach are able to out-think competitors, be more efficient and generate market share gains that yield extraordinary shareholder returns. Regenerative organizations are not only held in high regard by employees, customers, suppliers and other stakeholders because they enrich the communities and stakeholders they serve, but also because they provide the products and services that outperform competitors.

One such case is Nucor, a steel company operating in a tough, low-margin, competitive, cyclic, and lay-off-prone industry. Yet Nucor has bucked the market norm of regular lay-offs by embracing a regenerative approach, looking after its people while making healthy profits. Let's explore this case in more detail:

 *Business Insight: Nucor - North American steel maker.* Nucor, has created a culture of shared values, deep loyalty, committed teamwork, high innovation and agility. It operates through self-organizing team-based networks where fresh insights and innovations are actively shared across the corporate network. Nucor's bottom-up decentralized living-systems approach has enabled it to be nimble in a difficult market. Rather than the market-norm of mega steel mills, Nucor focuses on mini-mills that recycle scrap steel and work collaboratively with local communities. Nucor invests more in its people than its competitors, and has higher margins to show for it. The role of the mill-manager is not to control the mill like a machine, but rather to create the conditions for self-organizing teams to flourish, to connect with employees, to listen, mentor and encourage. *"In spite of having the highest-paid workers in the steel industry, Nucor normally has the highest net profit per employee"*, notes Jay Bragdon, who has been monitoring Nucor's performance for many years now (Bragdon, 2016).

 *Dive Deeper:* For robust research comparing the shareholder capital return of organizations rooted in yesterday's mechanistic logic comparable to organizations applying a living systems logic, google-search 'The Global Lamp Index' and also see Jay Bragdon's book *Companies That Mimic Life.*

The key for Regenerative Business is that even though a healthy bottom line is where everything begins, the vitality of the entire ecosystem is the central tenet - not a nice-to-have perk, but something core to the organization's existence and ability to succeed financially. It's the fuel that drives regenerative companies to impressive results mobilizing stakeholders throughout the system in powerful ways.

 *Business Insight: Buurtzorg - Dutch Healthcare provider.* When Buurtzorg started out in in 2006 everyone thought they were crazy. A small group of nurses were fed-up with the stressful work environment for social workers and nurses in the Netherlands. They started Buurtzorg with self-organizing teams of 10-12 and a vision to give their clients (elderly people) the attention and care they deserved. This attracted nurses from across the Netherlands who were fed-up with controlling mechanistic bureaucracy and stress. They simply wished to be allowed to primarily focus on providing quality care for their clients in need. In the years that followed, Buurtzorg has grown to a company of 14,000 employees with spin-off companies such as physical therapy and catering, all innovatively created by the nurses who knew the market better than anyone. Buurtzorg far outperforms traditional social care companies providing richer client service while reducing overall efficiency and costs. They have accomplished a 50% reduction in hours of care needed and Buurtzorg has overhead costs of 8%, compared to an industry average of 25%. Why? Because something powerful happens when people feel motivated, empowered and personally engaged (Laloux, 2014).

This brings us on to the next DNA strand, the *mission and movement* of the organization.

## 2. Mission & Movement

**Objective:** *Make sure the organization is contributing to something bigger than the organization*

Organizations that have profit as their only motivation won't last long in the changing landscape of our world today. What employees crave - and decide by their engagement - is whether the organization has a mission they resonate with, so they can feel good about contributing their time and effort on a daily basis. Unlocking the brilliance of the workforce depends upon having an emotionally engaging mission. The 2018 *Workforce of the Future* research report conducted by PwC found that 88% of millennials (people born around 1980-2000) want to work for a company with values that reflect their own (PwC, 2018). Millennials will comprise 75% of the workforce by 2025. Having a mission-driven organization where people feel engaged and connected to its purpose and values will prove to be essential for organizational success.

A regenerative organization's mission is not a static statement defined and declared, and then stuck up on the wall or put on a PowerPoint slide. No, it's dynamic, it's alive, it *evolves*. As the landscape changes, the mission evolves to ensure the organization's maximum effect. Likewise, the employees of regenerative organizations are rarely seen as 'employees' but instead as valuable front-line members of the organization and it's mission and movement.

Let's differentiate between what we mean here by the words *mission, purpose*, and *values*, as they are words that are often handed around in today's world of business lingo.

A **mission** is the direction set by the company. You might call a mission its North Star - and it is core to the organization's strategy. It is also what we call a *transformative mission*, as a Regenerative Business's mission seeks to transform our systems from consumerism, disconnection, and degenerative business practices towards conscious living, sustainability, connectedness and life-affirming practices.

**Purpose** is what we embody – both personally and culturally. Having a sense of purpose is to conduct oneself, or live in a way, that is purposeful. We call it the *power of purpose* and we shall unpack this power of purpose in a moment as it's a crucial aspect of Regenerative Business.

**Values** are the core behaviors people within the organization abide by while delivering on the mission. Values are not external 'things' decided by the leadership team with the assistance of external consultants, changing every time a new CEO steps in – no, they're molded in to every fiber of the company DNA, actively used in everyday decision making. They are what guide the organization amid its evolving journey to make good on its Mission.

And then we have **Movement**, which is closely linked to mission for regenerative organizations. The *movement* represents the desire to transform society towards life-affirming futures. The movement is the motivation of the mission that reaches beyond the survival and thrival of the organization into societal transformation. There are plenty of good examples of companies working at being a movement as well as having a mission. Let's look at a few of these:

 *Business Insight: A plethora of organizations demonstrating the importance of Mission & Movement.* The menstrual wear company **Thinx** is helping revolutionize women's attitude to their body and menstrual cycles. An important part of the company mission is to educate about the empowerment of tracking your cycle and being in tune with the constant changes in your body. The company is bigger than its products – it is contributing to a revolution in consciousness. *Houdini*, the outdoor brand, sets an impressive standard for regenerative value chains and materials, and also sees its responsibility to educate and empower customers to become more sustainable and responsible when being outdoors. There's the water-pump manufacturer *Grundfos* that invests massively in ensuring people below the poverty-line get access to clean drinking water. It's not just about the 'business case', it's about the mission and the movement. They see it as their responsibility to provide clean water for everyone in the areas they operate in. *Tony's Chocolonely* is a chocolate brand that was started when the founder realized the extent of child slavery in the chocolate industry. Many kids are forced to work long hours in the cacao plantations without pay. Some so-called 'sustainable brands' - large corporates who win sustainability awards - often act slowly while profiteering. If you buy chocolate without the fair-traded logo (or something of similar standard) you can be pretty sure its traded unethically. *Tony's Chocolonely* invest massively in the entire value chain and have a dedicated mission to end slavery – when you open their chocolates their mission is the first thing you see: *"I exist to end slavery in the chocolate industry. My mission is to make 100% slave free the norm in chocolate. Together with you. Are you in?"* *Carcel* is a fashion company with a mission to employ incarcerated women, giving them a fair wage and empower them for a new path in life post prison while enabling them to take care of their family outside of prison. They have established close relationships with everyone from the inmates, to the prison officials, local authorities and sustainable local resource providers – alpaca wool for their operations in Cusco, Peru and silk for their operations in Chiang Mai, Thailand.

*Purpose* has become a bit of a buzz word these days and can often get watered down to mean very little, so let's zoom in on the core aspects of this *power of purpose* so that we can see how an organization embodying its purpose is key to Living Systems Culture.

Psychotherapist Vicktor Frankl, in his classic book *Man's Search for Meaning*, wrote that *"happiness cannot be pursued; it* ensues *as a result of living purposefully"* (Frankl, 2004). This is true for the organization's mission. A mission cannot be pursued in some outer sense, but ensues as a result of operating purposefully throughout everyday challenges in alignment with its values.

To understand the context of an organization's purpose, we must turn to further understanding the personal purpose within the individual. World-leading purpose specialist and best-selling author of *The Power of Purpose*, Richard Leider, defines a simple model that looks at purpose through 3 overlapping dimensions, to create the power of purpose within us as leaders (Leider, 2015).

# POWER OF PURPOSE

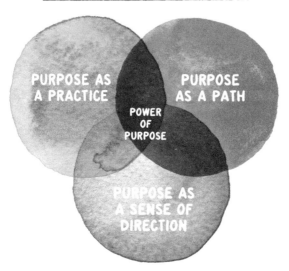

Source: Richard Leider

*Purpose as a practice:* This is a daily practice, a quality of attentiveness, how we are listening-in to ourselves, sensing into what feels right or not, learning to see beyond our constrictions and old habits that may be holding us back. This is linked to self-awareness and systemic-awareness. This 'purpose as a practice' is not 'what' but 'how' we attend to everyday interactions. It's not 'what' we do, but the 'way' that we do it.

*Purpose as a path:* The path is not only what lies ahead of us, but the wake we leave behind us, our legacy. How we traverse through life is our path. Leider speaks of the power of 'growing and giving' as core to our purpose path. Each day we may ask ourselves, how do I choose to grow today, how do I choose to give today? We self-reflect and deepen each day as we walk the purpose path.

***Purpose as a sense of direction:*** While travelling through life, we can cultivate our 'inner compass' to help us navigate amid a wind-tossed sea of distractions and conflicting desires. A daily discipline of gaining coherence within ourselves, grounding ourselves, connecting to our deeper self, so that this inner compass is easily accessible rather than buried under the stress and cacophony of day-to-day pressures.

As we cultivate our personal power of purpose as a leader, we also sense our resonance with the organizational purpose (its mission and cultural values it operates by), and learn to recognize the evolutionary nature of the organizational living-system. This is often very revealing, as it is through personal purpose, that Regenerative Leaders access the power of the organizational sense of purpose.

When the personal power of purpose aligns with the organizational sense of purpose, we unlock brilliance within ourselves, in our teams and through our inter-relations. Individuals find authentic meaning in work and feel energized and emotionally engaged through trials and tribulations. The organization thus becomes our vehicle for manifesting purposeful living in the world. Cultivating this resonant sense of purpose across the organizational living-system is an art. Our self and systemic awareness helps us detect when there is resonance or not. If the organizational sense of purpose feels forced our inauthentic, then the living-system dynamics will not flow as vitally or creatively as they could do.

*Business Insight: Whole Foods Market - an organic ethical supermarket chain.* Whole Foods Market is now an international operation with thousands of stores. Whilst its mission is to bring good quality food to its customers, core to its existence is contributing to the wider movement of healthy food and wellbeing. Co-CEO Walter Robb says: *"We are not so much retailers with a mission as missionaries who retail. The stores are our canvas upon which we can paint our deeper purpose of bringing whole foods and greater health to the world".* Every three years 800 store team leaders gather together for a

'Tribal Gathering' – a long weekend of networking, inspiration, education and a renewing of the deeper purpose, mission and movement that guides the organization.

*Business Insight: Triodos - an international bank that aims to make money a force for good.* Triodos's mission as a business is to provide finance for enterprises that enhance quality of life through providing benefits to society and the environment. It has 4 core values that are shared across all of its international businesses: Transparency, Entrepreneurship, Sustainability, Excellence. Through a mix of global and local activities these values are embedded into day-to-day behaviours. There is a global values workshop held three times a year where people from all countries are invited to attend three days in the woods for deep connection with the values, personal and organizational sense of purpose, and company mission. This helps cultivate resonance between people's personal purpose and the organization's purpose. Each country business takes responsibility for tailoring their own approach to ensuring this resonance of purpose. For instance, at Triodos UK there are values-workshops where people explore the practicalities of living the values amid day-to-day pressures.

We can guide the organization with a clear Mission and Movement, yet we cannot 'control' its way of evolving. Implicit in the Mission and Movement is an *evolutionary power of purpose* that is ever tuning in to its changing environment.

Regenerative Leaders are cultivating the leadership skills of sensing into the living-system; cultivating ecosystemic awareness so that they can better tune-in to the potential of what wants to emerge within the systems they are engaged in, at all levels: local (at a team level); organizational (across the living-system); global (in the wider socio-ecological-economic systems we operate in). The organization is a living-system that has its own evolutionary purpose which we can learn to listen-in to and serve.

This hits the nail on the head – the Mission and Movement has to be guided by listening-in to the living organization. Closely linked to Mission and Movement is the Regenerative Leader's ability to facilitate regular dialogues and check-ins to cultivate resonance between our personal purpose and organizational sense of purpose. This doesn't mean that each employee is forced to have a specific personal purpose but that there's coherence between the personal purpose and aspects of the organizational purpose. Many different individual purposes contribute to a vibrant living-system. In the case of Whole Foods Market, some employees may be passionately driven by making organic and healthy produce more accessible, others may be driven by offering a unique customer experience, while some may be driven by ensuring employees throughout the organization feel valued. All these individual purpose-drivers makes Whole Foods Market thrive. This unlocks immense power, magnetizing employees and leaders alike to do extraordinary things. Purpose is not something to be pursued or attained, it is something to be lived, it's a power that flows through us and through our organization's conversation with the world.

## 3. Developmental & Respectful

*Objective: Hold space for yourself and others to learn, grow, and develop in respectful ways*

For Living Systems Cultures to thrive, we need people on the ground who everyday create the cultural conditions conducive to life. Regenerative Businesses break away from fear-based, control-obsessed cultures and instead embrace respectful cultures where people feel safe yet courageous enough to explore, learn and grow. Too much energy is used in conventional organizations by people who try to fit in to norms, play it safe, follow bureaucratic procedures, and who dim down their true essence out of fear of being seen as different or not successful.

Robert Kegan and Lisa Lahey, two Harvard psychologists, have done an impressive amount of research in the field of developmental organizations, about what works, what doesn't, and why a developmental culture is important for next-stage organizations. One of their key arguments is the need to radically reduce the amount of energy people spend on pretending, covering up and hiding: "*In an ordinary organization, most people are doing a second job no one is paying them for. In businesses large and small; in government agencies, schools, and hospitals; in for-profits and nonprofits, and in any country in the world, most people are spending time and energy covering up their weaknesses, managing other people's impressions of them, showing themselves to their best advantage, playing politics, hiding their inadequacies, hiding their uncertainties, hiding their limitations. We regard this as the single biggest loss of resources that organizations suffer every day. Is anything more valuable to a company than the way its people spend their energies?"* (Kegan & Lahey, 2016).

Does that sound like something you have experienced?

The reality is, even in some of the most mission-driven social entrepreneurial organizations, if you dig a little deeper you may find a corrosive concoction of burn-out, stress, anti-social silos, cliques, toxic office gossip, power addiction, and a general lack of coherence around core values being lived in the day-to-day behaviors. It's as if the 'outer' focus on the exciting *mission* comes at the expense of the 'inner' authenticity and attentiveness of the company values and culture.

Often, in passionate mission-driven companies Founders and CEOs bring a ton of confidence and charisma that inspires devotion and loyalty to the movement; however, this – unwittingly – casts a shadow. In what the leadership specialist Simon Western refers to as 'Messiah Leadership' people become 'followers', subsumed by the CEO or Founder's zealous mission-driven dynamic. These followers become overly-dependent on the Messiah Leader, submissively dedicating themselves to a higher cause, but in ways that undermine their own personal development, which can create all sorts of problems *inside* the organization, such as a fragile 'inner' culture that is not authentically shining through into the 'outer' mission. This inner-outer incoherence can damage the organization if not handled carefully. The mission becomes more about 'outer' propositions, 'outer' sustainability, PR and brand, rather than about embracing a holistic life-affirming approach.

Regenerative Leadership is markedly different from Messiah Leadership, and it relates more to what Simon Western calls 'Eco-Leadership' where the leader is attentive to both the 'inner' and the 'outer', and the health of the entire interconnected ecosystem. The leader can drive the Mission and Movement forward with passion and dynamism and yet can also create the conditions for a thriving, developmental and purposeful culture.

*Dive Deeper:* For more on Simon Western's work on Messiah Leadership and Eco-Leadership, see *Leadership: A Critical Text*.

A Developmental and Respectful culture cultivates conditions for people to flourish individually and collectively. Every aspect of day-to-day relations, conversations, small group reflections, peer reviews, meeting conventions, informal social sharing and formal decision-making protocols aim to stimulate our conscious learning and development.

The question remains as to *how* to implement Developmental and Respectful cultures within an organization's system, and for that we turn to Kegan and Lahey, who have studied five different approaches and techniques that work well across different sectors and industries.

We summarize their key insights as:

1. *Create procedures for giving feedback and providing safe space for sharing:*

   It's important to have defined procedures for how we share feedback, critique and respectfully communicate these learning insights. We each take responsibility for our own learning and for helping others learn, as part of a learning culture. Some organizations combine quick feedback systems with more in-depth methods for best results. A company may use quick app-based feedback-systems of giving marks or thumb-ups or down on presentation techniques, meeting facilitation, and other activities. These quick feedback systems can help to assess general performance levels but are not really sufficient for true learning and growth, as that requires richer qualitative inputs. Hence, app-based systems are best used in addition to deeper qualitative processes where employees feel seen, heard and gain detailed input on how to improve and grow. These qualitative procedures can be deep listening in pairs, peer-to-peer coaching groups, or group dialogue, such as a 'fish-bowl' (you create a circle with the selected team sitting in the middle that share their learnings and insights while others around the outside of the circle listen, and later reflect back what they heard in non-judgmental ways). We share more about certain sharing methods in Part 3 of the book. Here is an example, taken from Kegan and Lahey's research on ArcLight Hollywood movie theatre company:

*"In one such conversation we watched three employees from the IT, marketing, and operations arms of the theatre business talk about why a new customer-loyalty program seemed to be stalling. The COO of the theatre division suspected that these three key players were not communicating effectively. So she asked them to describe how they were experiencing the situation. The fishbowl format enabled the wider theatre managers' group to listen to, learn from, and participate in the conversation. With careful facilitation by another senior manager, the three were able to express the ways in which they each felt shut out or shut down by the other two when decisions were made and information should have been shared. Each also identified some personal trigger or blind spot that had led him or her to shut down one of the others. They could then reach agreement in the presence of colleagues about how to proceed in a different way. Because dialogues like these are routine, people view them as a healthy exercise in sharing vulnerability, rather than a rare and threatening experience."* (Kegan & Lahey, 2016).

2. **Full transparency**

In some of the companies Kegan and Lahey researched, they have a rule of recording all meetings. If you have been talked about at a certain meeting you can easily find out what was discussed, listen to the recording, ask for more detailed feedback. Again, some companies use an app system where they give each other feedback during daily interactions that is made accessible to all. Not to encourage comparisons but rather to help facilitate a culture where we learn from each other regardless of position, age, and experience and that there's no shame attached to imperfection. We are all on a constant developmental journey regardless of hierarchical position in the organization. This can feel threatening to our ego to begin with, but as people see that the intent is to help each other grow and develop, not to blame or undermine, most employees and leaders alike then learn to embrace the feedback rather than overly-defend against it.

3. **Everyone is expected to show vulnerability**

A developmental culture doesn't work if only the new-comers are expected to share their mistakes, weaknesses, doubts and fears. All are expected to air their concerns, worries, ideas – and also if things are happening at home that your colleagues would benefit from being aware of: a divorce, death of a loved one, issues with a kid, a wedding coming up – we all have personal lives and in developmental cultures we're not expected to leave all of that behind when at work. This goes directly against what most of us have been taught to do in the workplace. Developmental organizations have on-boarding courses and continuous training where everyone is expected to dedicate a lot of time to their own development. It is this willingness to be open to learning, to show vulnerability, to embrace our blind-spots and grow that is key to a developmental culture. It reduces the energy spent on pretending and covering up.

4. *Nothing is static – dynamic non-equilibrium*

Another factor is that companies often rotate roles and positions to encourage the constant stretching of comfort zones and up-levelling of skills. People rotate teams and roles to ensure shared learnings, new ideas and perspectives and constant tuning in to growth and learning. For example, at the e-commerce company NextJump, a highly driven ambitious leader was appointed to the leadership team. She wasn't voted in for the next tenure (the entire company regularly vote for who makes up the leadership team). She felt mortified. Through receiving feedback, she learned that her colleagues felt she prioritized her own results over their collective growth. She was not playing her part in the developmental culture. In their eyes, she had become too obsessed by her own success. She learned from this, reflected and saw her blind-spot, and worked on improving. After months of a dedicated effort and inner growth she was voted back in to the leadership team.

5. *Failure is expected*

Developmental cultures encourage failure – you cannot grow and evolve if you have a fear of failing. The investment company Bridgewater uses a variety of tools and practices to help people learn how to embrace failures as growth opportunities. For instance, all employees record problems and failures in a companywide 'issues log' detailing their own contributions to mistakes. Logging failures is applauded and rewarded, as its seen as a vital part of the organizational learning. Not recording mistakes can be viewed as a serious breach of duty. When the culture celebrates your failures and your honesty about admitting them, it encourages people to try out new things and to learn in an open way. It creates the bottom-up conditions than enable organizations to innovate, adapt and evolve.

A developmental culture is essential for enriching the relationality across the system, the flow of feedback, the local-attunement, and the co-creativity. We enliven the living organization by cultivating the nutritious soil of its culture. The essence here is for the Regenerative Leader to cultivate a psychologically safe, yet stimulating space that allows for each person to evolve and develop authentically – letting go of trying to make everyone fit in to a mechanistic regime for how certain roles are performed.

 *Business Insight: Next Jump – a billion-dollar e-commerce provider.* Next Jump is one of the organizations that Kegan and Lahey researched in-depth. A typical day at Next Jump begins with people working in pairs – known as 'talking partners' (TPs). Each person in the pair shares, listens and co-mentors in an unstructured yet authentic way. It is part of the daily culture of Next Jump. The TP meetings cover three aspects: *meeting, venting, working*: The pair commits to consistently *meeting* up each morning; the sharing starts with each person *venting* whatever is on their mind, whether its work related or home-life, warts and all, so we have a safe space to vent frustrations and anxieties while learning to bring our whole-selves to work. After venting the conversation focuses on the work we are doing and the pair help coach each other to see constructive pathways forward on any given challenge, idea, process. Then, every week for one hour, two different pairs of talking partners and an experienced coach come together in what is called the 'situational workshop' (SW). The 4 explore challenges they faced during the working week, and through the sharing and coaching, are encouraged to reach a higher level of self-awareness, and explore different ways of responding to challenges to avoid reactivity and increase responsiveness. Then, monthly, there is another company-wide practice called 10x Factor. 10 people each give 5 minute presentations to the whole company about their personal contributions to the company, which includes their developmental contributions to the culture as well as other outputs. People give live feedback to the presentations via an app. As part of the developmental culture, there is also a Personal Leadership Boot Camp for on-boarding new staff and developing experienced staff. All these practices work in concert together to make growth and development an inherent part of the culture.

*Dive Deeper:* For more on developmental cultures, see Kegan's and Lahey's work at Harvard University, and their book *An Everyone Culture.*

Imagine the working cultures we could help facilitate if all people spent their time and energy on becoming whole and true to themselves, rather than siphoning off energy on presenting a well-cropped image, pretending, playing the game, projecting, judging, hiding, and so on. It is this vitality, the emergent showing of your true nature in the workplace, which is so fundamental for Regenerative Leadership.

We have to integrate our own shadows, work on ourselves, notice our triggers, gain perspective on our blind spots, all while holding space for a safe and trustful environment, so that others feel able to work on themselves. It's an ongoing journey towards wholeness.

The organization will never flourish in the 21$^{st}$ century world unless we become more human, more open, more alive, more responsible and more respectful.

## 4. Diversity & Inclusion

*Objective*: *Valuing diverse backgrounds and perspectives as part of an inclusive values-rich culture*

The mechanistic corporate culture we have created over the last century or so has led us to believe we all need to be the same, to fit in by acting according to a certain standardized norm of what it means to be successful. If you deviate from this norm you find yourself struggling to fit-in and may feel excluded.

In looking at how we best cultivate cultures of Diversity and Inclusion within our complex human organizations, we can apply the logic of living-systems: the Life Dynamics of Divergence and Convergence. We stimulate divergence in our organizations by opening-up ourselves, our team dynamics and our stakeholder relations so we work across boundaries of difference. We can purposefully ensure a rich blend of diversity – in terms of ethnicity, upbringing, gender, age, general outlook and business perspectives – through our embracement of social technologies like swarms, stakeholder dialogue sessions, and future-search workshops. Through convergence, we create a sense of inclusivity and belonging. The core values and behaviors we cultivate in our culture provide the cultural soil that brings together the rich diverse perspectives and orientations celebrated through divergence. It is this honoring of both the convergence through common values, and divergence through diverse perspectives that ensures the vibrancy of our organizational living-system.

Many of us have been working in mechanistic cultures that value certain stereotypes over others, and as a result, we have developed an unconscious bias. Unconsciously, we put people into boxes, assessing them at first glance, sizing them up as to whether they are part of the 'in-crowd' or part of the 'other'. Psychologically, this has been referred to as 'othering' when we view certain types of people as different from ourselves and further create a sense of separation from them by consciously or unconsciously excluding them from the in-crowd, from our clique, clan or organizational culture.

> "People in general are biased and see reality in the shape of their own homogenous environment, making us blind to inequality. According to research, it is not that privileged people don't want to deal with inequality: they are not able to see it. When we extend these research insights to the workplace, it means that those in privileged positions are blind to the lack of equal opportunities in getting hired, making contributions or advancing. We are also blind to inequality because it's systemic, hidden in our organizational processes and implicit norms."
>
> Tinna Nielsen, anthropologist

Over the last decade, there has been a rising interest in how to move beyond our unconscious bias, so that we respect and appreciate diversity in the workplace. Not only do we know in our heart that people of all perspectives, orientations, and backgrounds ought to feel included, it also makes really good business sense to cross-pollinate the living-system with a richness of ideas and perspectives. Research proves that diversity boosts a company's profit, growth and even creativity (McKinsey, 2015).

The increasing interest in creating cultures of diversity and inclusion covers the entire spectrum of human difference: gender, ethnicity, origin of birth, age, sexual orientation, disability, education, upbringing, political orientation, psychological orientation (introvert-extrovert, for instance), and the general outlook and perspectives we bring when engaging with everyday challenges.

The first step in embracing Diversity and Inclusion is to become aware of our own unconscious bias, the filters through which we see others. This helps us empathize and understand unconscious bias and behavioral patterns in others. From this perspective, we can engage in understanding the cultural assumptions and bias throughout the organization, and its ecosystem of stakeholders. This challenges our underlying norms and ingrained perspectives. It asks us to open up our perceptual horizon so that we value the different orientation of others. The more we engage with different orientations and value the diversity this brings, the more we dissolve silos and separateness. Rather than cliques of in-crowds and 'others' we cultivate inter-relations of difference that spawn innovation, creativity and compassion.

The psychologist, Daniel Kahneman, simplifies the human mind into two general systems: System 1 (unconscious) and System 2 (conscious). System 1 dominates about 90% of our behavior and decision-making, and this system is instinctive, irrational, emotional, associative and biased. Psychologist Jonathan Haidt uses the metaphoric image of System 1 as the elephant and System 2 as the elephant rider. The rider can understand the importance of equality and diversity and try to guide the elephant using rational arguments, yet it can never force a six ton-heavy elephant to behave inclusively without the right motivation.

Part of the reason we're, culturally, not making enough progress on Diversity and Inclusion is that we have so many hidden barriers around System 1 (the elephant) – this part of the unconscious mind still largely operates in a tribe mode, where we feel safe to be around people who are like ourselves and skeptical towards those that are 'others' (Nielsen 2016).

 *Dive Deeper:* Take a look on-line at Diversity and Inclusion experts Nielsen & Kepinski's *Inclusion Nudges* for a guide to creating inclusive environments in the workplace.

The 2015 *Diversity Matters* research report by McKinsey analyzed 366 publicly listed companies and showed that organizations with high levels of diversity amongst senior leaders out-perform organizations with low levels of senior leader diversity. As well as an ethical and moral imperative, Diversity and Inclusion is becoming a strategic imperative for organizations across the board.

*Business Insight: Gucci – a global fashion brand.* In February 2019 Gucci was in a media storm due to one of its sweater designs upsetting people, as it resembled blackface caricatures. One of their influential collaborators Dapper Dan, among many others, issued a statement saying: *"There is no excuse nor apology that can erase this kind of insult. The CEO of Gucci has agreed to come from Italy to Harlem this week to meet with me, along with members of the community and other industry leaders. There cannot be inclusivity without accountability. I will hold everyone accountable."* Immediately Gucci pulled the wool sweater from all stores, issuing a statement that read: *"We consider diversity to be a fundamental value to be fully upheld, respected and at the forefront of every decision we make."* A few weeks later Gucci launched a new global Diversity and Inclusion strategy in their realization that although they felt diversity and inclusion was key to their brand they had not been 'walking the talk' properly. The strategy includes: 1) Hiring global and regional Directors focused on Diversity and Inclusion, 2) Setting up multicultural design scholarship programmes, 3) Launching a global diversity and inclusivity awareness program, 4) Launching a global exchange programme to ensure key employees gets broad cultural exposure. This shows how our blind spots can often cause harm to others. It takes a dedicated effort to the leadership dynamics of self-and-systemic awareness to ensure we 'walk the talk' of company values. In our view Gucci responded quickly and responsibly, but time will tell how this programme transforms the organization and it's value-chain.

*Nature Insight: Nature banks on diversity.* Colonies – both bees and ants – with a lot of variation tend to survive and thrive whereas colonies with little diversity tend to collapse. Honeybee colonies with greater diversity are also less stressed as there's less competition between members as they get to occupy different niches. Biologist Tamsin Wooley-Barker explains: *"A harvester ant colony with more genetic diversity grows faster, survives longer, and reproduces earlier than less diverse ones nearby. That's because of their*

*wider range of foraging styles. Some workers start early, others late; some are active and intrepid, others slow and cautious. Collectively, the colony achieves longer, more effective foraging"* (Wooley-Barker, 2017).

 **Business Insight: The Social Capital Fund** A Danish capital and investment fund that specializes in companies that proactively include minorities. The Social Capital Fund invests and helps accelerate companies with a strong social profile – meaning companies that actively work to include those outside the normal labour market. People that may have a hard time finding a regular job due to a physical disability, a mental illness or a social challenge. The investment fund has proven the financial success of these companies – it makes good business sense to invest in diversity and inclusion. Not just for the government and for those that get employment but also for the financial health of each company.

Diversity and Inclusion is all about leaders becoming more self-aware, more conscious of their own blind-spots, projections, and unconscious biases, while opening-up and valuing difference systemically. The Logic of Life shows us that living-systems bank on diversity. Life doesn't thrive in silo-based monocultures. The geneticist Sir Ronald Fisher has demonstrated in his research that a population's capacity to evolve successfully depends on its level of diversity (Fisher, 1930).

All cultures need to be infused with different perspectives to truly innovate and reach new heights.

## 5. Self-Organizing & Locally-Attuning

*Objective: Unlock resiliency and agility through self-organizing principles*

While we do find hierarchies in nature, these hierarchies are not ones of power-and-control that stifle the freedom of individuals. In communities like hives, colonies and swarms, individuals are free to constantly adapt to the changing environment while operating within the community's constraints. These communities are highly adaptive and resilient, because they tap into the collective intelligence of the whole while embracing bottom-up self-organization.

Self-organizing ways of working are becoming more accepted across all sectors and sizes of businesses, with a variety of organizations applying formalized approaches for self-organization - such as Holacracy, Agile and Sociocracy - or working to develop their own home-grown approaches. Self-management is one of Frederic Laloux's 3 key characteristics of next-stage Tier 2 'Teal' organizations (the others being 'the journey toward wholeness' and 'evolutionary purpose').

> "In a self-managing organization, change can come from any person who senses that change is needed. This is how nature has worked for millions of years. Innovation doesn't happen centrally, according to place, but at the edges, all the times, when some organism senses a change in the environment and experiments to find an appropriate response. Some attempts fail to catch on; others rapidly spread to all corners of the ecosystem."
>
> Frederick Laloux, organizational specialist

The main shift towards self-organizing teams is from top-down power-based hierarchy towards 'heterarchic' roles/areas of responsibility. In heterarchic organizations levels of hierarchy are significantly reduced, making for a more networked organization. Cultivating relationship dynamics, listening and collaborating skills, personal accountability and facilitation, is all essential here. Hence, self-organizing ways of operating are coupled with a Developmental and Respectful culture. Without the trust, feedback, sharing and self-responsibility cultivated through a developmental culture, self-organization struggles to thrive. People need to feel able to share openly how they really feel, to learn from feedback, and operate in transparent non-political non-manipulative ways.

It can take time for people to become accustomed to the personal responsibility and accountability that comes with making decisions in groups without the boss to turn to or shoulder the blame if things go awry. Likewise, it can be equally challenging for the managerial mind-set to let go of control and provide the necessary trust and freedom for the teams to learn through failing. In a self-organizing system, the leadership team needs to understand that their role is primarily one of facilitation, space-holding and coaching.

Experienced coaching is vital in the early stages of the shift toward self-organization - the period of time when teams are learning to feel their way around as control relaxes and hierarchies loosen. Whether the coaches are employees or external consultants, they provide a means for teams to check-in every so often at local and regional levels and receive unbiased advice on how to best transcend tensions and challenges that inevitably arise.

 *Business Insight: Buurtzorg – Dutch Healthcare provider.* At Buurtzorg, there is a team of coaches on stand-by to help teams that need external advice or assistance overcoming a challenge or conflict. Conflict and tension are inevitable. The trick is learning how to transform it in constructive ways. In Buurtzorg the CEO doesn't dictate control from above – there is an app-system that allows him to tap into the collective intelligence asking for advice and feedback on new strategic initiatives. This allows the employees to either vote for or against new initiatives or provide their qualitative feedback from the field. This has allowed the business to quickly develop new business opportunities and spin-offs as its employees can suggest new and needed business endeavors. Like a catering service for sick people, for instance.

Instead of a separate innovation team coming up with new ideas behind their screens and in siloes, that then filter a new innovation through ranks of managers, that eventually gets presented to the board some months after the idea was conceived, self-organizing organizations are much more nimble and responsive. They allow for the organizational living-system to tap into the collective intelligence of those out in the field that know best, locally-attuned to different niches and specific client needs.

Regenerative Leaders learn self-organizing ways through experimenting and being patient, as they hold space for others to feel more empowered and take responsibility for their own decisions. The healthy challenges for Regenerative Leaders are met by training in communication skills, team dynamics, facilitation, deep listening, peer-coaching, open-ended questioning, conflict transformation, all helping team members rise to the challenge and opportunity of self-organization.

> "Self-organization is not a startling new feature of the world. It is the way the world has created itself for billions of years. In all of human activity, self-organization is how we begin. It is what we do until we interfere with the process and try and control one another."
>
> Margaret Wheatley and Keller-Rogers, leadership specialists

Key to this dynamic is the fact that each organization, team, and member is given the opportunity to explore ground rules that encourage a context where self-organization can thrive without too much direction setting from 'above'. These can be general behaviors set across the business to help guide the teams, much like a moral compass.

 *Dive Deeper:* For more on Burtzorg's and other's approaches to self-organization see Frederic Laloux's book *Reinventing Organizations*.

Self-organization requires a form of governance or *advice process* to provide clarity around how people within the organization are to make good decisions by *seeking advice* among internal experts rather than *needing a boss to tell them what to do*. The term 'advice process' originated at the energy giant AES with CEO Dennis Bakke. The multinational energy corporation created the conditions that enable small interacting teams to feel capable of making the right decisions in a complex ever-changing environment. Implementing an advice process allows anyone in the organization to make a decision, as long as he or she has sought advice from relevant parties affected by the decision and relevant experts related to the issue. Therefore, the person remains self-empowered, as long as they consciously listen to the information and input they receive, which does not mean all of the information will affect their final decision, but all will be considered.

An advice process is *not* consensus, rather it is a means to tune into the system and get various opinions and feedback on the table before making decisions. As Frederic Laloux notes, *"While consensus drains energy out of organizations, the advice process boosts motivation and initiative."* (Laloux, 2014).

*Business Insight: AES – a global energy utility.* When Dennis Bakke was CEO of AES, it was a worldwide energy giant with 40,000 employees in 31 countries and revenues of $8.6bn. He challenged the business establishment by proving that any business of any size or complexity can organize around multi-skilled self-managed teams to ensure a fulfilling and fun, yet challenging and developmental, workplace. Bakke notes: *"The advice process is my answer to the age-old organizational dilemma of how to embrace the rights and needs of the individual, while simultaneously ensuring the successful functioning of the team, community, or company…To get the most out of the advice process, people inside an organization must share all information."* (Bakke, 2005). At AES the advice process enables teams to work in a non-hierarchic networked self-managing way, making decisions locally without higher-level approval on a whole host of complex tasks including health and safety, day-to-day operations, budgeting and performance, quality control and stakeholder relations.

*Dive Deeper:* For more on the *advice process* at AES see Dennis Bakke's book *Joy at Work*, also you can visit on-line the *Reinventing Organizations Wiki* for general insights and further sign-posts on self-management processes and best-practice.

A healthy life-affirming organization meets people where they are at and therefore it is worth bearing in mind that not everyone wishes – or is ready for - self-organizing ways of operating. There are times when hierarchy is needed, and where clear levels of authorization are sought by particular members of the community. Some people simply find full-on self-organization too overwhelming and thrive better with clearer instructions and guidance. It is a fine-line between providing psychological safety and stimulating people to engage developmentally.

Regenerative Leaders can take hybrid approaches of hierarchy and heterarchy (flat self-organizing teams) and help sense in to what would work best in any given situation and context. The Harvard Business School leadership professor John Kotter has for some years been researching the value of having a hybrid approach in what he calls a 'dual operating system'. The dual operating system maintains the traditional power-based top-down hierarchy as per normal, but parallel with a highly networked, agile structure where 'volunteers' from across the organization work together in agile self-organizing ways. These volunteers come together regardless of their place in the hierarchy. They are energized by being allowed to work together in these dynamic ways and as Kotter says: *"when you find energized people producing effective change, you almost always find people who want to do just that, and feel that they have been given permission to do so."* (Kotter, 2014).

 *Business Insight: North Star Housing Group – a UK Housing Association.* North Star has a culture that supports both hierarchy and self-management to great effect. CEO Angela Lockwood has found that investing in the training and development of people is key to ensuring people are comfortable with knowing when is best to self-organize and when a more directive or hierarchic approach is needed. She calls it 'conscious directive management' - learning to become conscious of when we need to be more directive in our leadership style and when we need to be more collaborative. Lots of training is provided to help people with this. Personal development is key here - people taking personal responsibility for learning and developing their own self-management capabilities while being supported by company-wide training programmes. At North Star, there is a clear vision and set of values, and also 'Behavioral Guides' that help ensure people feel comfortable with how best to behave. Peer-to-peer coaching and learning is part of this – where every leader is also a coach, learning the necessary listening skills required. Respectful relating across the culture within and beyond the business, where all stakeholder relations are conducted in respectful 'adult to adult' ways, enables a blend of hierarchy and self-management to work in practice. As a result of this, North Star consistently out performs in its market and wins awards for customer service and employee culture.

Today, there are many case studies to take inspiration from when choosing whether our organizations ought to embrace a self-organizing approach out-right or dual-run on networks and hierarchy. There are examples of hierarchic organizations cultivating an adaptive agile culture where bureaucracy does not reign supreme, and there are also examples of organizations who have flattened their hierarchies and then found that employees still don't feel empowered to take decisions, because the power still resides at the top. It has as much to do with the culture and mindset that is nourished and practiced throughout the organization than it does with the hierarchic structure.

Former World Bank executive and renowned agile-business advocate Stephen Denning addresses this in his book *The Age of Agile*: *"One question that I ask workshop audiences is, 'How many layers can an organization have and still be Agile?' I get various answers, ranging from two to seven. Of course, it's a trick question. The right answer is that it doesn't matter how many layers the organization has. What matters is the mindset. For instance, the Microsoft Developer Division has multiple layers but it doesn't feel like a bureaucratic pyramid. Conversations are multidirectional. Anyone can talk to anyone. The right mindset creates the right spirit of conversation, curiosity, and fluidity. By contrast, a tiny singular-layer organization can be tied up in bureaucratic knots with a single layer. It's the mindset that creates the rigidity."* (Denning, 2018).

What is paramount for the regenerative organization's vitality is the capacity for people at all levels in the organization to feel empowered and be able to sense and respond effectively to local changes without too much bureaucracy. The role of the Regenerative Leader is to help facilitate the required level of trust and processes (like the advice process) to help unleash the local-attunement and thereby intelligence, capacity and innovation potential that lies within the units and the individual employees.

## 6. Ecosystemic Facilitation and Transformation

*Objective: Attentive care and understanding of the entire system in which the organization operates*

As we have gathered by now, fundamental to successful regenerative organizations is a shift from overly-mechanistic logic toward an ability to focus on the parts while also being conscious of the interrelating living-system dynamics across the entire organization and its ecosystem - what we call *systemic awareness* and *ecosystemic awareness* – themes that run throughout the DNA model and the 3 components of Living Systems Design, Culture and Being. *Ecosystemic awareness* is systemic awareness across the entire ecosystem (recall in Part 1 where we distinguished between the open-mind of systems-thinking, the open-heart of systemic awareness, and the open-will of ecosystemic awareness, whereupon we sense into the wider social and ecological system interconnections). Ecosystemic awareness enables us to become the Ecosystemic Facilitators we touched upon in Living Systems Design.

As Regenerative Leaders enliven the culture, they are also tasked to empower people across the business to spot opportunities and make decisions at the local level that benefit the whole. The Regenerative Leader cannot singularly focus on optimizing his own division as that may have damaging effects on the whole organization, which is why silo-focused KPI's can do much damage.

As Dennis Sherwood writes in *Seeing the Forest for the Trees, A managers guide to applying systems thinking*: *"The department you manage is part of a highly complex connected system, some aspects of which are within your own organization, many of which extend beyond your organizations' boundaries. You understand your department well, and you feel confident taking decisions locally. Nevertheless, a decision that is totally rational within your own department might be suboptimal for the organization as a whole, and so your local action on your own part of the system might be counterproductive overall"* (Sherwood, 2002).

We see this happening time and again. There are actions taken in one place in the organization, that look good in isolation, which do damage overall and go undetected due to a lack of ecosystemic awareness across the company's culture.

> "The world is a complex, interconnected finite ecological-social-psychological-economic system. We treat it as if it were not, as if it were divisible, separable, simple and infinite. Our persistent, intractable, global problems arise directly from this mismatch."
>
> Danielle Meadows, systems thinker

In theory, we might like to think that we can predict and control or 'change manage' certain outcomes through hierarchic top-down dictate, but in practice this becomes an illusion. Reality is something far messier (yet not chaotic), where complex processes of human relating can be nurtured and cultivated by taking the approach of an Ecosystemic Facilitator who sees the bigger picture, detects stagnant energy in the system, unlocks flows, and knows where special attention and effort is needed – so called acupuncture points (we explore Ecosystemic Facilitator tools in more detail in Part 3).

The concept of 'urban acupuncture' was coined by the Brazilian Mayor of Curitiba, Jaime Lerner. Lerner's approach was to heal the city through acupuncture-inspired interventions. Instead of top-down, one-way urban planning his approach was to listen to people on the ground and carefully implement ideas in areas where those efforts could create positive ripples throughout the larger system. Through this approach he transformed an incredibly fragmented, disconnected, poor town with many slums and a high crime-rate by creating pockets of local commerce, markets, green areas, and increased livability.

Just like an acupuncturist unlocks flow and stagnated energy by inserting needles in relevant meridian points, his approach was to unlock potential in the city one pinprick at a time, implementing creative approaches based on compassionate dialogue with the locals in the area sensing into their specific local needs and potential. The initiatives included a bench to rest on, a playground, a food-truck area, a park, improved sanitation, and a plan to thread electrical cables and water pipes through the handrails of the steep staircases that wind their way through the city's hillside favelas, bringing power and water to those communities at minimal cost. His urban acupunc-ture strategy worked wonders albeit he had to bear much criticism in the beginning as his approach was deemed too radical. Curitiba is now one of Brazil's richest cities and has attracted residents and investors thanks to his ideas, vision and implementation. Lerner fought bureaucracy for decades, constantly having to argue that these particular efforts could not necessarily be quantified or measured, or controlled top-down: yet that they would ultimately bring value as they empowered people on the ground to take responsibility for the health and vitality of their city.

Lerner believes that our obsession with measurable results has killed many great ideas. *"If only cities had fewer peddlers of complexity and more philosophers!"* he writes in his book Urban Acupuncture. *"Industrious mediocrity is gaining ground, along with merchants of complexity: the bean-counters and the inconclusive, never-ending researchers. But sometimes, just one stroke of creativity is acupuncture powerful enough to make progress."* (Lerner, 2016).

To Jaime Lerner Urban Acupuncture can be many things. The highline in New York, the Cheonggyenchein River in Seoul or *"the music that plays in a city's streets".* It's about bringing life to areas where energy has stagnated and facilitating the living system through community, happiness, sustainability and connection.

 *Dive Deeper:* Read the book by Jaime Lerner: *Urban Acupuncture, Celebrating Pinpricks of Change That Enrich City Life.*

For our purposes, Urban Acupuncture applies to an organizational context as well. Regenerative Leaders ought to ask themselves on a regular basis: *"Where do I sense stagnated energy? Where could I help unleash new energy by empowering key members?* Anything from a lounge-area that invites employees to relax and connect, green spaces indoors with lots of plants, a new initiative that facilitate partnerships across departments or with key stakeholders, a policy of ensuring maternity and paternity leave for all employees, or an initiative that encourages employees to spend 20% of their time to be creative, or getting outside the office more. What is key here is that the Ecosystemic Facilitator – the Regenerative Leader – cultivates the ability to sense into what will create the positive ripple effects for multiple win-win-wins throughout the living-system organization.

At the heart of Regenerative Leadership is Ecosystemic Facilitation - an artful undertaking that requires practice and patience. Our Living Systems Being (explored in the next chapter) aids this artfulness so that we sense-and-respond effectively, compassionately and wisely, learning as we go.

 *Business Insight: Waste Management – a large North American waste management company*. The company has been processing waste since its inception in 1968, and has steadily grown in size over the decades. A few years ago, according to financial analysts, the company's most valuable assets were its 271 landfills (Mackey & Sisodia, 2016). Over the years, sustainability has become more of a pressing issue for Waste Management's ecosystem – not just its customers like Walmart, but also increasing social and environmental pressures. The company has set about revolutionizing its strategy and operations to become fit for the 21$^{st}$ century. It facilitated stakeholder dialogue sessions with diverse parties across its entire ecosystem, not just suppliers, partners and corporate clients, but indigenous community leaders, environmentalists, and local pressure groups. Through this ecosystemic approach, the company was able to see how best to transform its ways so that it does not merely survive but actually thrives in the years ahead, in a way that benefits the entire ecosystem. It begun to realize that its next-stage purpose was to be 'North America's leading provider of integrated environmental solutions' and saw how it could handle waste in more circular and beneficial ways, treating waste as a valuable resource rather than a problem to be buried. As John Mackey and Raj Sisodia note in *Conscious Capitalism*, Waste Management *"generates about $13bn in revenues annually but estimates that the waste it handles contains about $10bn of value, most of it not yet extracted."* The company has invested heavily in its future, divesting away from landfills into materials recovery facilities and hundreds of waste-to-energy projects already generating enough to supply 1.1 million homes (Mackey & Sisodia, 2016).

Regularly bringing diverse people together from across the ecosystem is the best way to sense into future possibilities while ensuring systemic issues are transformed into opportunities. These ecosystemic workshops allow for continual prototyping and empathizing to occur, synergizing deeper understanding about the challenges and opportunities arising in our ever-changing business context. Just as the Mission & Movement of the organization is transformation-based, in that it seeks to transform the market and community it operates in, so too are ecosystem stakeholder relations, in terms of how they positively engage suppliers, partners, investors, customers and other stakeholders in the transformation to life-affirming futures.

The approach of Ecosystemic Facilitation can also be used at government level in the development and roll-out of new political initiatives or programmes. In May 2018, the Danish government appointed 11 Danish experts across sectors to work on a green growth strategy for Denmark.

This was launched in January 2019 and a few weeks later Laura moderated an event and panel debate with CEOs and ministers discussing how to move the recommendations in the strategy forward into implementation. Across the board – from city-officials, to public utilities, start-ups, data-experts, private companies – they all identified the main barrier to implementing the recommendations as key stakeholders being too protective and not opening-up enough. Many expressed a great desire to move forward together instead of wasting precious resources protecting assets and information. They agreed that they could all go further together by shedding the old protectionist ways and instead see each other as partners. As one of the utility companies present in the dialogue said: *"Instead of focusing our energy on how big a piece of pie we can secure for ourselves, we should collectively bake a bigger and better pie".* It was agreed that what was needed was a regular facilitation and dialogue to help this process of systemic collaboration and ensure successful implementation of a new Danish green growth strategy.

A quick self-check for Regenerative Leaders is to ask about any situation, decision or solution we face: *Is this regenerative or degenerative? What will be the long-term and ecosystemic implications of this decision?* When adequately informed about the wider ecosystem we are operating in – having listened to diverse stakeholder groups – we can then sense inward with an open mind, open heart, open will. The more we do this, the more we learn to cultivate the capacity to sense if something is regenerative or degenerative.

And so to summarize this chapter on Living Systems Culture: For Regenerative Leaders to succeed in nurturing healthy living-systems cultures they must constantly practice the leadership and life dynamics addressed in Chapter 5: Working inwards and outwards, seeking input and cross-pollination while consolidating and anchoring - all simultaneously.

Recall the music metaphor we used at the beginning of Part 2: The *Logic of Life* is like the musical instrument, the *Life Dynamics* and *Leadership Dynamics* are like the notes the Regenerative Leader plays to create the right rhythm, and the components, *Living Systems Design, Living Systems Culture,* and *Living Systems Being,* are like the strings inherent in the music of life. How the leader prepares to play the musical instrument and pluck the strings with precision and presence is all important. This is where the art of holding-space comes in.

To adequately hold-space for dialogue, tensions, rich conversations, eco-system workshops, and more, the Regenerative Leader is required to spend adequate time preparing ahead of each stakeholder dialogue, to 'let go' and 'let come' (as Otto Scharmer would say applying his presencing technique) so we are able to see beyond our own perspectives and agendas to truly empathically connect across relational boundaries. Not marching in to a meeting with your fixed agenda; but rather co-create transformative life-affirming outcomes from rich dialogue that respects the other.

This brings us to the importance of our quality of 'being' – how we show up and nourish our relationship with our inner nature and encourage others to do the same. This is the focus of the next DNA Component: *Living Systems Being*.

"The people who hold the contradictions and resolve them in themselves are the saviors of the world. They are the only real agents of transformation, reconciliation and newness."

Richard Rohr, author

# Living Systems Being

This chapter will be a controversial read for some in the world of business, but to us the concepts covered here is where great leadership begins and ends.

Too often leadership courses, methodologies and business school programmes overlook the inner components of leadership, or address it in a vague and superficial way. Yet, it is the understanding of the deep, reflective, inner work and the understanding of human-to-human behavior where the art of truly great leadership is found.

Living Systems Being is all about how we show up as individuals in the Age of Regeneration. How we reclaim the parts that we lost journeying through the Age of Separation.

# LIVING SYSTEMS BEING

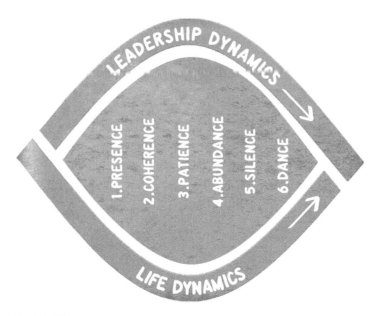

© copyright Hutchins & Storm

The DNA strands for the third component of Regenerative Leadership –
Living Systems Being – are:

1.  Presence: Nurturing a deep relationship to your inner self (inner nature)
    and your relationship with others and the world (outer nature)

2.  Coherence: Being aligned with your authentic self and acting in accor-
    dance with your own inner guidance system

3.  Patience: Being at ease with and open to the unfolding nature of life,
    not being reactive, defensive, pushy, or judgmental

4.  Silence: Allowing the space of silence to nourish you and your interactions

5.  Abundance: A frame of mind that opens you up to life's rich possibilities,
    keeping you curious, creative and compassionate

6.  Dance: Tapping into the rhythm of life - its playfulness, change, sea-
    sonality, depth and emergence

In exploring these DNA strands of Living Systems Being, we draw from neuroscience, biology, biophilia, meditation, ancient wisdom, adult developmental psychology, and research into stress, wellbeing, creativity and innovation. Ultimately, this component of leadership is about the foundation on which inner strength depends. It is about how you commit to showing up amid everyday busyness.

All of what we cover here can be cultivated through the practices we explore in Part 3. Now, let's dive into each strand in more detail:

## 1. Presence

*Objective: Nurturing a deep relationship to your inner self (inner nature) and your relationship with others and the world (outer nature)*

Presence is an *inner* quality of calmness uncluttered by the thoughts that take us out of our reality. Presence is also an *outer* attentiveness that is both receptive and responsive. When we are present, we are no longer reactive, tense or anxious, and instead we are relaxed, open and connected. Others around us can sense this calm aliveness. Our presence enhances the lives of others, and we contribute to a generative space that invites others to feel more open, relaxed, seen, heard, and unguarded. It's vital for Regenerative Leaders to cultivate an atmosphere of presence.

Giving ourselves, and our relationships, our full presence is the most precious gift we can offer the world around us.

As we explored in Part 1 stress and burnout has become a global epidemic. A stressed brain operates in high-beta, fight-or-flight mode, which means increases in body tensions, underlying anxieties, outbursts of anger and constant worries about the past and future. High beta brain waves strip us of our inner guidance system, our connection to our inner wisdom. It makes it impossible for us to be present with ourselves and those around us. We become unable to be open to life, and have difficulty seeing new potential or sensing the appropriate direction.

Presence is at the heart of being regenerative and the key to allowing the emergence of new ideas and visions. The inability to be present - always or often operating in fight-or-flight mode - limits feelings of compassion and thwarts the ability to make sound strategic decisions, access creative abilities, and sense into the living-system. Presence allows a deeper knowing to emerge in the leader, where *"what to do just becomes obvious"* (Senge et al. 2004).

Presence is our way into Regenerative Living and Leading.

As we explored in Chapter 6, spending time in nature – or even looking at pictures of nature – calms us and helps enhance our presence. Meditation teacher and Way of Nature founder, John P Milton, notes that by being fully present in nature, surrendering to the awesome embrace of life, we find our presence – an effortless union of inner nature and outer nature.

In Chapter 5, we mentioned how leadership specialist Otto Scharmer addresses the concept of presence in his Theory U model, revealing our two modes of either being present or being absent in our interactions. Scharmer calls 'absencing' an architecture of separation; and 'presencing' an architecture of connection. The more self-aware we can become of how it feels when we are presencing rather than absencing, the more we can realign our attention with our deeper intention to be present, true and authentic.

*Absencing* often feels disconnected, our minds racing with many different thoughts at once, our bodies eager to move on and act, and emotionally we seek to criticize, judge and blame. Whereas *presencing* feels calm and connected; we seek to sense, understand and embrace what is unfolding.

This is a life-affirming way of approaching life and requires a high level of self-awareness – a pervasive theme throughout Regenerative Leadership. In cultivating self-awareness we can notice how often we find ourselves absorbed by fear-based projections and speculations, and where we become more focused on winning arguments rather than achieving the right outcomes. *Does that sound familiar?*

Many leaders become obsessed with being seen and heard that they bulldoze their way forward in meetings – a behavior that stems from a fear of losing influence, position, or respect. As Tony Parsons, author of *The Open Secret*, poetically puts it: *"In our rush to find a better situation in time,*

*we trample over the flower of beingness that presents itself in every moment ...*
*Presence is our constant nature but most of the time we are interrupting it by*
*living in a state of expectation, motivation or interpretation."* (Parsons, 1995).

In terms of business, cultivating presence pays great dividends, as we find
more respectful relationships, compassionate interchanges, and higher quality
performance in ourselves and those around us. As Regenerative Leaders who
cultivate presence, we shape our environment through our words, actions
and the vibe we bring to our interactions. We cultivate our architecture of
connection by becoming self-aware of how we are attending to each evolving
moment. The more we notice whether we are relaxed, open and generative
or whether we are stuck in habit, anxiety, projection and separation, the
more we can bring ourselves back into coherence with the Logic of Life.
When we sense we are going into a reactive, tense mode of being, we can
catch ourselves and re-center, and if need be, withdraw from the situation,
go for a walk, take deep breaths and come back to our state of presencing.

True success comes from a strong inner connection and a strong presence
with all that we are, without judging, criticizing or turning to outer things to
calm us or build us up. As we learn to cultivate a strong inner connection,
we feel more content in business and in life. We become better leaders.
Presence with self also allows us to heal the deep split between our own
inner and outer dynamics that we explored in Part 1.

Too many of us chase outer success and recognition in ways which mean we
never feel truly satisfied nor happy. In our attempt to fill the void we judge
other people more, become more critical, hunt for more outer success and
consume more. We become addicted to titles, power, and money when we
prioritize 'outer' action and ignore 'inner' connection.

A strong inner and outer presence reveals to us the essence of our person-
ality, of our very being. We know things spontaneously, cutting through the
noise of distraction within and around us, tapping in to our true essence and
knowing that it draws from an inexhaustible source – the Living Systems
Field. By tapping into the Living Systems Field we 'activate our super-nature'.
This gives our awareness a depth, taking our self-awareness and systemic-awareness to a deeper, richer, wiser dimension.

> "Great leaders are awake, aware and attuned to themselves, to others, and to the world around them…they seek to live in full consciousness of self, others, nature and society."
>
> Richard Boyatzis, leadership specialist

Tapping into our super-nature enables the shift in consciousness from separateness to interconnectedness – an alchemic transformation that deepens our essence, our sense of who we truly are, beyond ego-projection into a deep knowing of our sense of place and purpose in the world.

Today there is a great deal of pressure around finding one's purpose. We believe that this 'purpose' is not necessarily one defined goal and, ultimately, our purpose is really to be present with who we truly are and allow the essence of ourselves the space it needs to emerge through us. We remove the pressure to find a grand purpose in life and, instead, explore the essence of who we are, every day and every moment.

It can be a fun endeavor – not another burdensome 'leadership practice' but rather the mindset of having fun with noticing our true essence in any given moment. When we are at ease with ourselves, without pretending, playing roles and living up to degenerative ideals of successful project manager, designer, team leader, executive - we can embrace life as an exquisite learning experience that is teaching us how to be more courageous, compassionate and wise. With this approach, our organizations become a vehicle for manifesting this courage, compassion and wisdom in a world that desperately needs it.

Remember: We are all constantly creating the world we live in through our way of being – our behavior creates ripple effects far wider than we can imagine. The world needs grounded, present, wise leaders that practice and value their deep relationship to life, in doing so, inspire others to do the same!

 *Dive Deeper:* If you would like to read more about practices of presence in nature, see John P Milton's book *Sky Above Earth Below*. For more on how presence relates to next-stage leadership see Peter Senge's et al., *Presence*, Joseph Jarworski's *Synchronicity* and Otto Scharmer's *Theory U*.

## 2. Coherence

*Objective: Being aligned with your authentic self and acting in accordance with your own inner guidance system*

Coherence is a result of acting in alignment with our authentic truth and enables us to lead from the inside out. When we are acting from alignment we are rooted in our essence, in touch with our deeper sense of self.

We can sense in ourselves when we speak and act from a place of coherence or incoherence. People who are in alignment with their inner truth feel to others like they are 'rooted', 'grounded', 'trustworthy' and 'wise'. However, when people start to worry about fitting in, or how best to speak the corporate lingo, or play the political game, incoherence starts to slip in, and we are forced to navigate frantically without the strong inner anchoring. A negative spiral ensures of more insecurity and anxiety, yet more incoherence.

We have probably all experienced incoherent behavior - speaking words that are not truly ours, presenting ourselves in a certain light, saying yes to projects we are not truly aligned with, or navigating decisions or processes on other people's terms. In some regards this is quite natural, and yet by noticing it, we can gain self-mastery over these ego habits. Incoherent behavior often feels anxious, saddening and stressful to ourselves; others often subconsciously pick up on our feelings, which feel to others like we are untrustworthy and inauthentic. People might find us 'insecure', 'nervous', 'edgy' and 'ungrounded'. The truth is, many of us have simply not prioritized exploring our deeper essence and purpose, hence we may feel like we are having to play a role and be someone we are not just to get through the day. It's like a survival mode, but it's actually life-denying.

Coherence is an essential core quality of being an Ecosystemic Facilitator as it allows us to embrace paradoxes and polarities and hold space for the tension that arises in life. Standing strong in who we are regardless of the circumstances and turmoil that may be around us. The stronger the inner connection, the more clarity leaders have to deal with complexity within an emergent living-system.

All living systems – from cells, to our bodies, to our organizations, to Planet Earth – constantly seek coherence. It is inherent within life. It is the convergence dynamic of the whole working across the divergence of the parts. Coherence happens when the interconnected parts of a living system (personal or organizational) integrate and align with the other parts, acting as a coherent, authentic whole. When the living system attains inner and outer coherence (what systems theorist Ervin Laszlo calls 'supercoherence') it is consciously aware of how it interrelates within itself and beyond itself, seeking harmony with life through its conscious intent and quality of attentiveness. This 'supercoherence' is the mastery of self-awareness and systemic-awareness; it is flow – the optimal human experience.

> "Striving effectively to regain supercoherence requires more than finding technological solutions to patch up the problems created by our incoherence…It requires reconnecting with a mind-set, a mind-set based on a profound sense of belonging to each other – the rediscovering of the power of love. This rediscovery is timely, and it is not mere fantasy: it has its roots in our holographically whole, non-locally interconnected universe."
>
> Ervin Laszlo, systems and quantum theorist

Scientific studies, such as the work at the HeartMath Institute, conducted with electrodes covering the entire body show that through simple practices we can shift our physiological and psychological coherence. A technique called Heart Entrainment (which we explore in Part 3) encourages our brain-waves to entrain themselves on the deeper waves of the heart, and when this entrainment happens, neurological and nervous systems throughout the body gain coherence.

This changes us both physiologically and psychologically. *Physiologically*: our tissue repair rates improve, stem cell reproduction increases, senses awaken, synapse connections in the brain enhance, and left and right brain hemispheres inter-relate more readily. *Psychologically*: we open-up more and are more receptive and responsive, we cultivate a feeling of flow, where we are simultaneously relaxed yet alert, present yet calm, and our capacity for empathy, for generative sharing, deep listening, non-judgement and trans-forming tensions, all greatly increases.

In short, when we are coherent with ourselves we become better leaders.

## 3. Patience

*Objective: Being at ease with and open to the unfolding nature of life, not being reactive, defensive, pushy, or judgmental*

Impatience is rife amid today's hurry-up-and-get-on-with-it culture. In many corporate settings there's a constant pressure to act and do, which fuels our impatience. We want everything done today and the norm is to fill our schedules and to-do lists with too much.

We need more patience to build an empowered, rich, creative, nourishing workplace that delivers high quality results, not those rushed by impatience.

Patience is what increases our capacity for flow, presence, and coherence, while impatience undermines the natural rhythm of things and reduces our capacity to notice subtly-lit synchronistic pathways, make the right deci-sions, get the great ideas.

> "Nature does not hurry, yet everything is accomplished."
>
> Lao Tzu, ancient philosopher

With patience, we do not push, strive or hustle; rather we are at peace with how the natural rhythm of things is unfolding. It's about allowing softness a greater space within us, not soft as in weak, but a gentle open attitude to accept what is. This does not mean that we are passive, careless, or lackadaisical. Yes, sometimes we need to meet a certain timeframe, and so discernment is the helpful sister of patience. It's about letting go of staring obsessively at Gantt charts and letting go of a fixation on certain outcomes in certain ways at a certain time.

The Regenerative Leader allows a patient spaciousness within their day-to-day interactions, to help sense into the natural flow of things, to roll with the waves, to swim with the stream. We remain fully attentive, knowing when best to act, to pause, to give space, or to cut through entanglement. Just as we cannot push or demand a flower to bloom – it will happen in its own right time - we cannot force people or projects to prematurely unfold. For the flower, the individual and the project there is a process one must go through to have the right result emerging in the right time. When we sow a seed the plant full of ripe and ready fruits can't be in our hands the next day. In organizations impatience often stifles flow and weakens relationships yielding poorer results by forcing things too early.

In our desire (no matter how noble and well-intended) to push through things and encourage people to work fast, we feed irritation, separation, sadness, disappointment, and frustration. We have all experienced the impatient controlling manager who wants things done at his or her pace in his or her way, which completely strips the process of a space for creativity, innovation, trying new things, empowerment and excitement for all involved. In such instances, leaders miss out on letting things emerge and evolve into their full potential.

If you are the somewhat controlling project manager type where could you loosen up and soften more; to allow a process to emerge into its full potential and trust the people you work with to find their flow?

"Softness is when I surrender to what is and at the same time keep moving forward. It is when I surrender to what is without giving up. And if I need to let it go, I will."

Carrie-Anne Moss, story-teller

Patience comes with learning to be comfortable with the uncomfortable, with not-knowing how things are going to unfold, yet knowing and trusting that things will unfold as they ought to, naturally. Again, it's not carelessness or *laissez faire* but a less tight, less controlling, less micro-managing grip on processes and people. It's the ability of the Regenerative Leader to be the Ecosystemic Facilitator who senses when the flow is just right, or when a tension can transform itself, or best be stimulated by simple nudging interactions (listening to different opinions, offering advice, having a pause or taking a break).

Patience is, so to speak, a midwifing of the pregnant tension; becoming comfortable with the uncomfortableness of the tension as it becomes full, birthing what is right for the given moment, just as it should be, on time, in flow. It's an honoring of the natural rhythm, an adherence to the Logic of Life.

Both of us - Laura and Giles – have rather impatient, strong-willed, relentless driven leader-profiles. There's a saying that you teach what you need to learn yourself right? We have both served as leaders for decades and studied at business schools where the impatient laser-focused leader who always had a plan ready for every eventuality was the celebrated role-model. A few years back Laura's patience was tested to the fullest when she sustained a minor traumatic brain injury in an accident in the Summer of 2015. For months she was nauseous non-stop, had double vision, couldn't sleep, yet was tired around the clock, couldn't cope with light or sounds. It was a nightmare that didn't seem to end. Instead of surrendering to the situation she couldn't control she used the little energy she had trying to project-manage her own recovery. This was *not* possible. Over months she slowly accepted that she needed to surrender and allow in a new way of flowing, accepting, being with what is. Accepting the tension, the fear and the not knowing. Slowly learning to trust, go within and see life in new ways. Slowly life started to reveal golden nuggets and a deeper inner wisdom emerged.

This inner wisdom in us all is buried by impatience and revealed by patience.

## 4. Silence

*Objective: Allowing the space of silence to nourish you and your interactions*

Our world has become overwhelmingly noisy. Going through our day many experience a bombardment of our senses – from billboards, traffic, and people. At home we often distract ourselves by having a TV or radio on in the background, picking up the phone as soon as we feel slightly bored.

A study conducted by researchers at the University of California showed that each day most of us are bombarded with the equivalent of 34 gigabytes of information – this is enough to overload a laptop within a week. Through our phones, the internet, email, tv, radio, newspapers, books, social media, and the urban landscape, we receive 23 words per second each waking hour (Bohn, 2012).

Between 2014 and 2018 the average worker sent 40 emails a day and received 90 (Radicati, 2018). This is only a global average – many of us receive far more. In fact, before Giles left his corporate career he would receive around 200 emails a day during busy times, in addition to the endless meetings, webinars and conference calls he had to attend to. That's what many leaders are required to deal with in many of today's organizations - it's utter insanity.

Contemporary philosopher, Matthew Crawford, has researched and written extensively about this rising bombardment of our attention in what he calls the *Age of Distraction*. As we addressed in Part 1, our minds and nervous systems are not wired to filter and process this amount of input and stimuli, and the overload is what makes us physically and emotionally ill, burned out, and depressed. This 'noise' makes it harder for us to listen to our inner guidance system and act with compassion and clarity.

Today, in order to thrive, we must cultivate time where we can tap into an inner space for stillness and quiet. It is this that enables our bodies and brains to regenerate their ability to respond to challenges with clarity and wisdom. For many, silence is scary and takes courage to explore. *What will arise in my own thoughts and space if I am not scrolling my social media feed, reading emails or internet shopping?* Yet, it is evident that in today's society we crave silence. The rising demand for silent meditation retreats is testament to that.

Our leadership seminars and retreats always include elements of silence – and on our skype calls together (discussing this book among other things) we often tap into a moment of silence to kick-off the meeting and conclude it. We do this to cultivate a space where we are in tune with the truest essence and meaning of our work and partnership and not immediately get carried away with all the things to do and discuss. We do it to hold space collectively for what wants to emerge through us. We are now both used to silence as part of our daily lives (although it hasn't always been like that) and we make a dedicated effort to keep those sacred silent moments throughout the day.

Pythagoras, the ancient Greek mathematician and philosopher, had a school where he would only accept students who had spent a minimum of two years in silence prior to arriving. He believed the mind had to be cleaned of any old programmes and conditioning in order to be able to receive a higher order of truth not infused with ego. He believed that by constantly cleansing the mind in silence, he and his students could open up to fully comprehend the deep wisdom in life. He knew that the aha-moments and strokes of genius come to us through the Living Systems Field, which we best access in silence. Many scientists, including Einstein, Humboldt, da Vinci and Bohm swore by silence and solitude.

Many great thinkers report how genius ideas access their minds when they take a break. We have probably all experienced those moments of clarity and insight in the shower, while walking in nature or sitting on a train looking out the window. Great ideas are rarely forced.

Let us not confuse silence as only the cessation of sound – silence, like patience, can be experienced as a feeling of spaciousness inside. By opening up to life in silence, we quieten our minds and sense the stillness innate within life. This silence is always here for us to tap into. Spontaneity is born from this stillness. Creativity spawns from this silence.

Many organizations have incorporated silence as a component into their meetings and everyday behaviors at work. At the American media agency, Sounds True, there is a minute's silence at the beginning of every meeting and at the Danish energy corporation, SEAS-NVE, it's also custom to integrate silence into all meetings.

It takes practice to let go of the head-chatter or inner strategizing about how to get our point across in meetings and instead sense into the here-and-now and invite in presence and systemic awareness, so we can be in service of the meeting and its higher purpose rather than directed and controlled by our own egos.

For many a culture of silence in the workplace and in meetings becomes a cherished way of revitalizing the workday. Those organizations we have worked with report that this new *modus operandi* for meetings means they're far less tired and exhausted when they leave work – they've given their brains and nervous systems a chance to catch up during the day.

In the summer of 2018 we both attended a silent retreat for systems think-ers from all over the world in the Catskill Mountains, up-state New York. Peter Senge (*The Fifth Discipline*), Raj Sisodia (*Conscious Capitalism*), David Cooperrider (*Appreciate Inquiry*) also attended as well as 30 other leaders from around the world. The first day we had discussions, shared meditations and allowed talking over dinner. Then, on the second, third and fourth days, we spent the entire time in silence and held regular collective silent medita-tions. We are both used to longer times of silence so we were not worried about entering this space but, for many of the people there, silence was a rare activity. You could sense the anxious nervousness and excitement on the final day, when coming out of silence, and sharing in the circle – most had had revelations and deep moments of clarity. There were many tears and a collective sense of wonder as to why our lives have become stripped of this profound, yet so simple ingredient.

This access to clarity, connection, certainty and a sense of being grounded deeply within comes simply from presence and silence with oneself.

For successful leadership, it's paramount to regularly access the depths and wisdom that silence provides, to make space to explore these inner chambers that silence reveals.

In silence, you can integrate shadows and demons (we all have inner demons and shadow projections) and thereby reduce the need for spending energy on hiding or neglecting parts of our psyche and persona.

We are in desperate need of leaders who dare sit with themselves and others in silence and hold space for what wants to emerge in a calm and compassionate manner.

*Dive Deeper:* Laura gave a TEDx talk in 2017 on *How Silence can lead us to a more sustainable world*, about what her 2 years in silence taught her about leadership and the sustainability movement and how we can never have outer sustainability without the inner dimension that silence cultivates.

## 5. Abundance

*Objective: A frame of mind that opens you up to life's rich possibilities, keeping you curious, creative and compassionate*

The main reason people work themselves to the ground, fight competitively and politically for promotions, worry about people stealing their ideas, and spend vast amounts of energy on positioning themselves, ultimately boils down to one thing: fear. Fear of missing out, being excluded, not being seen, heard, valued. Not being a success in society's eyes. As we have touch on before, culturally we are addicted to the external validation due to an impoverishment of a strong inner connection.

This is why it is key for Regenerative Leaders to facilitate an abundance mindset instead of one of scarcity. Abundance is a way of living and leading that we can bring into our relationships and culture that enlivens a regenerative way of being. It invites in trust, catalyzes win-win-win situations, and unlocks collective flow.

Abundance is a shift away from the scarcity, zero-sum mind-set that infuses organizations with a sense of lack, mistrust, skepticism, anxiety and impatience, which starves the co-creative dynamic that is required for presence, coherence, patience, and silence. Through cultivating an abundance mindset, we can break free from patterns of scarcity and control and see everyone within our organization as part of the same community – not divisions or teams we fight against or withhold information from out of fear they will outperform us. We can practice inviting in, listening to, sharing, and celebrating diverse perspectives. We co-create, co-develop, explore together, and learn together, across boundaries, transforming degenerative cultures in to regenerative ones.

The old adage 'knowledge is power' has us caught up in a scarcity and control-based mentality that reduces collaboration and co-creativity. It purports that gold hides in tightly closed pockets inside the organization and you better protect your assets as people can steal from you anytime. This prevents ideas from flowing freely across the system and, as a result, the wisdom is held back, protected, controlled. We fear someone's stealing our ideas, criticizing us, making more money than us, getting more recognition than us, and so we hold back instead of opening up.

The energies of this scarcity mindset can manifest into feelings of envy and jealousy, such as finding it difficult when someone else is sharing their success or recounting a happy moment. Perhaps someone has just been invited to speak at a conference or to a meeting and you would have liked that invitation. Or a colleague is receiving praise, a promotion, or sharing something about themselves that invokes a pang of jealousy.

Such reactions are a natural part of our human condition, and we ought not suppress or reject those feelings or aspects of ourselves, as they will then only fester in the shadows causing even greater harm. Accept them and take them as a hint there's an inner craving calling for your attention. Don't project them on to the other and create separation. Instead, own them and transmute them into gold through greater self-awareness and, ultimately, self-mastery.

With a mindset of abundance, we are not immune or adverse to negative feelings or reactions. Instead we allow those (pangs of jealousy, in this case) to inform us about something within ourselves, perhaps a lack of confidence or self-worth, and in this fraction of a moment, we can either contribute to a co-creative regenerative dynamic or let the pang take over our behavior and allow a degenerative dynamic.

Never compare someone's summer to your winter – it will strip you of your presence and drain you. Instead, see the world as filled with potential and others' successes as proof that what you desire is possible. Their title, promotion, love-life, pregnancy, or best-selling book does not mean that possibility and dream is now taken away from you. Despite what this zero-sum, dog-eat-dog, hyper-competitive culture we've been living in for decades depicts, that's not how life really is. Someone else's win is not your loss. An abundance mindset is practicing letting go of feeling worried that someone is going to steal our thunder, our results, our budget allocations – or whatever it may be.

"From our immersion in scarcity arise the habits of scarcity. From the scarcity of time arises the habit of hurrying. From the scarcity of money comes the habit of greed. From the scarcity of attention comes the habit of showing off. From

> the scarcity of meaningful labour comes the habit of laziness. From the scarcity of unconditional acceptance comes the habit of manipulation."

Charles Eisenstein, author and activist

Often, we feel scarcity sneaking in when we haven't prioritized filling up our own cup of coherence first; when we're out of balance or stressed, tired and anxious, it is easy to see our fears projected everywhere. Again, self-awareness and self-mastery are key here, so that when challenges inevitably come our way, we may see them as crucibles for us to sense the tensions within ourselves, and those tensions can be turned into gold if we listen to their teachings. Through the lens of abundance, we can see where we have old inner wounds that we need to tend to instead of letting them repeatedly cause suffering for ourselves and others. The essence of being able to shift beyond the scarcity mind-set lies in our ability to pause, to become self-aware of how we are feeling, explore where the jealousy comes from and to cultivate our presence and self-compassion as situations unfold. Then we are able to shift from reactivity, where we may seek to defend, judge or be on-guard, in to a more compassionate, grounded and nurturing way of responding.

> "Between an event and our response, there is a space. In that space lies our power to choose our response. And in our response lies our growth and our freedom."

Viktor Frankl, psychiatrist

If you read this thinking, *"this 'abundance' concept is an odd thing to raise in a book on leadership and business"*, then ponder on the amount of harm a scarcity fear-based culture does to our well-being, creativity, innovation, team-spirit and organizations' ability to perform well in today's landscape.

Leaders and employees in successful regenerative organizations cannot afford – or accept – the energetic drain a scarcity mindset causes. That's why abundance is key for Living Systems Being and Regenerative Leadership where our goal is to generate more value than we take.

# 6. Dance

*Objective: Tapping into the rhythm of life - its playfulness, change, seasonality, depth and emergence*

The final DNA strand of Living Systems Being is the ability to dance between it all – the highs and lows, the excitement, the sadness, the winter and the summer – with the help of many of the qualities and behaviors mentioned above. Nature works in cycles and seasons, and we are all cyclical beings in need of the processes that all seasons bring: The lightness of spring, the intensity of summer, the letting go in autumn, and the deep restoration of winter can teach us to loosen our grip and allow a flowing dance through the seasons, the tensions, the waves, the births, deaths, and rebirths constantly unfolding in our lives.

Look up at the moon constantly waxing and waning, look at the ebb and flow of the tide, the trees changing their colors. For most of the time on this planet, our lives have been dependent on tuning in to these cycles as they contained wisdom critical for our own survival and thrival. Humans are inherently wired to be in tune with the natural seasons of life, yet today most of us are disconnected from this cyclical approach.

Over time we have created a culture where we expect to be in constant spring and summer. We want the non-stop great ideas, the execution, the rewards, the performance, without factoring in the need for regeneration and restoration. We have become afraid of the dark depths of a winter-phase, and its stillness of regenerating and slowly preparing the soil within and around us for the next round of fertile ideas. We have forgotten how to deeply nourish our roots.

When we neglect the phase of winter and restoration we weaken our bodies, psyches, emotional resilience, our ideas, and our performance. Winter is not just a literal season that comes once a year. Every day we can honor the seasonal rhythms, and next-stage regenerative leaders help ensure a work culture where all seasons are celebrated, not just the spring and summer.

In our busyness, we often favor the masculine qualities of planning, focusing, controlling and progressing, while we neglect the feminine qualities of nurturing, reflecting, systems-sensing, pausing and going within. In Part 1 we explored how the Journey of Separation witnessed centuries of patriarchy which has prioritized rational-analysis, reductionism, competition, separation and silo-thinking over intuition, compassion, collaboration, relationships and systems-thinking.

It is now time to find the balance and integrate what we lost on our journey through separation between human and nature, masculine and feminine, inner and outer, left brain hemisphere and right-brain hemisphere. It's time we learn to dance through it all and weave it all together.

**Regenerative Leaders are weavers of a new way.**

In a world where more and more jobs are replaced by robots and Artificial Intelligence, we depend more than ever on our ability to innovate and be creative. The increased acceptance of creativity as the main driver for a company's future success means that companies now recognize that creativity and flow are critical x-factors. Yet, many organizations do not understand how to nourish a fertile and rich culture for creativity to flourish.

A 2012 Adobe study on *the global creativity gap* interviewed 5000 adults across the US, UK, Germany, France and Japan, and showed that 80% feel that unlocking creativity is critical to economic growth, yet 75% feel under pressure to prioritize being productive rather than creative at work and very few believe they are living up to their own creative potential.

*So how do our organizations realize their full creative potential?* By cultivating a culture that integrates all seasons, that plays with yin-yang tensions, that honors the inner and the outer, the feminine and the masculine, by embracing play, meditation, integration-time and individual creative expression in the workplace.

The challenge is that so many of us are programmed to think that play and meditation – two parts of the same creative spectrum – cannot be associated with good work. We feel guilty, soft, not serious enough, even shameful, when we're either too playful or take a pause to unplug and renew.

Yesterday's logic measures success and achievement through long hours in the office, being busy, frenetic, sacrificing family time or holidays to 'get the job done whatever it takes'. Yet, today's science shows us that play is a profound biological process, one which enriches brain plasticity, personal and team resilience, and makes us smarter and more agile (Brown, 2010). Play invigorates and energizes us, releases endorphins, makes us more abundant and optimistic – it helps cultivate a culture of prototyping, learning and exploring new ways. Play lifts us out of the mundane and makes us see things from new perspectives – you can call it the pathway to new inventions.

"Sometimes when a situation is really heading south, a moment of imaginative play is the only thing that provides enough distance to see the way out of a predicament."

Stuart Brown, founder of National Institute for Play

Learning to dance with the rhythms of life, the highs and the lows and to see the gold in every phase and season will allow you to tap into your creative potential and teach you to accept it all – the light and the dark.

It is through the celebration of every season that continuous adaptation, learning, renewal and reconfiguration occur. This is how we can achieve wholeness. This requires Regenerative Leaders to create space for the unforeseen to emerge, for sensing-in, for introspection and reflection, and for generative meetings without agendas that creatively explore the art of the possible.

We then learn to let go of tightly holding on to the river banks and swim with the stream, to ride the waves and use the undercurrents; tuning into the Logic of Life while finding our organization's unique rhythm. Building a thriving, innovative and creative culture with room for wholeness and authenticity requires from us that we cultivate these conditions conducive to life – an acceptance of it all and the ability to dance rhythmically with all that comes along.

"The notes mean nothing themselves: the tensions between the notes, and between notes and the silence with which they live in reciprocal indebtedness, are everything. Melody, harmony and rhythm each lie in the gaps, and yet the inbetweenness is only what it is because of the notes themselves. Actually the music is not just in the gaps any more than it is just in the notes: it is in the whole that the notes and the silence make together. Each note becomes transformed by the context in which it lies."

Iain McGilchrist, neuroscientist

We cannot stress enough how important the DNA strands of Living Systems Being are to next-stage leadership and organizations. This is where great leadership begins and ends. In fact, neglecting these qualities is exactly what is causing so much havoc to our inner and outer worlds.

What we covered in Living Systems Design is fundamental for our survival as a species: How we redesign the way we produce and consume, yet if we only focus upon Living Systems Design we fail to become truly life-affirming. We need the inner as a prerequisite for the outer success in our transitioning to the Age of Regeneration.

The next-stage of our evolution as a species on this planet depends on our ability to reclaim what makes *Homo Sapiens* (wise beings) truly wise, by applying our collective genius to co-create thriving regenerative cultures.

Building flourishing regenerative cultures requires we dare look at how we live our lives and transform our ways of BEING by embarking on a journey in to our deep inner wisdom and nature.

"As above, so below, as within, so without, as the universe, so the soul"

Hermes Trismegistus, ancient Greco-Egyptian sage

INTERLUDE

# We Are the Ones We've Been Waiting For

"You have been telling people that this is the Eleventh Hour, now you must go back and tell the people that this is *the* Hour. And there are things to be considered ...

Where are you living?
What are you doing?
What are your relationships?
Are you in right relation?
Where is your water?

Know your garden.
It is time to speak your truth.
Create your community.
Be good to each other.
And do not look outside yourself for your leader.

Then he clasped his hands together, smiled, and said, "This could be a good time! There is a river flowing now very fast.

It is so great and swift that there are those who will be afraid. They will try to hold on to the shore. They will feel they are being torn apart and will suffer greatly.

Know the river has its destination. The elders say we must let go of the shore, push off into the middle of the river, keep our eyes open, and our heads above the water.

And I say, see who is in there with you and celebrate. At this time in history, we are to take nothing personally, least of all ourselves. For the moment that we do, our spiritual growth and journey come to a halt.

The time of the lone wolf is over. Gather yourselves! Banish the word 'struggle' from your attitude and your vocabulary. All that we do now must be done in a sacred manner and in celebration.

We are the ones we've been waiting for."

**HOPI ELDERS' PROPHECY**, ORAIBI, ARIZONA

# PART 3

# When the Rubber Hits the Road

"Vision without action is merely a dream. Action without vision just passes the time. Vision with action can change the world."

**Joel Barker, futurist**

# Applying the Regenerative Leadership DNA

*So, what now?* If what you have read in this book resonates, then it is only natural for you to be questioning the next steps: *This all sounds great, yet... also a little overwhelming – where do I start?* We hear you.

After all, we've covered a dizzying number of topics that sweep across the landscapes of science, psychology, economics, history, biology, biomimicry, circular economy, biophilic design, adult developmental psychology, neuropsychology, systemic-awareness, to the witch hunts, the dynamics in ant colonies, patience, the power of purpose, and so much more. We have journeyed through the root cause of our current crisis, taken the temperature of the landscape in which leaders are navigating, and have covered the entire DNA model of Regenerative Leadership.

It's only understandable if you now feel overwhelmed – or maybe a little skeptical: *This will never work in my organization, this is too idealistic – and not very realistic.*

Again: We hear you.

This is why Part 3 of this book is focused on application, integration and implementation of everything we have covered. We give you concrete tools to assess how your organization is currently performing according to our

DNA model, how to cultivate your own Ecosystemic Facilitator skills, we answer the kinds of questions and concerns we think you may have at this point, and we give you suggested exercises and practices to take your leadership to the next level.

Shedding the old, mechanistic, and life-denying methods of doing business can be challenging, as our society has become habituated by them. And for many, continuing with the status quo is much easier, safer and more comfortable than carving out new regenerative ways. But our current ways are not fit for the future – our current ways of doing business are degenerative, not only weakening you inside but also weakening your organization's vitality and the vitality of the ecosystems it depends on for survival. But this should all be clear to you at this point of the book.

> "We are racing to protect not just our portfolios, not just our grandchildren, but our species. So get to it."
>
> Jeremy Grantham, investor

Carving out new regenerative ways of doing business is the reason we have written this book. We want to help leaders by offering them proven alternatives to the current degenerative practices that dominate many organizations today. If you sense the inkling that something has to change and long to learn new ways, this part of the book will help you take the first steps on the journey toward Regenerative Leadership. And remember the research we mentioned in Chapter 5 – it only takes 10% of a collective to start changing their behavior for the entire system to start shifting. That seems feasible and doable, right? We think so.

There are two important things we want to stress before we dive into the practical application of the Regenerative Leadership DNA:

## 1. There is no cookie-cutter recipe

No special formula, no magic bullet, no one-size-fits all approach. That would be missing the entire point of embracing the Logic of Life. For when we start to see organizations as living-systems, full of life, and ever-changing, they will not fit in to a neat and tidy matrix, 10-step process or organization chart.

## 2. Rome wasn't built in a day

Be patient. With yourself. With your team. With the world. But be persistent. And remember to have fun for heaven's sake! Life is about finding joy, love, and excitement – about enjoying the journey. There is no 'end destination' to reach, to say you've made it and all is sweet, job well done! Yes, it can be useful to have milestones to keep you and your team motivated, but the journey, the learning, the unfolding *is* the destination.

Let's get started. Have pen and paper ready by your side as this part of the book is all about rolling up your sleeves, reflecting, and getting a little creative.

# The DNA Diagnosis Wheel

*How Aligned is Your Organization with the Regenerative DNA?*

The Diagnosis Wheel is a high-level assessment tool that allows any individual or organization to reflect on each and every aspect of the DNA Model and assess where your organization is currently at in relation to each of the 17 DNA strands. This tool provides an overview of how well you are performing and where to pay more attention going forward.

The DNA Diagnosis Wheel consists of a select number of questions for each of the 17 strands of the DNA. Each answer receives a point on the rating system, and the points will show how the organization scores. *More on this below.* But first know that, anyone can use the DNA Diagnosis Wheel. It does not matter if your organization is a manufacturer or service provider, a multinational corporation, a B-Corp, a start-up or mom and pop shop.

This tool allows you to take the temperature and assess where to prioritize your efforts to have more impact, be geared for the future, build more thriving cultures and generally prepare your organization for the Age of Regeneration.

# THE DNA DIAGNOSIS WHEEL

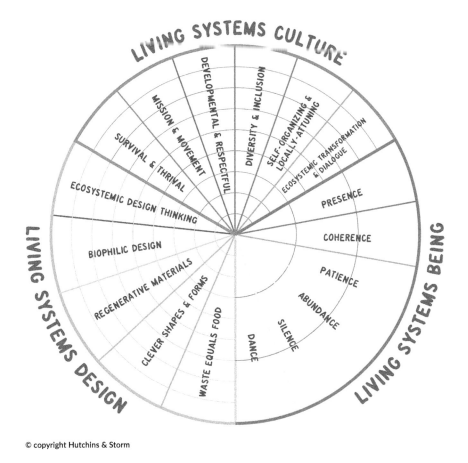

# How to

For each of the 17 DNA Strands, you mark your organization's performance by giving points from 0-3 on each of the Diagnosis Wheel Assessment Questions.

The points per answer are given as follows:

**3 Points:** Yes – this statement is true for us. We are performing well in this area, excellent, life-affirming, truly regenerative

**2 Points:** To some extent but plenty of room for improvement

**1 Point:** No, this is not something we adequately address

**0 Points:** On the contrary our actions in this area are degenerative

In order to receive the most authentic and accurate results, we ask that you take your time and answer each and every question honestly and subjectively. Take the time to ponder and reflect on how you feel your organization deals with each of these questions. If you do not know, or feel you don't have enough information or can't be subjective enough for a specific area, ask the question to someone else in your organization. In doing so, you will learn more about the ways in which your organization operates and its capacity for transformation. It may also be that not all areas are relevant to your organization and that's OK – biomimicry for example may not apply to a non-design organization. Then you just skip the question.

Once you have answered each question, and scored each appropriately, add up the marks to fill in the corresponding DNA Strand in the Diagnosis Wheel. If you score a total of 5 points for Biophilic Design you color in 5 sections.

We have provided a completed Diagnosis Wheel to the right to give you the gist of how that looks like. On the webpage for this book *www.regenerativeleadership.co* you can download and print more wheels – or you could just get going and use the one in this book.

# THE DNA DIAGNOSIS WHEEL

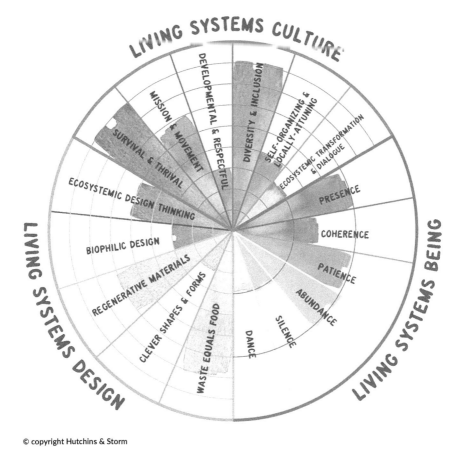

© copyright Hutchins & Storm

The above example of a completed Diagnosis Wheel shows you that although the organization is performing well in terms of circular economy and regenerative materials, you're missing out on the potential of tapping into biomimicry, bio-inspired innovation and using nature as a solution catalogue in general. Also, when you look to the right side of the wheel you see that this organization is not really nourishing the inner dimensions of Regenerative Leadership. In this case, we would suggest the leader explore the components of Living Systems Being and also see how to nourish the culture aspects of thriving organizations. See the toolbox in Chapter 11.

We suggest using the Diagnosis Wheel regularly. We have found that running this particular diagnosis every three months is a great tool to take the temperature and track progress.

# DIAGNOSIS WHEEL ASSESSMENT QUESTIONS

## LIVING SYSTEMS DESIGN

### 1. WASTE EQUALS FOOD

*See all resources as valuable nutrients to be recycled, upcycled, reused, and reintegrated into the value chain*

a. **Cradle to cradle**: My organization embraces the principles of a circular economy and cradle-to-cradle (or has a mindset of recycle, reuse, and design for disassembly).

**POINTS:**...............

b. **Life-cycle Assessments:** We have value-chain wide social and environmental impact reporting and a detailed 'value-chain footprint' per product/service (this could, for example, be Life Cycle Assessments on all products and services).

**POINTS:**...............

c. **Strategy for net positive impact:** We have a clear operational plan to get to 'zero negative impact' and then beyond into 'net positive' impact for all products/services/operations.

**POINTS:**...............

**TOTAL POINTS:**...............

## 2. REGENERATIVE MATERIALS

*Use regenerative materials and products in all designs and purchases*

a.   **Design expertise on regenerative materials**: Our product and service designers have knowledge about toxic non-biodegradable materials and we mainly use non-toxic biodegradable materials and resources in our production and development.

**POINTS:**...............

b.   **Organizational know-how & awareness**: In our organization, we have procedures in place to ensure regenerative behavior around resource consumption.

**POINTS:**...............

c.   **Sourcing of resources**: We have strict procurement policies and/or procedures in place for sourcing regenerative and/or sustainable products and service materials and office supplies, like office cleaning products, printing paper, canteen cutlery, factory uniforms, etc.

**POINTS:**...............

**TOTAL POINTS:**...............

## 3. CLEVER SHAPES & FORMS

*Seek inspiration from nature's time-tested shapes, forms and structures*

a.   **Biomimicry**: Our designers and partners actively use biomimicry or bio-inspired innovation in their product or service design – or we source bio-inspired products and services.

**POINTS:**...............

b.  **Nature as source for inspiration**: It is an encouraged behavior in our organization to apply nature's inspiration in our workshops and brainstorm-sessions.

POINTS:...............

c.  **Nature as a model & mentor**: We have an organizational habit of looking to nature for sustainable design advice on patterns, structures, forms and solutions that we integrate in our systems-product- and design-processes.

POINTS:...............

TOTAL POINTS:...............

## 4. BIOPHILIC DESIGN

*Design in ways that .allow people to reconnect to the nature within and around them, and therefore enhance wellbeing*

a.  **Access to direct or indirect nature**: Our built environment (offices, factories and other buildings) encourage a connection with nature. Such as a direct connection with nature (access to outside areas in nature for hosting meetings or areas inside where plants grow in beds or potted plants on desks, presence of water-flowing) or an indirect connection (views of nature through windows, pictures of nature on the walls, nature's ambient sounds playing in the back-ground, etc.).

POINTS:...............

b.  **Nature inspired interior design:** Our office environment has plenty of natural light, natural air flows, natural textures, natural colors, and natural patterns.

POINTS:...............

c.   **Awareness around biophilia**: Our key decision-makers, architects and designers are aware of the psychological and physiological effects of biophilia and Biophilic Design principles as part of the core product/service/place design approach for the organization.

POINTS:...............

TOTAL POINTS:...............

## 5. ECOSYSTEMIC DESIGN THINKING

*Facilitate the flow of life through the stakeholder network and think holistically at every step of the design process, sensing the entire evolutionary dynamics at play*

a.   **Awareness around ecosystemic design impact:** It is ingrained within the culture of our organization to always have the bigger ecosystem in mind when designing products and/or services – we consider the effect our designs have beyond their immediate utility.

POINTS:...............

b.   **Living-systems partnerships:** We actively seek partnerships across the value-chain to help tackle the ecosystemic challenges the organization faces, and for the execution of new initiatives, projects and products.

POINTS:...............

c.   **Organizational integration of ecosystemic perspectives:** Our designers and leaders regularly take time-out from the immediacy of the task to gain an ecosystemic perspective and tap into the field of stakeholders potentially affected or influenced by our product design and/or services.

POINTS:...............

TOTAL POINTS:...............

# LIVING SYSTEMS CULTURE

## 1. SURVIVAL & THRIVAL

*To thrive the business has to deliver healthy financial results*

a. **Profitability:** Our organization has a healthy P&L and/or sound financial forecasts enabling investment in the culture and value propositions of the business.

**POINTS:**...............

b. **Priority of long-term investors/shareholders**: Our organization has a proactive desire to engage long-term investors/shareholders who have an interest in the sustainability and thrivability of the organization while we phase out short-term investors (if you don't have investors/shareholders then assess whether you are mainly focusing on short-term wins or also prioritizing the long-term success of your organization).

**POINTS:**...............

c. **Geared for success in the future:** Our organization is already gearing our offerings toward a market with increasingly conscious customers, higher priced raw materials, stricter rules on working conditions, sustainable ethical sourcing, etc.

**POINTS:**...............

**TOTAL POINTS:**...............

## 2. MISSION & MOVEMENT

*Make sure the organization is contributing to something bigger than the organization*

a. **Purpose-driven organization**: Our organization is driven by a strong sense of purpose that goes beyond the organization's financial success.

**POINTS:................**

b. **Lived values:** The mission of our organization is supported by a core set of strongly-lived organizational values.

**POINTS:................**

c. **Engaged employees:** The majority of employees are strongly committed to and passionate about the mission of the organization and the bigger movement we seek to help mobilize.

**POINTS:................**

**TOTAL POINTS:................**

## 3. DEVELOPMENTAL & RESPECTFUL

*Hold space for yourself and others to learn, grow, and develop in respectful ways*

a. **Culture of openness and sharing**: Our organizational culture celebrates healthy vulnerability, sharing lessons learned, and it is the norm to help each other learn and grow.

**POINTS:................**

b.  **Dedicated developmental culture:** We have dedicated processes in place for ongoing development like 360-feedback, peer-to-peer learning, coaching and check-ins to offer feedback and advice – not just annually but regularly as part of how we work and collaborate.

**POINTS:**...............

c.  **A culture of wholeness:** Our organization is one where all are encouraged to be themselves – arriving at work and feeling at ease without the need for toughening up, wear a mask or play a role to fit in.

**POINTS:**...............

**TOTAL POINTS:**...............

## 4.  DIVERSITY & INCLUSION

*Valuing diverse backgrounds and perspectives as part of an inclusive values-rich culture*

a.  **Diversity is a dedicated priority:** In our organization diversity is a strategic priority. This influences all decisions across new hires, leadership team, board, partners and external experts.

**POINTS:**...............

b.  **Celebration of differences:** In our organization we celebrate and respect differences in skillset, talents, backgrounds, perspectives, culture, nationality, age and gender.

**POINTS:**...............

c.  **Strong focus on inclusion**: In our organization we have a strong sense of belonging and inclusivity across the organizational culture – there are no in-crowds, 'old-boys-networks' and glass-ceilings that exclude some but not others, all are welcome everywhere.

POINTS:..............

TOTAL POINTS:..............

## 5. SELF-ORGANIZING & LOCALLY-ATTUNING

*Unlocking resiliency and agility through self-organizing principles*

a.  **Distributed Leadership**: In our organization our decision-making is characterized by a healthy level of distributed leadership where people at all levels can make appropriate decisions without the need for top-level approval.

POINTS:..............

b.  **Self-organizing teams**: In our organization there is plenty of examples of cross-functional non-hierarchic teams working on challenges and projects in self-organizing ways – employees are not locked into certain teams or departments but can easily work across.

POINTS:..............

c.  **Involvement of all in the organization**: In our organization people from all levels of the organization are regularly engaged in key decisions, whether through workshops, dialogues or off-sites. Strategic decisions are rarely made by a few behind closed doors and then disseminated top-down through the hierarchy.

POINTS:..............

TOTAL POINTS:..............

# 6. ECOSYSTEMIC TRANSFORMATION & DIALOGUE

*Attentive care and understanding of the entire system in which the organization operates*

a.  **Ecosystemic consideration in decision-making processes:** In our organization, all parts of the business and stakeholder ecosystem are regularly connected through workshops, cross-company initiatives, etc. to help ensure decisions are not made in one area of the company which affect another without having all parties involved or considered.

**POINTS:**...............

b.  **Tapping into insights from the wider ecosystem**: In our organization, we often involve stakeholders outside of the organization – suppliers, customers, experts, pressure groups, community representatives – in collaborative stakeholder workshops or future-search workshops to collectively explore future potential.

**POINTS:**...............

c.  **Stakeholder partnerships and dialogue:** Our organization has a number of collaborative partnerships across the value-chain where the economic, social and environmental benefits of each partnership create win-win-wins that are known and reported transparently to each party.

**POINTS:**...............

**TOTAL POINTS:**...............

# LIVING SYSTEMS BEING

## 1. PRESENCE

*Nurturing a deep relationship to your inner self (inner nature) and your relationship with others and the world (outer nature)*

- In our organization, we have a culture where time for reflecting, pausing, meditating, perhaps going for a walk, or taking time-out to renew between tasks and meetings is encouraged.

**TOTAL POINTS:...............**

## 2. COHERENCE

*Being aligned with your authentic self and acting in accordance with your own inner guidance system*

- In our organization we encourage an environment where we each take the time to sense if our actions, behavior and decisions are aligned with who we are. We practice self-awareness, constantly tuning-in to ourselves to notice when we are off-center.

**TOTAL POINTS:...............**

## 3. PATIENCE

*Being at ease with and open to the unfolding nature of life, not being reactive, defensive, pushy, or judgmental*

- In our organization, we encourage patience through attentiveness, pausing, sensing into when to act and when to wait. Sleeping on it is encouraged in decision-making processes.

**TOTAL POINTS:...............**

## 4. SILENCE

*Allowing the space of silence to nourish you and your interactions*

- In our organization it is viewed as normal practice to tune-in to silence a few times a day, maybe in a dedicated quiet room, and/or as part of starting and ending every meeting with a moment of silence.

**TOTAL POINTS:..............**

## 5. ABUNDANCE

*A frame of mind that opens you up to life's rich possibilities, keeping you curious, creative and compassionate*

- In our organization we believe in win-win-win scenarios – our culture is not dominated by a zero-sum, competitive, scarcity mindset.

**TOTAL POINTS:..............**

## 6. DANCE

*Tapping into the rhythm of life – its playfulness, change, seasonality, depth and emergence*

- In our organization we fully embrace that everything ebbs and flows and has a natural rhythm – we don't push things through to fit hectic schedules and we ensure that we collectively hold space for the restorative winters as well

**TOTAL POINTS:..............**

You now transfer the Total Points per DNA Strand and color the sections on the Wheel accordingly (2 Points total = 2 sections in the respective DNA strand colored). You now have a high-level analysis for you and your organization, which covers all three aspects of *Living Systems Design, Culture, Being*.

## Upon completing the DNA Diagnosis Wheel Analysis

With your completed DNA Diagnosis wheel, you have a more holistic picture than what most reporting tools offer. These traditional tools are still indeed valuable, however they rarely go beyond mechanistic parameters like resource consumption, electricity use, employee turnover – things that can be measured, quantified and verified. Those elements are important to assess yet to build truly thriving organizations, the overall culture, atmosphere and lifestyle aspects also need to be included in these assessments.

We often use this tool in our workshops and seminars, proving time and again how much it is able to help leaders, designers, and teams gain a holistic understanding of how everything is interconnected internally as well as externally. It's also immensely valuable as a tool to kick-start deeper conversations in teams to explore how we do things and how and where we could improve.

The DNA Diagnosis Wheel includes the inner dimension of an organization in the right-hand side and often leaders are blind to how much damage a neglected right-hand side truly does to our work culture, innovation ability and performance. Including the inner dimension is crucial when assessing the organizational performance.

We recently talked to a regenerative intrapraneur (someone from inside a large organization working to transform it from the inside-out). She had become very frustrated with the large global firm she worked for. The organization talked a good story on sustainability and provided services that helped other organizations become more sustainable, yet when it came to the organization's own internal culture and practices, the DNA Diagnosis Wheel Analysis clearly demonstrated they had major gaps in their procedures for recycling, paper use, office supplies and also the inner wellbeing of the company showed developmental culture gaps.

Once you've completed the DNA Diagnosis Wheel, the next step is Ecosystemic Mapping, which builds on the Wheel Analysis but can also be carried out alone. Here you will gain further insight on the inner and outer aspects of your organization. As explored in the Regenerative DNA model, learning to become a true Ecosystemic Facilitator that applies an ecosystemic mindset is key to cultivate thriving cultures.

# Ecosystemic Mapping

*What does your inner & outer stakeholder landscape look like?*

An Ecosystemic Map helps give you an overview of your entire living-system and identify the system dynamics at play. We find doing both a personal and an organizational Ecosystemic Map to be a very useful step towards becoming an Ecosystemic Facilitator – but you can, if you wish, also integrate all in one map. This exercise will provide you an overview of your personal and organizational ecosystem and will highlight stagnated energy, blocked flow, and areas of potential new growth and opportunities.

Once you start reflecting on whether relationships are actually thriving or not, you start to see how areas (people, practices, places) in your ecosystem landscape influence each other either positively or negatively and where you are missing out on opportunities. Every time we do this exercise in workshops, the participants experience revelations, as there is a remarkable difference between mapping your ecosystem down and seeing it on paper than thinking about your ecosystem in your mind's eye.

An organization – and an individual – with a thriving ecosystem is illustrated by relationships that contribute to synergistic win-win-wins, little to no stagnated energy, and a rich flow that benefits the learning and development of all stakeholders involved. Yes, there may be occasional tensions, perhaps even conflict, but these can contribute to richer outcomes if addressed respectfully, rather than by toxic behavior which undermines the learning and growth of others and yourself.

If the relationships become stymied by judgement, projection, fear, manipulation or suppression, then the organization becomes unhealthy and degenerative. Likewise, if people are simply being too polite, superficial and agreeable without actually voicing their true feelings then things inevitability get out-of-synch, tense, or false. People can – even if only subconsciously – sense if you're wearing a mask. Every relationship will inevitably bring tension and learning, and it is a healthy relation when each party feels able to be true to themselves, to open up, be honest and frank, give feedback, listen and share from the heart.

A healthy regenerative relationship dynamic is not all sweet rose-petals. Nor is a healthy regenerative relationship too intense with too much developmental feedback or over-emotional sensitivities. A healthy regenerative relationship is learning to respect boundaries, sharing in ways that speak our truth in respectful ways, helping others grow and learn, all while getting the-job done in the day-to-day thick of it.

Now, we are going to map our organizational and personal relationships, and sense which feel regenerative and which do not. This is subjective and ever-changing, that's the point, but the activity of mapping them out and feeling in to these relational dynamics can be very powerful and revealing in and of itself.

### How to

We suggest you start off with one map for your organization, and a separate map for your personal relationships, even though there is obviously inter-relation between the two maps. As you get used to Ecosystemic Mapping, you may like to put it all together in one map. But for now, let's make it two.

We have provided instructions for both Organizational Ecosystemic Mapping and Individual Ecosystemic Mapping, plus examples to illustrate each.

## Organizational Ecosystemic Mapping

This mapping will enable you to sense your organizational relations – both inner (within the organization) and outer (beyond the organization). As an Ecosystemic Facilitator, this will guide you to identify the areas of unfulfilled potential, stagnated energy, or acupuncture points (we addressed this in chapter 7 illustrated with the Brazilian Mayor Jaime Lerner who actively used urban acupuncture to revitalize his city).

## Step 1

Start with a blank sheet of paper. In the center of the paper, draw a small circle to represent the organization. To the right of the circle, plot all relevant 'inner' stakeholder relationships and dynamics that influence the inner organizational landscape (see example list below). On the left side of the circle, plot all relevant 'outer' stakeholder relationships and dynamics that influence how the organization engages with its outer world (see list below).

Next, draw thoughtful connections from the inner and outer stakeholders to the small circle. Make the lines in different colors, thicknesses, textures, each to how regenerative or degenerative you sense the relationship is at this moment in time. Be creative – zig-zags, dots, waves – do what feels right for you. There are no rigid rules here, only guidelines to assist. When we facilitate Ecosystemic Mapping at workshops and seminars, we often suggest using vibrant colors for the healthy thriving relationships, and the thicker the line, the healthier the relationships are. For degenerative relationships, you might use grey tones or dark colors, and again, the darker and thicker the line, the more degenerative they are.

*To the right: Inner Stakeholder Relationships & Dynamics*

- Departments or business units: Finance, Procurement, Marketing, HR, R&D etc.
- Executives within the business: C-suite or other leaders with great influence and visibility
- Team members
- Informal leaders & other key influencers
- Mission – general sense of purpose, sense of belonging, clarity of mission
- Culture – team spirit, general atmosphere, levels of toxicity, authenticity, feedback, sharing, etc.
- Employee job satisfaction (in many organizations this is actually measured through regular surveys. Feel free to draw on these surveys and also use your own subjective judgement)

- Dedicated physical spaces to withdraw and meditate, sit in silence or access to green outdoor areas
- Stress levels – busyness, anxiety, fear levels across the company
- Honoring of employee's family life and need to design their own work-week: working from home, sick-days (kids or yourself), maternity/paternity policies

As you begin to draw lines and make your own connections, you will end up with a mixture of specific names of departments, functions, culture, or people and general headings like 'stress levels', 'life-balance', 'atmosphere'. Again, every map is different and we don't want to prescribe rules here. This is your map. Plot in every area, person, place that comes to mind.

### To the left: Outer Stakeholder Relationships & Dynamics

- Customers (write the actual name of key clients, where possible)
- Suppliers (write your key suppliers here + maybe a shared headline for the smaller suppliers)
- Environment and ecological systems (if you use large amounts of water, cotton, steel or other natural resources you plot that in too)
- Investors & Shareholders
- NGOs
- Partners & Collaborators
- Competitors
- Expert advisers, consultants, coaches, etc.
- Government bodies and regulators, key political influencer & politicians
- Media
- Communities

## Step 2

For each and every area/organization/person ask yourself this question:

***At what level (good/ok/poor) is the relationship area thriving, healthy and regenerative?***

*It can be responses like*

- **Good** – creating healthy regenerative and sustainable value
- **OK** – reasonable, tolerable but causing stress to some extent and could be improved
- **Poor** – not at all healthy

Then you color out the relationship from the small circle to each of the left and right-side areas, depending on how you feel they create regenerative value. You will begin to further connect the dots between all the areas and have the chance to contemplate how they affect each of the other areas on your map and then draw the connections between them.

When you have mapped it all out and drawn the interconnections between them this overview gives you a pretty good indication of where to prioritize your efforts – where to unlock potential and release tension. Let's dive in to a concrete example to help illustrate the potential findings of Ecosystemic Mapping.

## EXAMPLE 1: Ecosystemic Map for an example organization

This example is of a service provider, a specialist consultancy that has rapidly grown to a few hundred people with an HQ in Europe and regional offices in North America and the Far East.

When we did this exercise with them it was clear that the left-hand side, the Ecosystemic Map looks quite promising. Their partner relations are thriving. There is great activity and energy, with many positive spin-offs, and new areas developing and growing. The work being delivered is adding a lot of value for their clients and for wider society and the environment. The organization has healthy synergistic relationships with NGOs and the media, and is viewed as a leader in the fast-evolving space of sustainability business consultancy. Its impressive how quickly it's grown.

# EXAMPLE OF ECOSYSTEMIC MAP

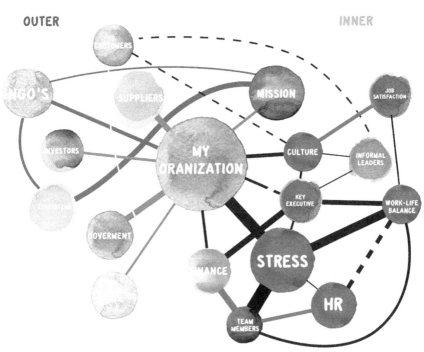

© copyright Hutchins & Storm

Yet, as we can see from the map above we cannot consider this a Regenerative Business, because its focus is skewed toward the 'outer', which is a sure sign that the underlying leadership consciousness is still largely mechanistic. This becomes apparent when we look at the right-hand side – the inner dynamics of the company. Here we see a lot of dark, thick lines, tension and stress. When exploring this in depth with them it seems the turnover rates among employees are on the rise, and over the last six months the company has experienced over a dozen major burnouts, both among seniors and juniors, with many more being on the edge. The culture is dominated by high levels of stress, internal competition and fear of failure in a high-speed environment, and its undermining the business's potential.

When we did this mapping exercise with them the inner friction had slowly started to show in the outer landscape as well. The quality of client deliverables was starting to be impacted, negative customer ratings surfacing for the first time, and employees were starting to leave the company and spread the word that the company "is not a great place to work for". The 'inner' toxicity is spreading to the 'outer'. The foundational reason for the inner toxicity is that the leadership consciousness is too mechanistic and rigid. Senior leaders focus too much on winning clients, executing, expanding, and becoming a market leader while running the business as a machine, with minimal regard for the inner dynamics and assurance that the organization adapts, learns, and thrives.

In our discussions with them we made it clear that the company will either crash and burn or get sold to a larger rival (giving the founders a pay-out while ultimately failing the people, wider stakeholders, and the mission of the business). Or they could embark on a journey of transformation towards Regenerative Business that will ask that all leaders begin working on their self-and-systemic awareness and dedicate efforts towards nurturing a Living Systems Culture. The company will need to discover ways to enliven the culture through divergence and convergence and ensure that both inner and outer aspects of the business become life-affirming.

Simply put, by applying the Regenerative DNA Model throughout the organization, not just in terms of circular economy, life-cycle assessments, and the financial bottom-line, this company can soon operate as a Regenerative Business. In this example, we would advise the company to begin by examining the DNA strands covered in Living Systems Culture and Living Systems Being.

> "Mapping the ecosystem of our organization was actually slightly overwhelming as it clearly showed how we are not always walking the talk. We think of ourselves as a sustainable company but looking holistically, this is not true at all. It has uncovered valuable insights I can't wait to get back to address."
>
> Participant feedback from a Regenerative Leadership Seminar

## Step 3

Reflect on the organizational map. Yes, the action of Step Three is to step back and reflect for a couple days. Take your time. You can bring your map to work, where it is possible to sense into certain connections on the map, such as having a meeting with a stakeholder relating to a part of the map we have colored. Other insights may come in different environments or with different interactions. With time, you can gain a more telling perspective on the dynamics of the living system than what you may have initially mapped.

It is a challenge to objectively observe anything when we are in the thick-of-it; therefore, Step Three is designed so that you can detach yourself from everyday relational tensions, personal perspectives or judgements on how individual people and parts are behaving. Attend meetings and see if you can objectively observe relationships, power-plays, motives, behavioral drivers. Slow down, lean back, pause, notice, observe, sense. Rather than seeing each interaction as a transaction, start to see everything as dynamically interrelating, whether it be the ripples that are triggered in a chat next to the coffee machine that then spread into the next meeting or some office gossip that influence decision-making. Be curious and explorative. What is really going on beyond our own judgements and projections? Take yourself out of the dynamics at play and observe. What is the atmosphere actually like here and what and who is affecting it?

After Step Three's vital time of reflection, exploration and digestion, you are ready to step in to the role of an Ecosystemic Facilitator, ready to address the whole 'gestalt' (the overarching field, all its relationships, the parts and the whole) of the organization-as-living-system along with all its stakeholder relations. Ready to start engaging yourself with the living-system – using the insights from the DNA model – to start addressing the challenges. We have more suggested practices in Chapter 11 to help you with this.

Ask yourself the questions: *Where can we unlock tension, potential or change in order for the living-system to become truly life-affirming?* Identify key people, key stakeholders, key action points. These people may be across the entire ecosystem, some within the organization, some far removed and yet still influenced by or influencing the ecosystem. These will be your first ports of call, and maybe even your allies or fellow Ecosystemic Facilitators to enable organizational systemic transformation.

## Individual Ecosystemic Mapping

This Ecosystemic Mapping is for you personally and allows you to zoom in on key relationships and areas in your life right now. It will give you an overview of how well your family, friends, partners, colleagues, mentors, and other personal areas, are thriving. Keep in mind that we are all different. The goal here is not to suddenly have x-number of friends or attend x-number of network meetings – if x-number is not what makes *you* flourish. Some of us are introverts and need an ecosystem map where the connections to nature, silence and alone-time are the strong healthy areas. Others may need a plethora of friends and social activities to thrive. The Individual Ecosystemic Map is a chance for you to gain perspective on your ecosystem and to sense into what fulfils you, what is draining you, and where you might wish to transform relationships in order to live a richer life (spoiler alert: if you thrive there is a high probability that you can deliver thriving leadership and work performance as well).

### Step 1

Start with a blank sheet of paper. In the center of the paper, draw a small circle to represent you. To the right of the circle, plot all relevant 'inner' relationships and dynamics that influence your life (see example list below). On the left side of the circle, plot all relevant 'outer' relationships and dynamics that influence how you engage with the outer world (see list below).

### To the right is

- Close family
- Extended family
- Close friends

- More distant friends or acquaintances, or work relations that also have a personal/friend aspect
- Love & Romance
- Stress levels
- Mood & Happiness
- Health – eating, exercising, bodywork
- Retreat, silence, reflection, stillness
- Time in nature, spiritual/contemplative practice
- Time on holiday, travelling or engaging in hobbies

*To the left is*

- Bosses
- Colleagues – peers
- Employees
- Professional networks
- Mentors & Coaches
- Education: Courses, evening classes – where we learn new skills and insights
- Your purchases (everything from clothes to groceries) – are they sustainable and responsible or do they add toxicity to society and the environment due to their design and consumption?

## Step 2

As with the organizational mapping above, you start drawing your relationship connection to each of the areas mentioned above. Where the lines are thick and colorful the relationship is abundant, thriving, regenerative. Where its black or grey the relationship is in a lesser state, and is undermining not only your general well-being but also your ability to be a regenerative force for good (think: *what ripple effects am I personally creating across my ecosystem?*). Thin lines are a weak connection, thick a strong connection – either strongly regenerative or strongly degenerative.

*EXAMPLE 2: Ecosystemic Map for Anonymous female executive, 45 years old*

This map is of a 45-year-old female executive – we will name her Lotta – with two kids and a partner. She loves to exercise and has always been very active and social. She enjoys being the center of attention and meeting new people; however, in the past year or so she finds herself feeling very exhausted and tired and doesn't have the energy to nourish her network of friends. Nor does she prioritize time with her partner and children. She hates meditation and prefers high-tempo adrenalin infused exercise, none of that 'boring yoga' or 'hippy dippy' stuff is what she would say.

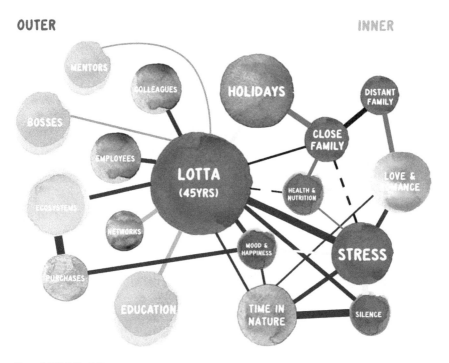

Spending time alone in nature is not her idea of fun. In fact, the mere thought of it makes her anxious and nervous. Her kids are doing well at school, but the energy in her marriage is stagnating. It's not thriving to say the least. She is very outgoing, with a need to be very active across different professional networks, and also very active on social media. She is well respected amongst her peers, yet has a bit of a reputation for being self-absorbed. She is defensive when it comes to any critical feedback, and doesn't get the support or applause she used to which makes her frustrated. While generally liked by her employees she is sensing more and more distance from them these days. She's often responding to their questions with impatience, seeing them as burdensome and even a disturbance. She has started to get more and more annoyed recently, especially with some of the young new joiners who have failed to deliver upon her high standards.

She feels disconnected on the inside, and anxious. She has started to feel fragile and vulnerable which she does not accept. She is losing her temper more easily with her kids and finds herself overreacting in many situations. Something is off, it makes her even more anxious to not feel in control, yet she has no idea what to do or where to start, apart from taking holidays, but that is not really changing anything as soon as she's back in the mud. Only a very temporary escape. She also realizes she spends too much money on things she doesn't really need. She has no idea where her products come from or how they're made. She admits that buying things makes her feel momentarily better but sees how her purchases pile up without bringing any real joy.

Lotta did her Individual Ecosystemic Mapping in a Regenerative Leadership Seminar, and while mapping it all out it became crystal clear to her that she was lacking intimacy and presence in her close relationships. She could see how this behavior was starting to rub off negatively on her relationships at work and in all parts of her life. The mapping gave her insight into what she had avoided looking at for a long time.

*So, what did she do?* Again, Rome wasn't built in a day and the journey of Regenerative Leadership is no quick fix, but an ongoing process of striving for wholeness and life-affirming approaches in all aspects of our lives. She started, based on our advice, by allocating a little time every day to breathe deeply and just be: Connect inward, to take walks in nature, and get comfortable with being alone and just sitting in silence. At first the silence was admittedly terrifying. Her brain could not stop the never-ending worries and realizations that surfaced. It was highly uncomfortable.

She started to talk more open-heartedly with her partner and became more conscious of how she was showing-up in each of her conversations with others – including the junior employees – during everyday busyness. She now sees that the cause was her inner unease and anxiety – itself fed by too much doing, planning, executing – that fueled her outer stress, impatience, and frustration in relation with others.

She also admits that the parts of her that dreaded being alone in nature are actually starting to really benefit from it. She feels a softening inside and has allowed herself to sit with some of her inner anxiety while being in nature and just observe it, even if the emotions lead to her crying. A release is happening for her, a healing, a slow but constant metamorphosis. And she has decided to seek out a life-coach to help her with this shift she senses she is going through.

## Step 3

As per before, now is the step where you take time to gain perspective on your map. You might give it the space of a couple days or a whole week. It's time to be curious, explorative, sensing in and seeing the dynamics of your relationships. What is causing tension, what nourishes you, when do you feel the most content, how are different relationships affecting your energy levels?

After dedicated time of reflection, observation and digestion, you will have new perspectives on the flows of relational energy, where the energy is stuck, where it feels alive, where it's a bit dead or blocked, where you may be leaking time and energy. By observing your own map, you can assess if there are underlying power-dynamics or acupuncture points to be aware of, along with key people within your ecosystem that can help you enliven it. You become the Ecosystemic Facilitator of your own life.

What needs to change for you to live a life coherent and aligned with who you truly are and desire to be? Then dare to let go of what no longer serves you while welcoming in what you desire more of.

> "Mapping my inner and outer ecosystem was eye-opening. Honestly, slightly uncomfortable at first but it has given me so much awareness of the energy I, as an individual, am bringing forth wide and far across my ecosystem. I want all my employees to map this out when I get back as a thriving culture starts with how my employees are actually feeling and whether they are showing up in alignment with what's important to them."
>
> Participant feedback from a Regenerative Leadership Seminar

## Journeying together towards the Age of Regeneration

The journey towards Regenerative Business is not a solo-ride. For Regenerative Leaders a 'stronger together' mind-set is key. We succeed through our thriving relationships – co-workers, suppliers, communities, relevant NGOs and partners, even competitors.

The two practices just covered – The DNA Diagnosis Wheel and the Ecosystemic Mapping – can be carried out whenever you want. You don't need a dedicated team but we advise you start facilitating these sessions within the organization as it can be a means for rich and transformative discussions.

The reality is that the systemic problems we now face as a human civilization affect us all and can only be dealt with by working together. Working together, collaboratively and respectfully, is part of having an 'abundant mind-set' – embracing every day developmentally and seeing every interaction as an opportunity for growth and synergy. It's a journey full of twists and turns, tensions and trip-wires. Humans are political emotional beings of immense complexity. Rich diverse human relations make up the messiness of the living-organization and its ever-changing ecosystem of stakeholders.

Again, we don't believe in 10-step formulas to success – that's an illusion in a world as complex as ours and we are all so different that no one size will ever fit all. But we do know that the Diagnosis Wheel and the Ecosystemic Mapping will help you cultivate your abilities to embrace the inner and the outer, the self and systemic awareness dynamics along with convergence and divergence. It will help you train your ability to sense in to yourself while sensing in to the system and detect areas for growth and potential.

And if we could leave you with just a couple of things after having read this book – these two tools would be plenty to get started. Once you get the hang of it you can always dive deeper into every DNA strand and explore the depths of each that this book simply can't encompass in its pages.

The next chapter is dedicated to addressing different kinds of concerns and questions you may still have – consider the next chapter a written coaching session where we address some of the issues that are often raised by leaders keen on getting started. And then the last chapter of this book is a range of different tools and practices to test and try out in your life and organization to help you become a Regenerative Leader.

"Whatever you do, or dream you can, begin it. Boldness has genius and power and magic in it."

Johann Wolfgang von Goethe
statesman and writer

Photo credit: Tom Vining

# Frequently Asked Questions

We spend much of our time advising and teaching leaders from all walks of life about this new Regenerative Leadership DNA model and next-stage leadership in general. From our work, we have through the years compiled a list of the most commonly asked questions we receive as people embark on this journey to becoming a Regenerative Leader. In this chapter, we share those questions and offer our reflection and guidance. In our reflections, you will find practical and real-world application of the tools and techniques we have shared in this book, to help you get accustomed to new regenerative ways.

We recommend liaising in person with an experienced leadership and organizational coach to aid you on this journey; however, here we address some of the most common question you may have upon embarking on this journey. It makes for a good start as you venture out.

## QUESTION 1: Doubts about transforming a mechanistic multinational corporation

*"I doubt this approach of Regenerative Leadership would ever fly in my old-school organization. We are 500 employees in our HQ office alone and then with 25 offices all over the world, some of which are factories, and in cultures that think very differently than we do here in our European office. The business*

*is run like a machine and has been run like that since its inception many years ago. There are rigid KPIs, power-based hierarchies, zero acceptance of failure, it's very risk-adverse and male dominated.*

*Regenerative Leadership seems appealing indeed but how will this ever work in an organization like mine?"*

## Our Response

It is very natural to feel over-whelmed by the change needed to shift toward a Regenerative Business, and easier, in fact, to dismiss the possibility of the organization being open to such change. It can feel like a mountain too impossible to climb. *Where to start? How to persuade the C-level suite? Will they deem it too soft or fluff before they even engage with the business examples?*

We have found that you can take one of two approaches, depending on your position and influence on those with the power to make transformative change happen.

Let's first assume you are either a part of the C-suite, on the board of directors, or a senior who has strong leverage with one or more executives. First, sense which of the C-suite members will be more open to exploring transformative change. Next, draft a high-level business case that covers both the push (we have to change to stay competitive and resilient in this VUCA world) and pull (we know we have an innate obligation to contribute to a better world) factors. Include examples of other large organizations that are embarking on this journey.

Research some of the inner and outer benefits that come as a result of this journey – new innovations, business agility, stress-reduction (and therefore a reduction in paying for sick-days etc.), improved culture, higher motivation and creativity, efficiency savings and effectiveness improvements, stronger brand and improved reputation amongst stakeholders, greater ability to attract talent, etc.

By all means refer to the cases in this book. Research them in-depth – their approaches to transformation, their challenges, wins and successes. To get you started, here is a list of examples of large incumbent organizations with factories as well as offices that have successfully embarked on a regenerative journey – many of them are already mentioned throughout the book in our Business Insights. They all have interesting lessons learned that you will be able to draw upon.

- Iberdrola (large incumbent energy company)
- Gore & Associates (multinational manufacturer)
- Nucor (large steel manufacturer)
- Patagonia (outdoor fashion retailer)
- Interface (global carpets manufacturer)
- Novo Nordisk (pharmaceutical manufacturer)
- United Technologies Corporation (conglomerate of different manufacturing brands)
- Henkel (world leader in applied chemical and adhesive technology)

None of these companies are full-blown regenerative, yet each one is transforming their outer value propositions and stakeholder relations along with their inner culture in order to thrive in the years ahead.

Your second option – say if you are a middle manager, who feels unable to directly influence the top-level executives, yet have a team of people reporting to you, and have influence across different parts of the business – you can start by exploring how you might change the way you engage with your own team.

You can open a discussion around Regenerative Business with others on the team and other middle managers across the business. Perhaps an informal discussion with some of your team members and then an informal discussion (over lunch perhaps) with one or two of the next-level up in the business, may give you a sense of the appetite for change. You may well be surprised and heartened that others in the organization are up for real change towards life-affirming futures.

You can explore which leaders above you may be interested in reading this book or having a conversation with you about preparing the organization for the future. Again: beginning from an angle of securing the future success of the business, securing top-talent, being agile and responsive, innovative and creative is a *great* way to start a conversation in an old-school environment.

We suggest gathering a mini-case for change, reasons for needing to change (explored in Part 1), examples of others leading the change elsewhere (take from the Business Insights in Part 2). Emphasize the benefits of addressing the DNA strands in the model and offer concrete practices to get started (see Chapter 9 and 11).

## QUESTION 2: Too drained and exhausted to catalyze any change

*"I'm stressed and exhausted by my current organization. Reading your book resonates and now I crave a new way, but simply do not feel like I have the energy to change my organization – what to do?"*

### Our Response

You are not alone. Hundreds of thousands of people across organizations of all shapes and sizes also feel stressed and exhausted, but we want to share with you that the tide *is* changing, a tipping point is being reached. Leaders worldwide are realizing that something radical has to change to address the complexity of the systemic problems we now face.

Take each day as it comes. If you are able to have control of your own schedule at work, then block out some time here and there for your own personal regenerative practices – you can find inspiration in Chapter 8 on Living Systems Being or in the next chapter on personal practices. Perhaps some time after lunch, for an hour, go to a local park, sit and breathe deep. Take a notebook or journal with you.

Do the Personal Ecosystemic Mapping exercise to help you get an overview of where your energy gets drained the most and which areas in your life you could start giving more energy and attention to. That's entirely within your control, and helps you regain empowerment. You may be a little burned out. Focus on building yourself strongly from the inside out. Explore your options but take it slow and with compassion towards yourself. Prioritize time to just be with yourself and use this time wisely, to let go of all the noise, the phone, social media, the to-do lists, and stress, and to sense deeper inside yourself. Give yourself some space to just be.

Once you have gained some energy and recovered some of your inner stamina, you will be in a different space entirely and can start reflecting on whether it excites you to start to pull together a high-level case for change inside the organization (see our response to the first question) or whether it's time you explore other career options in other organizations.

You can start to share this case for change with those around you that you trust and who may also feel that another way is possible, desirable and essential. Again, Rome wasn't built in a day. Don't rush things or over-burden yourself. Otherwise, you will falsely believe you solve your misery by pushing and striving – in your case, space to slow down is a much better option.

## QUESTION 3: Feeling stuck in the old rigid corporate machine

*"I feel trapped in my high-flying corporate role with a good salary, good career options and the prestige that comes with it. I'm the breadwinner in my family, and there's no way I can leave my job, even though I know in my heart something needs to change. The personal and organizational Ecosystemic Mapping exercise has clearly shown me that things are unbalanced in my life at the moment, nor are they life-affirming within my organization. What do I do?"*

### Our Response

There are essentially two paths ahead of you:

1.  You can become an intrapreneur, not to be confused with an entrepreneur. An intrapreneur is someone who seeks to make change happen

within the organization. Start by diving deep into the DNA Diagnosis Wheel to assess areas where improvement is needed and then start constructing a business case for change. Invite influential stakeholders for coffee – people who may be open to these ideas (as discussed in question 1's response),

2. You can leave the organization and find another job that is far more in-line with who you truly are. This may seem like a big jump, but allow yourself to be open to exploring new opportunities.

The choice of path is up to you. Of course, you could also decide to do nothing, and stay with the perceived comfort of where you are currently at, yet continuing with the status quo stress. We don't advise you do that – it will drain your energies and appetite for life more than you might imagine. Rather, tap into a deeper desire by helping transform your organization into a force-for-good in the world, or move to an organization that better represents who you really are, and provides the stimulation for you to step in to the Regenerative Leadership journey.

## QUESTION 4: Best approach to getting started

*"I think I can get the right kind of support and momentum to initiate a process towards Regenerative Business & Leadership. Our organization is ready for this but how and where's best to start?"*

### Our Response

First step is about informing critical internal stakeholders about the potential of Regenerative Business. Arrange to meet these stakeholders informally first, perhaps for individual chats over coffee, to gauge their interest. Then, set-up a more formal one-hour meeting to present the landscape of VUCA, the necessity for next-stage Regenerative Business, and relevant business examples from others on this journey. See if you can engage and turn-on these stakeholders, and then gain the mandate for spending some time assessing the potential – even if in a small way to begin with.

The second step could be hosting an internal workshop with key stakeholders focusing on doing the Diagnosis Wheel Analysis and diving deeper into your organization's performance related to all 17 DNA strands. Facilitate a discussion around the insights gleaned from this process of assessing Living Systems Design, Culture and Being. Discuss the organizational strengths and weaknesses in relation to the Regenerative DNA Model and which areas require attention for the organization to thrive. Outline which areas you would like to prioritize first, explore business cases for these areas – for example, if you see great potential for a more dedicated living-systems partnership in your product development processes, you start outlining how other global organizations have done this and start testing options with relevant teams. Or if the DNA Diagnosis clearly shows a lack in developmental processes you can start diving deeper into this with the help of external coaches and some of the resources we have provided in this book and on our website *www.regenerativeleadership.co*

Carve out areas with low-hanging fruit – areas that have been neglected yet can get early executive buy-in to kick-off initiatives.

Know that you can't do it all at once, so decide where to focus energy first, get the small wins and start mobilizing an inner movement of *Regenerators* who get excited about journeying toward a Regenerative Business. Also, draw on the organizational practices covered in the next chapter.

## QUESTION 5: Tension and resistance toward change

*"I'm pretty sure my team will be critical toward these new practices as it requires inner work that many shy away from. It requires people to engage, collaborate and show up in new ways and I foresee some will have a hard time opening up, giving feedback, embracing silence, etc. How do I best address this resistance my team may have to the 'inner' practices?"*

### Our Response

Resistance to change is only natural. Change can be uncomfortable and demanding, yet it's what provides growth and development. The journey we are on is one of learning to transform lead (tensions) into gold (deeper insights), this provides the alchemy we now need in these transformative times.

As with much of our human endeavor, it's more effective to air the shadows, tensions, and frictions than to let them grow increasingly bigger and more burdensome. Why not ask what makes the individual team members uncomfortable about the 'inner' practices, and address these worries and uncertainty. Emphasize the benefits of Regenerative Business and how it's about creating cultures where all individuals let go of masks and inauthenticity, redirecting that energy to learning and growing, so the individuals and the team can flourish more authentically.

Remind everyone that this is *not* the next popular 10-step change management programme introducing new ways of measuring performance. What you are introducing is a co-creative value-adding culture to address the stress and friction we see across the organization and wider society.

A great exercise to get the discussions started is to collectively go through the DNA Diagnosis Wheel. Filling out the wheel and answering the questions together often provides insightful reflections and curiosity to try these approaches.

## QUESTION 6: Applicability to all industries

*"Is it possible for all organizations to become regenerative or is it simply impossible for some sectors and industries to transform to this Age of Regeneration you talk about?"*

### Our Response

Yes, it is indeed possible for all industries to start gearing their activities in a more regenerative direction. Any organization has the ability to transition into a life-affirming ecosystem. Today all the needed solutions and technologies are available that allow for a transition across all industries – even in the chemicals sector, farming, fashion, office supplies and transportation. Although it may require investments into new materials, procedures and technologies, the sooner an organization makes the transition, the better for its mid-and-long term organizational health.

Embarking on the transformation to Regenerative Business too late could mean the death of your company.

Remember Kodak who did not take digital photos seriously soon enough or Blockbuster who didn't take to streaming in time? You don't want to end up in the 'Those who didn't see the writings on the wall' Hall of Fame. You have the choice to be either a leader or a laggard in your sector. Recall the Business Insight of the global carpets manufacturer, Interface, which transformed its operations from high-polluting operations to sustainable practices while increasing innovation and staff empowerment – and became a market leader at the same time? Also, the UK Housing Association, North Star, that in the midst of tough market conditions revolutionized its culture to become an award-winning employer and market-leading service provider.

It's not necessarily easy to transform, but that is why our organizations need Regenerative Leaders with courage and conviction.

## QUESTION 7: Hierarchies and Regenerative Leadership

*"My organization is held together by hierarchies and is very top-down, so how can we work with Regenerative Leadership? Do we need to eradicate the hierarchies?"*

### *Our Response*

First, let's be clear – hierarchies are not all bad. We find all sorts of 'archies' (structures) in nature, including hierarchies; they are part of *life*. Human organizations, with all their messy complexity, do need clear lines of responsibility and accountability, and often hierarchies help provide this. Therefore, the problem is not hierarchies per se, the problem is those hierarchies that are based on power, control, fear, and mechanistic management. The problem is hierarchies that stifle and undermine human potential. It is absolutely fine to have layers of hierarchy if people respect each other both ways and provide adequate space for everyone, at all levels of the organization, to develop, learn, and grow in their own way.

You can reflect on how the top-down structure in your organization works in practice.

Is there flexibility, empowerment, empathic sharing, deep listening, trust in others, personal accountability, and respectful relating? How are people valuing the work culture in your employee feedback? As we explored in the Living Systems Culture DNA strand 'self-organizing and locally-attuning', layers of hierarchy can create bureaucracy and dis-empowerment and this is what undermines the organization's capacity to adapt responsively to change, and undermines people's capacity to thrive. It may be that a good first step for your organization is to explore 'hybrid-systems' where pockets of cross-functional non-hierarchic teams apply agile self-organizing approaches. The people work in self-organizing non-hierarchic ways when engaged in the cross-functional activities, but for all other purposes, they report into the traditional hierarchy. This can help people experience and understand the benefits of less hierarchic ways of working.

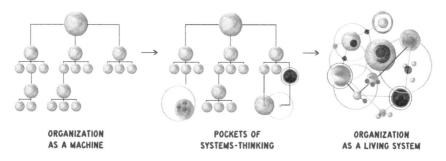

ORGANIZATION
AS A MACHINE

POCKETS OF
SYSTEMS-THINKING

ORGANIZATION
AS A LIVING SYSTEM

© copyright Hutchins & Storm, inspired by Biomimicry for Creative Innovation

Another tool you can explore is to cultivate an 'advice process' for your organization that allows people the empowerment to make their own decisions without needing to seek approval. This can be a great way to test out self-organizing ways of working without having to completely destabilize the traditional hierarchy.

# QUESTION 8: Feedback

*"Do we really want to give feedback all the time? It sounds very stressful."*

## Our Response

Cultivating a Developmental and Respectful culture is a necessity of Regenerative Business, and giving feedback is one aspect of this. The more people get comfortable with giving and receiving feedback with authenticity and respect, the more accepted it will be in everyday culture. Creating a feedback culture goes hand-in-hand with cultivating a 'coaching culture', where people feel equipped and supported to coach each other, even when difficult conversations are needed.

This is where training in how to give respectful feedback can be very useful. In fact we wouldn't advise starting new feedback processes without an internal course in coaching techniques. Perhaps it's worth revisiting the Culture DNA strand 'Developmental and Respectful' again and maybe dive deeper into the other literature we mention on this.

You do not need to move from a culture of minimal feedback to a culture of constant feedback and 360 evaluations – that's not advisable, and can be stressful for people, rather than respectful. The overarching aim is to provide working cultures where people can feel able to engage in their own journeys towards wholeness while contributing to a more vibrant life-affirming business. It does not matter what the frequency of feedback is, as long as people feel able to have proper conversations so issues are cleared up and learnings are continuously gained.

# QUESTION 9: Strategy processes for the Regenerative Leader

*"Will the traditional strategy process need to change or can we still do 3-year plans and Q1-Q4 targets in the context of Regenerative Leadership?"*

## Our Response

The mechanistic managerial mind-set is used to a 3-year plan, with a linear timeline of where we are at now and where we want to get to. There are useful aspects to this planning, and there is no harm in utilizing a linear strategy, as long as we also adequately supplement it with a systemic strategy that constantly assesses the changing dynamics in the inner and outer landscape. A regenerative strategy is one that takes into account all the inter-related stakeholder relations within and beyond the business, and the emergent ever-changing nature of life. This is where purpose and strategic intent become vitally important.

You can ask yourself if the Mission and Movement of the organization is clear. Is the underlying 'power of purpose' that we addressed in the DNA strand of Mission and Movement embodied by a threshold of people across the business? It is this power of purpose, along with the core values, that will enable the unfolding 'evolutionary purpose' of the business to navigate the volatility ahead. As a Regenerative Business, you need a left-brained hemisphere (linear traditional strategy) and a right-brained hemisphere (ever-changing systems strategy) to integrate into a regenerative strategy process.

We encourage you to combine some of the traditional strategy tools like SWOT analysis and scenario planning along with the DNA Diagnosis Wheel and Ecosystemic Mapping. Also, try out some of the practices we cover in the next chapter like running stakeholder 'swarms' where diverse parties from across the ecosystem actively contribute in to the strategy process. At all times, you must ensure that the strategy is serving the Mission and Movement of the organization and not becoming a one-sided focus overly serving financial returns and short-term shareholder value.

# QUESTION 10: KPI's and Quarterly Targets in Regenerative Businesses

*"What will replace KPIs, quarterly targets, and yearly budgets in regenerative organizations? Is measuring performance all bad?"*

## Our Response

Measurement and metrics are by no means all bad. Yes, we may have become overly inured in measuring and controlling all things, yet the old adage 'what gets measured gets done' has some truth in it. KPIs can be designed and deployed in regenerative life-affirming ways. In fact, in recent years there has been widespread take up of 'holistic KPIs' and 'systemic balanced score-cards', which take into account all stakeholders and a whole-life perspective.

These can be coupled with more iterative sense-and-respond approaches, where teams constantly sense into the changing landscape and adjust accordingly without becoming enslaved to top-down inflexible objectives and budgets. This is where your Ecosystemic Facilitator skills come in, to sense where the organization is flourishing and where it's not. We can use the dashboards and metrics to aid us, and also, we rely on our own insights and temperature checks gleaned from Ecosystemic Facilitation embedded across the business. Recall the Business Insight of Pukka Herbs, where key people from across the business came together every few weeks to sense into the vitality of the organizational living-system? That can be a good way of ensuring we're not overly-consumed with mechanistic KPI's, and that we continuously cultivate ecosystemic awareness.

# QUESTION 11: Is competitive behavior all bad?

*"Our business prides itself on having a competitive culture and beating the competition. Is this competitiveness all bad?"*

## Our Response

Competition is part of life. Competition can be healthy and life-affirming, when taken within a systemic context. If the organizational culture is one of ruthlessly exploiting, undermining and controlling others, then this kind of dog-eat-dog competition stifles creativity, collaboration and organizational vibrancy, instead infusing it with a scarcity mentality. Yet, healthy competition can stimulate creativity and help discover and refine our individual and collective potential. What matters here is the intent behind things. Are we trying to exploit for self-maximization (whether personally, at a team level or organizationally) or are we competing in a healthy way that seeks to improve the way we do things, the value we offer our clients and the way we do business?

Competition can contribute to greater divergence (through learning from competitors, innovation competition quizzes, adapting in competitive landscapes, etc.). Or competition can stifle divergence (hyper-masculine dog-eat-dog ruthlessness that creates an 'in crowd' us-versus-them mentality, where collaboration across silos is reduced and diverse perspectives are undermined). You can learn to sense when competitiveness is creating a healthy dynamic within the living-system, and when it's actually undermining the health of the system.

These were some of the most frequently asked questions. You may still have doubts, and again we stress: Start small. But do start.

In the next chapter, we will offer tools and practices – both personal and organizational – to strengthen you, your teams and your organization on the journey towards the Age of Regeneration. Together with the Business Insights and the DNA Model in Part 2 and the Diagnosis Wheel and Ecosystemic Mapping in Part 3, you have what you need to start your up-stretch into Regenerative Leadership.

REMEMBER THE
WISE SAYING THAT
A JOURNEY OF A
THOUSAND MILES
BEGINS WITH A
SINGLE STEP...

"A rock pile ceases to be a rock pile the moment a single man contemplates it, bearing within him the image of a cathedral."

Antoine de Saint-Exupéry, writer

# Toolbox for Regenerative Leaders

Here we provide the practices, tools and techniques that will support you on your journey of becoming a Regenerative Leader. These tools help you at both personal and team/organizational levels so that you can cultivate conditions for life-affirming business.

Let's begin with the tools that help you, personally, as a leader, to enhance your Leadership Dynamics of self and systemic awareness. Then, let's look at some tools that enhance the Life Dynamics of divergence-convergence-emergence for your organization-as-living-system.

## PERSONAL TOOL BOX

### 1. JOURNALING

Getting yourself a notebook, specifically dedicated to your own reflections and learnings – a 'journal' – is a very easy thing to do and a very important step. Journaling will train the critical skill of self-awareness.

You can begin by taking some time each evening, perhaps on the commute ride home, or after you have put the kids to bed – before you crash for the night. All you will need is five minutes to reflect on the day just passed. Scan through your day and notice if there are any feelings of tension (an interaction that did not sit well with you) or if you are still holding some anxiety or frustration about something someone said or didn't say. Also notice the moments when you felt aliveness and engagement. Write down in your journal whatever comes to you – what made your heart sing, what created some stress, what you are still holding on to, and such like. This may consist of you just letting it all out, ranting on paper or you might feel able to reflect on insights you gleaned from the events of the day, and gain perspective on what happened while sensing into the learnings for you. Perhaps some of the challenges may illuminate a blind-spot or shadow-aspect within yourself, or help identify what it is you need to work on more as you develop and grow.

Recall the quote from Richard Barrett in Chapter 5, "*you need to own your reactions and make yourself accountable for every emotion, feeling and thought you have. Please understand this. Nobody ever upsets you. You upset yourself.*" By becoming more conscious of your own triggers, reactions, biases, shadow-aspects, habits, and fears, we can gain perspective on them, and work on transmuting the shadow-aspects into gifts (lead into gold) as we integrate this learning into our way of living and leading more consciously. This is our *journey towards wholeness* each day, a learning journey, with our journal being our way of reflecting and gaining perspective. Keep this journal solely for this use, and use different note-books for general meeting notes, to-dos, daily actions, etc. Keep this private journal 'sacred' for your own developmental work as a budding next-stage leader.

Richard Leider's work on the 'power of purpose', explored in Chapter 7, notes that successful leaders are purposeful, and practice living purposefully by self-reflecting at the end of every day by asking themselves '*how did I grow today and how did I give today*' – everyday is an opportunity to practice '*growing and giving*'.

# 2. QUIET TIME

It is important that we regularly renew ourselves, quieten the mind, and make space and time to be still, pause, connect and reflect. Here are some suggested practices that may help you create space for self-reflection.

### 1. RESTORE SOME OF THE IN-BETWEEN TIMES

You may notice how most of us have a certain addiction to constantly checking our phones. Instead, practice being present. The brain needs 'idling time', so if you have a commute to work by bus or train, try one day a week without access to multimedia. Switch your device to airplane mode, or off completely, and practice just being present.

### 2. SPEND SOME QUIET TIME IN NATURE

Silent moments outside refreshes the body and mind so that we can be more creative, agile, clear and able to deal with life after this small respite. Venture out to a park, by water, in the woods. Even if only for 10 minutes, each day. Make it part of your daily sacred empowering practice. A walk after lunch perhaps. And again, experiment with switching your phone off for some of these walks, so you properly switch-off and just be.

### 3. PROTECT 'THINKING TIME' AT WORK

Bill Gates used to (and maybe still does) take whole weeks away from the workplace just to focus on new ideas and new thinking. By blocking out certain times every week where you do not have any meetings or activities 'to do', simply time 'to be', you can reflect, pause, and allow a wider perspective to enter the mind. A successful theatre director dedicated Friday mornings to 4 hours for 4 subjects that needed thought. It was in her calendar and her staff learned not to disturb during that time. A good way to get started is to put appointments with yourself in your calendar, which are boundaries to protect your precious thinking time. You can call them: 'strategy', 'planning', 'thinking time', whatever feels appropriate for you. Be the boss of your most precious resources: time and thinking.

### 4. BE A MODEL FOR OTHERS

Leaders set the model within organizations for what is accepted behavior. If you are seen to value self-reflection and time to simply refresh and renew, it gives others permission to do the same. Let half an hour nap-time, meditation, and such like, be the new norm and watch the change in culture.

## 3. DEEP LISTENING

How we listen to our inner-self and to others during our day-to-day conversations is the ground from which everything else unfolds. If, due to our frenetic busyness, we are unable to adequately sense-inward and listen to ourselves, we get lost, un-centered, tossed this way and that by whims, reactions, and urges. This will come through in our presence and behavior and infect the atmosphere of those we are interacting with – whether around us in the office or remotely connected to us through email, zoom, conference call, social media, etc. The more we cultivate deep listening the more centered we become in ourselves and within our conversations with others.

There are three levels of deep listening:

1. Deep listening inwards with our own self
2. Deep listening with another, in a one-on-one conversation
3. Deep listening amid groups – we refer to this third level under the heading of 'quality conversations through dialogue' in the section Organizational Toolkit, yet it builds upon these first two levels of deep listening.

### DEEP LISTENING TO OUR OWN INNER-SELF

A useful deep listening practice is to sit in silence for a few moments and sense inward. This simple 3-minute practice can be done anywhere, anytime of day. Here are four steps simple steps:

1. Ask yourself a question about a situation that happened during the day, or something that is not sitting right within you.

2. Simply sit with this question, and breathe deeply through the belly a few times. And sense into your belly area

3. Ask the question again, and this time sense into your heart area, while breathing deeply through the chest area, where the heart is. Then just sit, be still and see if you can sense your heart beating. Perhaps you may even be able to notice the space between the heart beats.

4. Then allow your body to relax, and get comfortable with just sitting, with no question, no expectation, just being present in the moment, as you breathe deep, and relax, for a few moments.

This 3-minute exercise repeated every day (or as often as you can) increases your capacity to sense inward, listen within, and connect with yourself.

## DEEP LISTENING WITH ANOTHER

You may be familiar with 'active listening', where we empathize with the person who is speaking to us, and we ensure we give bodily ques such as affirmative nods or 'yes, ah ha', and body postures to show we are actively engaged. Deep listening is a step beyond active listening.

Here is a simple 3-step practice:

1. FIND A PARTNER TO PAIR UP WITH

   A team member or stakeholder or even spouse or neighbor. Sit opposite each other, get comfortable, relax, and warmly look at each other in the eyes. We aim to maintain this eye contact throughout this exercise. One person is going to speak first, for 5 minutes, and the other person is going to listen without interrupting. Then we are going to swap over, with the other person speaking for 5 minutes. (You can make the time of speaking and listening whatever you wish, though no less than 3 minutes or more than 10 minutes).

## 2. THINK OF A QUESTION TO EXPLORE

This exercise allows us to explore personal reflective questions such as: *What would I like to change about my life? What are my greatest fears?* Or, we can explore work related questions such as: *What is really concerning me at work? How would I start to place steps of change towards Regenerative Business? What is the real purpose of this organization, to whom ought it be serving?* Once the pair is clear on the question they are going to speak about, they agree who is going to speak first for 5 minutes, while the other listens attentively and fully.

## 3. SPEAKING AND LISTENING FROM THE HEART

The listener should refrain from any bodily queues that could influence the speaker such as smiling, frowning or nodding or any verbal expressions. We listen with a blank yet open and warm expression and maintain eye contact throughout. We remain aware of how present we are while listening, catching ourselves when caught up in distractions, or thoughts about what is being said. We keep bringing our attention back to *fully* listening. This act of listening is a form of meditation in itself as it helps us free ourselves from noisy head-chatter, fully receptive to the other person. The speaker will, either consciously or unconsciously, sense this deeper awareness, and this will provide a sense of authenticity and trust between you both, so that a deeper more heart-felt sharing unfolds. When we are speaking it is important for us to feel into our heart and gut to sense what wants to be spoken through us with regard to the question. We speak spontaneously and freely as we go with pauses and spaces for stillness as-and-when it feels right. It does not matter if the speaker says little or gets into a flow and pours out a lot, nothing is right or wrong here and all is beyond judgement.

We do this exercise in all our workshops and seminars. And it always creates a strong bond between two strangers. You immediately feel you have something special with that person with who you've done deep listening with. You feel more compassionate, trusting, open to that person – yet it was only an investment of 10 minutes!

In organizations where they have implemented this as part of their common practices it has created impressive results in terms of improved culture, trust and healthy vulnerability.

## 4. PRESENCING WITH THE HEART

Presencing with the heart is central to both self-awareness and systemic-awareness. These next two tools, heart breathing and heart entrainment, can be used separately or become part of the same practice – a practice which greatly helps our presence and coherence.

**Heart Breathing:** There are two simple steps to this practice.

### 1. CONSCIOUS BREATHING

Whether you are sitting or standing, become aware of your breath. As you breathe in and out, feel your lungs move up and down and your stomach in and out. Feel the breath in your nostrils, cool as it comes in, warm as it goes out. Breathe in deeply from the belly area a couple of times. If the situation allows, we can place both hands over our heart area, one hand above the other, so one is covering the lower heart region and the other the upper heart region of our chest area in a gentle way. If the situation does not allow, then we can simply imagine we are placing our hands over our heart area and bring our attention into our heart region as we do so.

### 2. HEART BREATHING

With our imagination, we breathe in and out through the heart area (as if breathing through where are our hands are places over our heart). Do a few rounds of this heart breathing, breathing in and out deeply and consciously as we focus on the heart area. This 'heart breathing' amplifies our heart-awareness while helping our 'bodymind' coherence within us (improving our sympathetic and parasympathetic nervous system network alignment along with left and right brain coherence).

We may notice a subtle shift in how we feel, perceive and attend to what is emerging around us; a simple yet profound shift in conscious from head to heart occurs within us no matter how fleeting.

## HEART ENTRAINMENT

Let's find a space where we can be free to relax uninterrupted for 4 minutes – this could well be the office toilet or nearby park bench. When comfortable, we start with the two-step practice of heart breathing, as above.

Then engage in these further two-steps:

1. **RECALL AND RELIVE A MOMENT OF LOVE**

   When we feel ourselves breathing deeply and calmly in and out through our heart region, we use our imagination to recall a memory and feeling of something we really love (this might be, for instance, a memory of a pet we once had, a walk in nature, playing with our children, a special memory of a time in our lives when we felt really happy and alive – it does not matter what it is, only that it invokes a feeling of love within us. It is this feeling that we are sensing-in to.) While still doing our heart breathing, conjure up this feeling of love, and re-live this loving feeling with our imagination, feeling it in our heart.

2. **MAGNIFY THIS FEELING OF LOVE THROUGHOUT OUR ENTIRE BODY**

   Then, we allow this feeling to start to expand from our heart region throughout our body. While we are heart-breathing, feel this loving feeling spread into our legs and arms, our toes, fingers and spine, our neck and head, all over our body; allow ourselves to indulge in this feeling, immerse ourselves in it, as we continue with our heart breathing. Feel every cell in our body being washed and cleansed with this feeling of love.

   This simple exercise will subtly shift our consciousness. Less grasping, more openness. Less judgement, more empathy.

Combining these two exercises of Heart Breathing and Heart Entrainment shifts us physiologically and psychologically – if we had electrodes over our body while doing the exercise, we could see the changes on a screen. It is amazing how this practice of *Presencing with the Heart* brings us back into alignment – more balanced, more present, more coherent, more aware, more alive, more wise.

## 5. BODY SCAN (OR YOGA NIDRA)

Find a quiet space where you will not be disturbed for 10 minutes and can feel safe and comfortable enough to lie on the floor. Make sure you are warm enough during this exercise as when you relax, your body temperature is likely to drop, so it may be worthwhile having a blanket to put over you, or an additional layer of clothing.

1. To begin, lie down, make yourself comfortable, and relax. Practice 3-4 rounds of deep belly breathing.

2. Now, feel the weight of your body on the floor. Continue to remain aware of your breathing – in and out of your lungs.

3. The next thing you will do is a 'body scan' (which is based on the ancient practice of *Yoga Nidra*). We have provided a written instruction here, for this Yoga Nidra body scan, yet the best way to comprehend this exercise may be to watch a video on-line by googling 'Yoga Nidra' – there are plenty of good resources on the web, and you can also visit our website *www.regenerativeleadership. co* for further links. What follows here is a written instruction, so you can read the whole process, and get the gist of it. It's a wonderfully rejuvenating practice.

Feel the body lying on the floor; the weight of the body and the floor beneath us. Feel the sensation our clothes against our skin, and feel our lungs rising up and down as we breathe. Bring awareness to our breathing, notice our lungs filling and emptying. Notice any tensions and sensations, becoming intimately aware of how the body is feeling overall. We can take a couple more deep breaths and then bring our attention into our left foot, with specific focus. Let's really feel into the left foot with our awareness, feel the sensations in the foot. We imagine what it's like to be inside our left foot.

We then move through our different body parts with our awareness starting with the big toe on our left foot, then moving to each individual toe, then to the sole of the foot, then the ankle. We move our attention to our shin on our left leg, then to the calf, up to the front of the knee, and the back of the knee, up our thigh to our left hip, and then up the left side of our body to our armpit. Next, we sense our left shoulder, our biceps, then triceps, our elbow and then our left forearm, wrist, palm, back of the hand, thumb, first finger, second finger, third finger, fourth finger, and fifth finger.

Then, we bring our attention to our right foot and start with the big toe and move along the toes, the sole, ankle, up the leg, thigh, hip, side, armpit, arm, hand and fingers as per the left side, ensuring we touch each part with our conscious awareness catching ourselves when we drift off, always bringing our attention back to the body.

When we have finished the right side, ending with the right fingers, we then bring our awareness into the base of our spine and our buttocks, and then we move our awareness all the way up the spine, sensing all over our back as we move up the spine, up to the neck. Then we focus on the neck, back of the head, top of the head, forehead, left eye-brow, right eye-brow, nose, tip of the nose, left cheek, right cheek, left ear, right ear, lips, tongue, chin, throat, collar bone, left side of the chest, right side of the chest, diaphragm, feel it moving up and down with our breathing. We bring awareness to our heart area, to our stomach, to the organs in our stomach region, then lower abdomen, down to our sex glands and base of the spine.

Then we feel our whole body, we feel its aliveness as we breathe into every part of our body. We do a quick body scan to feel all around the body, notice the subtle energy flowing freely, and feel every part of our body alive with this energy; then we take a few deep breaths and simply relax into this feeling for as long as time allows us.

It is quite normal to drift-off or fall asleep while doing this exercise, and if our schedule allows, that's fine as it is rejuvenating. The more we practice it, the more proficient we will become at remaining in a conscious yet deeply relaxed, spacious state without falling asleep. This stimulates changes in our brain wave patterns and also our entire bodymind coherence. It also helps us tap into the Living Systems Field, and become more aware of our somatic, intuitive and emotional intelligence.

## 6. OPENING TO NATURE

This activity involves going outside and sitting on the ground for five minutes or more, so it's important to dress appropriately.

Here are 4 simple steps:

### 1. FIND A TREE THAT ATTRACTS YOUR ATTENTION

Then, sit down next to its trunk, making ourselves comfortable. It is best if we sit up, with our back and spine reasonably straight yet remaining relaxed and comfortable with our hands gently resting in our lap or at our side. Legs can be crossed or stretched out, which ever we prefer.

### 2. GET COMFORTABLE AND SENSE INWARD

Once we are settled comfortably, we can undertake a few rounds of deep belly breathing, on the inhale feeling the fresh air filling our lungs, and on the exhale releasing any nagging thoughts. Then, with our eyes closed or slightly open, sit and feel. Don't think, feel. Feeling our body sensations while we sit is easier said than done as our ego-chattering mind will no doubt try and distract us. Notice these thoughts and gently and repeatedly bring ourselves back to simply feeling, taking some deep breaths if we feel we need to relax further into this sitting meditation.

As we allow ourselves to relax and our head-chatter starts to wane (which may take a few minutes), let's bring our attention ever-more intensely into the sensations of what we are feeling, whether in our gut, heart, legs, arms or the sensations on our skin, or the noises and gusts of air around us.

3. SENSING INTO THE TREE'S ROOTS, TRUCK AND BRANCHES

Let's bring our awareness into the tree as a living being behind, beneath and above us. First, get present with the tree as a whole living-system, its entirety. Sense its solidity, and its reach downwards into the soil and upwards into the sky. Then, we can more specifically focus on roots radiating out into the earth below us, and the branches reaching out in the sky above us. First, let's focus in on the roots:

A. IMAGINE THE ROOTS RADIATING OUT IN THE SOIL UNDER US

With our imagination, let's sense the roots spreading into the soil beneath us, deeper and deeper they go. We can then use our imagination to go further into the earth beneath us, all the way into the molten core of our planet, if we wish. Then, we bring our awareness from deep beneath us back up into the roots of the tree and into our buttocks sitting on the ground next to the tree, and then into our body, up our spine, back and into our chest and heart area. As we undertake some deep belly breathing, sense a direct connection from our heart to the centre of the Earth beneath us. We are rooted, connected, at one with our planet.

B. IMAGINE THE TREE'S BRANCHES RADIATING OUT INTO THE SKY ABOVE US

With our imagination, lets sense the branches, twigs and leaves radiating and reaching out into the sky above. Sense the clouds and vast expanse above us, taking our awareness up further in to the stars and space that lie beyond our atmosphere. And then bring our awareness back down through these twigs and branches, back into the tree and also into the top of our head, down through our neck and into our chest and heart area. Sense our heart area connected with the sky and universe above us.

Let's just sit here for a couple of minutes with this relaxed awareness of the feelings within us and the world all around us. We sense the expansiveness of the universe above us, and flowing into us from above; and the rootedness of the earth below, grounding us as we sit and breathe deeply through the belly.

These personal tools are gentle and easy to undertake, yet powerful, especially when practiced regularly. These tools provide the necessary presence and coherence within ourselves to enable us to cultivate the self and systemic awareness (and ecosystemic awareness) essential to Regenerative Leadership Consciousness.

These personal practices act as the foundation for the organizational practices, which we now explore.

# ORGANIZATIONAL TOOLBOX

## 1. SILENCE AS A REGULAR PRACTICE IN MEETINGS

We spend so much time in meetings and most are draining energy and creativity and not very productive. *You can probably relate, right?* There's the one who over-talks with little awareness of or curiosity toward hearing others' points of view, then there's the silent introvert who says little if anything, and there's the one who always agrees with the one with the most 'influence', and so on and so forth. Now, instead, imagine landing in the room, settling in energetically, grounding everyone, and gaining focus on how the meeting could unfold most authentically and productively.

A powerful yet simple way of using silence to create thriving cultures is by making it the new norm to start every meeting with a moment of silence. Encouraging a culture of silence to start meetings restores the energy and power dynamics, especially if you combine it with the meeting practices provided below, of taking turns and making sure all have a say (often it's the introverts that hold back nuggets of wisdom that they don't feel comfortable sharing in a classical noisy extrovert-driven meeting culture).

The Danish consultant, Bastian Overgaard, works solely on advising organizations on building meeting cultures with integrated silence, and he advises to start with a couple of minutes of silence and then three-quarters of the way through the meeting, anchor the meeting with another couple of minutes of silence. His clients report improved energy levels and more efficient meetings; they have noticed how they no longer leave the workplace drained and with an overstimulated brain but that they feel much more energized and alive. The pockets of silence nudge them to only share what's essential, rather than over-talking. This practice of silence in meetings also helps create greater respect and trust between employees.

## 2. CONSTRUCTIVE FEEDBACK

Giving and receiving feedback is a reciprocating gift that nourishes both the giver and receiver. It is not about critically judging the other, a veiled form of one-upmanship, nor trying to get the other person to see your point of view. Feedback is about authentically wishing to help the other by providing useful insights into what has gone well and not-so-well from our empathic perspective, therefore allowing the receiver to identify areas of learning and development. We can all feel apprehensive and defensive about receiving feedback no matter how constructive it is to our development, and so creating an empathic atmosphere is important.

Give feedback in pairs. Find someone who is willing to give and receive feedback with you, and sit across from one another. It's good for both of you to try and remain relaxed with friendly eye contact throughout the sharing. Choose who is going to give feedback first, and who is going to receive.

Then, the one who is giving the feedback begins with a positive 'what went well' feedback comment to help create an open, sharing and friendly environment. Continue with constructive feedback 'what did not go so well' or may be 'an opportunity for learning.' Its important to frame our words carefully and constructively, empathizing with how it feels to receive such feedback, positioning it as a useful insight to help the other.

Three 'positives' and two 'learning areas' per feedback session is enough for us to digest and work with. Feel free to do less. If you have a couple of insights that's fine – one or two good insights is more useful than verbose ill-thought through feedback. Giving examples or referring to specific situations or conversations rather than generalities helps the receiver better perceive the area of potential learning.

It is best if the receiver simply listens and takes notes to allow the giver to go through all comments without interruption, yet the receiver can ask for clarification or further expansion, as opposed to starting to justify why what was done was done – this is not about justifying ones actions, as important as that may seem to our ego, this is about taking on-board someone else's perspective and insight.

Once one person has had an opportunity to share both positive and constructive feedback – and feel heard – the pair can rotate, with the receiver now becoming the person giving the feedback and the other person listening, clarifying and taking notes.

The more we build-in regular cycles of feedback within our teams, the more we are able to sense-and-respond, adapt and learn  We can start to embed informal yet artful spontaneous feedback as part of our normal daily undertaking of business. This deepens the authenticity and wisdom of both the giver and receiver and also the wider team's relational dynamics.

## 3. FUTURE BACK TOOL

This is an exercise that can easily be done with a colleague (or coachee) or with a small group of people from your team. All you need is a quiet, private meeting room which is long – for instance, a boardroom, with a long table and several chairs along the length of it. You can also do it at home, in a long room or corridor, or out in a field or park.

Keep in mind that in the instructions that follow, we assume you are in a meeting room with a long boardroom-style table in it, long enough for eight or so chairs to flank each side. This exercise has been used by us in many different situations to great effect. It draws upon foresight, scenario-planning, and back-casting tools, which are often used as part of strategy planning and also draw upon Professor Peter Hawkins's Systemic Coaching 'future back outside in' method.

This exercise is simple, yet powerful. Try it out on yourself first, and then try it out on someone you are coaching or a member of your team, then with your leadership team, and then with different stakeholders, either individually or in a small group.

The instructions here assume you are with one of your team members, and are guiding them through the exercise, much like a coach and coachee.

### STEP 1

Sit at one end of the table with your team member/coachee at the same end as you.

Ask your team member to reflect on the question: *To whom or what is your work serving?*

Invite them to take as much time as they wish and to not feel restricted in their response. They may share all sorts of things – serving their family, serving themselves, serving the organization, the organization's clients, the communities affected by the work, perhaps even humanity, or the wider ecology of the planet, or their children and their children's children. There are no right or wrong answers. And it is healthy if the person reflects on both the personal and the organizational – as it is only natural that our work serves both. It is an invitation for the person to sense-in to what the underlying motives and drivers for their work are, the obvious ones and also those that lie beneath the obvious. If you wish, you could also have some A3 paper and coloured pens to hand, so that the person can start to draw a high-level map of who their work is serving (an option here is to undertake the Ecosystem Mapping exercise if time and situation allows).

Spend five or more minutes on this, asking open questions, that encourage your team member to open-up and go a bit deeper around "*To whom or what is your work serving?*"

You are the 'space-holder' or coach for this session, and you will be listening deeply to what is said and not said – the body language, the emotions, and such like – which may encourage you to ask certain questions that explore aspects where you detect it would be useful to probe further. Naturally, it is good if you have already received some training in coaching, and yet many of us, when given the right space and time, can with practice become good at simply listening and asking open questions while providing a safe-space for the other person to feel able to share authentically and openly.

## STEP 2

Invite your team member or colleague to inquiry into how the organization feels, to come up with words, expressions, emotions that describe how the organization feels, as a living-system. For instance, does the organization feel vibrant and energized, or busy and impatient, or slow and bureaucratic, etc.

Invite your colleague to express the atmosphere in the office, the characteristics, the general culture – how would they describe it. Again, there are no right or wrong answers, and this is not about trying to see our organization in a good light or an overly-critical light, but to gain an open honest perspective on how the organization really is, giving ourselves a chance to stand back, pause and reflect for a moment. It may be that words or expressions like – busy, hectic, a bit slow at making decisions, entrepreneurial, bureaucratic, oppressive, creative, too impulsive, a bit cliquey, etc. – come up.

Again, through deep listening and the use of open questions, invite them to go further with what they mean by these expressions, and to keep exploring what the organization feels like for a few minutes.

If you wish, you can use some A3 paper and colour pens and invite them to draw how the organization feels, or write words that describe it (this could be an opportune time to undertake the organizational Ecosystemic Mapping exercise if time and situation allow). When this feels done, pause for a moment, and relax, sit with it for a while.

## STEP 3

Explain that this long table represents the future ahead of us, the next 10 years, the chairs along the sides are the years ahead. You stand up and invite the other to stand up and walk with you to move out of the present and move into the future 10 years from now, as you walk to the other end of the room. At the other end of the room, you are now standing in the future – at the other end of the table.

While you are both standing at the other end of the table – in the future – ask your coachee to reflect in silence for a moment, here from the future, 10 years from now.

What might the future be like for the organization? How might the world be? You may wish to refer to some of the trends we know about the future – increasing digitization, AI, robotics, electric cars, increasing population, aging population, smart grids, increasing awareness of organizational impacts on society and the environment, etc. – yet also explain that we have no real idea what the future will be like in 10 years' time.

All we do know with some certainty is that 1) the future will be very different from the present 2) issues around sustainability, climate change, sustainable food production, ecosystem degradation, social inequality, essentially every one of the 17 SDG goals will become higher priorities over the next 10 years. We can say, without much shadow of a doubt, that our organization will have to address these systemic issues in a way that is core to its business, central to its operations, an essential part of its 'licence to be in business'.

Pause and reflect in silence on all this for a moment. And then invite your colleague to sense-in to how the organization needs to be in this 10-year future moment, and to sense-in to the transformation the organization needs to embrace over the next 10 years in order to be able to not just survive but truly thrive in 10 year's time. What do we need to do differently? Where should we dedicate more energy? Are we on track in terms of our R&D? What areas of our business have to transform?

## STEP 4

After a couple of moments silent reflection, invite your coachee to share what may need to transform from the present down one end of the table and towards the future, here at the other end of the table. And what does this mean for the 'inner' and 'outer' – the inner culture, in terms of how the organization feels, and the outer, in terms of how the organization engages with the clients, communities, suppliers, investors and wider world it participates with.

## STEP 5

Now invite your coachee to look from the future back to the present, to look from this end of the room back down the table to where you originally sat, where the present day is.

Ask the question: *What is the future calling of me and my work today?*

Spend some moments of reflection and deep listening on this. Inquire on how your colleague may wish to courageously move from current ways of being and doing, into ways that work systemically across the business and wider ecosystem, to catalyze the organization's necessary transformation so it thrives in 10 years' time.

When it feels right, go back to where you were sitting, back into the present, and both sit down, reflect, share and capture any insights in your notebooks/journals.

This exercise of walking in to the future can be powerful for all in the room and provide insights beyond what other traditional tools offer. We create a generative space and wider perspective to sense in to what the future asks of us instead of linear planning, foresight and strategy based on current norms and today's limitations.

# 4. QUALITY CONVERSATIONS THROUGH DIALOGUE

Often in today's busy business environment we feel we do not have time to engage in deep reflective dialogue with the people we work with. We are all too busy, rushing from one meeting to the next; endless meetings in which we sit round tables with a sense of separation from each other, perhaps even competing for air-time, to push our point across, to get ourselves heard, or switching-off hiding behind our laptops and smartphones as the conversation fails to engage us adequately.

At the heart of our organizational culture lies the complex responsive processes of human relating we explored in Living Systems Culture, and our meetings and conversations are what enliven these complex processes of relating. Yet, let's be honest, many of our meetings and conversations are inefficient and ineffective. While many of today's organizations pride themselves on relentlessly focusing on efficiency and effectiveness, when it comes to meetings many miss the mark completely.

The 'new norm' of business requires a step-up in the quality of conversations. This is where deep listening comes in, and the practice of Dialogue. Dialogue recognizes the importance of conversation as a listening, feeling, learning, sharing dynamic. The famous quantum physicist David Bohm in his later years became passionate about the benefits of Dialogue as a way to enhance the richness of human communication, and he formulated an approach to Dialogue which has since been adapted and enhanced by several practitioners. Based on their extensive experience of working with Dialogue, Chris Laszlo and Judy Sorum Brown, in their book *Flourishing Enterprise*, provide some guidance:

- Begin with a powerful question, for instance, 'What draws us toward the goal of becoming a regenerative business?'
- Shift from knowing to wondering. It is okay to be uncertain, to question and explore as this opens up exploratory ground, rather than holding-on to preconceived definitive perspectives;
- Shift from statements to thought-provoking questions that draws out interest in the other;
- Shift from certainty to curiosity, develop a genuinely curious interest about the topic and what is emerging, letting go of any pre-conceived notions about what is right or not;
- Speak only for ourselves and about our own experience, from a grounded heartfelt presence of where we are right now;
- Resist the temptation to get sucked into to-and-fro 'tennis match' debates, exploratory questions can help dissolve a debate;
- Listen (inside and out) with intense curiosity while suspending our assumptions, giving up the ego-need to hear ourselves speaking or hear someone agreeing with what we have said, and notice any internal tensions forming in ourselves without allowing them to disrupt our dialogue;
- Allow for silence, silence can be productive and generative while allowing us to take in what has been said and let-go of urges to react;
- Listen generously and deeply;
- Seek and welcome difference without getting sucked into debate, as difference sharpens our collective exploration and learning;

- Speak with a fresh voice, resist saying what we might normally respond with, remaining silent if need be until we have something genuine to offer, and do not interrupt others;
- Bring 100% of ourselves with complete presence, letting go of distractions and frustrations.

Dialogue is a regenerative way of speaking and listening that enables us as Regenerative Leaders to work through inevitable tensions and divergent perspectives in respectful and developmental ways.

The next practice – Way of Council – further builds on this Dialogue tool.

## 5. WAY OF COUNCIL

Through the ancient practice of Way of Council groups of people can come together to share in a communal atmosphere of non-judgment and acceptance. In Council, people sit in a circle and commit to being fully present, freed from distractions, judgements or opinion forming, listening intently and sharing open-heartedly with each other without preparing or rehearsing our responses.

Included, is a talking piece (which may be a stick, a stone, a ball or whatever feels appropriate). The person holding the talking piece is the only one allowed to speak, while everyone else around the circle listens with complete attention and presence. Then, when the talking piece is put back in the centre or passed around the circle, the next person to hold it speaks, knowing they will not be interrupted or judged.

Here are the basic ground rules of Council:

### 1. SPEAKING

When speaking in Council, we speak from our heart and gut, not from our head. We do not rehearse what we are going to say while the others talk. We allow what comes up within us to come out, just as it comes. We talk from the 'I' perspective, about what is going on for me, not using words such as 'you' or 'they', and we do not bring in blame or projection on to others. We simply talk about what is going on for us, how we are feeling and the challenges or opportunities we are experiencing. We are also conscious of the time available for the circle, by being concise in our speech and not rambling too much or speaking for too long.

## 2. LISTENING

When listening, we listen with our whole bodymind, being present in the here-and-now, so that our attention is fully absorbed in listening generously and open-heartedly to what is being said. The act of listening in such a deep and fully present way is beneficial in-and-of-itself as the act of listening to another helps us remain present. We continuously bring ourselves back to the act of fully listening each time our attention wanders.

## 3. THE TALKING-PIECE ACTS AS A BEACON OF ATTENTION

Our attention follows the talking piece and we give whoever has it our full attention. We practice mindfulness while listening and speaking. Being self-aware when our attention wanders, bringing it gently back to whoever has the talking-piece.

## 4. NO CRITICISM OR JUDGEMENT ABOUT OTHER'S SHARING

We do not critically analyze what another has just shared when it's our turn to speak, yet we may refer to another's comment in terms of how it affects 'me' and my feelings. So we share how what has been said relates to what is going on for 'me' without getting dragged into me-versus-you judgements or criticisms.

## 5. VOLUNTARY CONTRIBUTION

Silence is always permitted while holding the talking-piece, and we can pass it on without saying anything at all if we wish. There is no pressure of any kind to have to say anything if we do not feel like it.

## 6. WHAT IS SAID IN THE CIRCLE STAYS IN THE CIRCLE

General themes may be captured and shared by means of informing our work in general, but people's specific sharing remains confidential and not specifically quoted beyond the circle without permission. Learning to respect the confidentiality of the circle is an important learning for us, teaching us to respect each other's perspectives while becoming more self-aware of our tendency to gossip.

As a practice, Council is applicable to all social interrelations from family discussions to executive board meetings. For indigenous cultures, where collective decisions are regularly made through this circle, it is acceptance rather than consensus which is paramount – an empathic understanding of the differing views occurs even if everyone is not in agreement with the final decision. This way resentment does not build up and then corrode the community. Differing opinions are healthy and ought to be celebrated as it is diverse opinions within a community that provide for the resilience needed for long term viability.


# 6. STORY CAFÉ AND WORLD CAFÉ

This is a simple yet effective way of hosting small groups (story café) or large groups (world café), so that diverse perspectives (divergence) are aired and shared through a process that provides the opportunity for alignment (convergence) and also for new insights to form (emergence).


## STORY CAFÉ

Gather a small group of stakeholders – no more than 15 people – around 2 or 3 tables of 4-5 people per table, and start by discussing a topic that everyone feels involved in. The discussion itself follows a Dialogue approach, in terms of listening intently and sharing in an open and heartfelt way.

Let's say we start with the discussion: *Share a time when we felt fully alive in our lives.*

Once everyone is clear on the question or topic being discussed, start the process with a couple of minute's silence (perhaps some deep breathing, as well) to help develop presence and coherence. Then each person, in silence, jots down their own story.

After three minutes, the first person shares their story while the other three listen attentively, without interruption – like we practiced in the deep listening exercise.

After three minutes we move round the table with another person sharing their story and the other three listening attentively. Repeat, until everyone has shared.

There is no need to sell our stories or present them in inauthentic ways, although to start with there may be that tendency, as we wish to make ourselves look good in front of others, but as we gain experience in this kind of sharing our desire to put on a show dissipates as our deeper authenticity starts to come through. As we get more comfortable with this authentic sharing, we may wish to discuss questions related to the challenges in our organization, for instance, sharing what makes us feel really alive in our work-place and how we might encourage more of it.

## WORLD CAFÉ

The only difference is that it involves a larger group, more than 15 people, and more than two or three tables of people. After a couple of rounds of discussion amongst the tables, people are free to leave their table and join another table where space allows. A table host stays on the table, but all others are free to move around to experience slightly different sharing with different people. The questions evolve as the session develops. The hosts then share the insights with the overall group.

What is provided through the Story Café and World Café approaches is that people feel heard in a deep way, with everyone able to share their insights, and the table hosts then sharing key insights with the whole group. Something new emerges out of the divergent perspectives of the individuals and table groups.

# 7. OPEN SPACE TECHNOLOGY

Open Space Technology is a method for running self-organizing meetings of small or large groups (it has been run effectively for groups of 2,000 people before). The originator of Open Space, Harrison Owen, explains that this approach works best when there are the following conditions present: complexity, diversity, conflict, and urgency.

Each meeting has a trained facilitator and a meeting sponsor, but no specific agenda. The meeting sponsor starts the meeting with an overriding 'meeting purpose.'

Then, the facilitator explains the Open Space process, which is essentially about everyone creating the agenda themselves and then exploring the issues in self-organizing groups. When key issues or aspects of the agenda start to form amongst the different groups, certain people passionate about particular issues come forward as sponsors for different topics.

These topics get posted on the meeting bulletin board or digital 'wall' (a shared space or folder for people to access on-line), and the topic sponsors then say a few words about the topic, issue or question of inquiry, and people in the wider group choose which topic group they wish to join.

People post comments and explorations on the topic wall as the discussions unfold both virtually and in face-to-face groups. People are free to move between groups cross-pollinating as they go. Each group then collates the key findings and instantly publishes them digitally so everyone can see the findings and go through them as a whole group. Over a matter of a couple of days, all the most important ideas, data, recommendations and questions for further study, along with immediate action plans, are published for all participants and for the entire organization and its wider stakeholders to see.

# 8. SWARM WORKSHOPS

A 'swarm' is rather like a 'hackathon' in that it brings diverse people together, yet has a formal process developed by a small group of creative social entrepreneurs to help multiple stakeholders co-create solutions with potential to make a more life-affirming world.

We refer to Dan Burgess, the co-founder of Swarm, for his insights on how a swarm should be best designed and hosted.

Before the actual swarm takes place, a significant amount of effort is under-taken in a 'shaping phase' to explore and articulate the challenge based problems requiring attention. This can be honed through a series of inter-views with a diverse variety of stakeholders, through on-line questionnaires, informal chats, walks, meets, and other information gathered. Then, a group of people, those who can participate in person for the two to three day swarm, are recruited. The group must ensure a good balance of dynamics, a range of skills and perspectives, and specific prototyping skills useful for the problem being explored (such as web coding, service design, business modelling, etc).

Finally, the participants of the swarm receive and digest well-honed briefs on the challenge-based problem along with relevant associated information a few days before the swarm, so they can hit-the-ground-running once the swarm starts.

The swarm is ideally hosted in a place conducive for co-creativity with access to nature where possible. The swarm itself blends creative collaboration, experiential learning and collective intelligence in an open, playful yet vibrant and intensive space. Participants self-organize into small sub-groups quickly immersing with the problem, accelerating into a 'prototyping phase' with the support of people who can construct, design and shape-up prototypes.

The two to three days are also inter-dispersed with plenty of reflection time, feedback, sharing and inspiration through talks, films and energizers, with emphasis on deep listening, play and fun, as well as time in nature. Wholesome food eaten together and music make up the mix. People may find the swarm experience is all at once uncomfortable, testing, and exhila-rating as we all embark on our own personal and collective learning journey over this intensive couple of days.

After the swarm, there is a 'sense-making phase', where the insights and solutions are gathered and reflected on, fed back to the attendees and stakeholders, allowing opportunities for further insights, sharing, reflec-tions and builds. This process very much brings into play the life dynamics of *divergence* (gathering multiple perspectives, opening up), *convergence* (consolidating, sense-making) that then leads to a new prototype or project *emerging*.

Organization specialists Henri Lipmanowicz and Keith McCandless point out that today's operational conventions of agenda-led meetings, presentations, managed discussions, status reports, and such like, are often designed to control and direct rather than to include and engage. It is by introducing tiny shifts, in the way people hold meetings, workshops and conversations, transforms decision-making and in turn unleashes the latent creative potential of people, which leads to better decisions, more innovation, and healthier culture.

Story Cafes, World Cafes, Open Space Technology, Swarms and other forms of collaboration sessions all aim to bring together, include, engage and empower people in ways that encourage listening, ideating and co-creating in self-organizing ways that transcend traditional hierarchical decision-making processes. This is the life-blood of adaptive, emergent, regenerative business.

There are, of course, more tools out there many of which we recommend such as Appreciative Inquiry, Stakeholder Dialogue Interviews, Art of Hosting, Social Presencing Theatre, and more. If you are interested in reading about these further Giles has also written about these tools in his book *Future Fit*.

With the personal and organizational toolkits provided in this chapter, you are equipped and ready to embark on the journey of becoming a Regenerative Leader, taking yourself and your organization to the next-stage of human consciousness.

"THIS COULD BE
A GOOD TIME!
THERE IS A RIVER
FLOWING NOW
VERY FAST...
WE ARE THE ONES
WE'VE BEEN
WAITING FOR."

–HOPI ELDERS

# Epilogue

> "In times of great winds, some build bunkers,
> others build windmills."
>
> Chinese Proverb

We live in a time of great upheaval. It's as though you can feel an old era dying and a new one being born. With this process of death and rebirth comes inevitable birthing pains, tension, and challenges. It is a simultaneously hugely rewarding yet challenging time to be a leader.

True leadership is about realizing that the current way no longer works and it's time to move on to a new way. True leadership is about daring to cross the threshold from the old to the new even without having all the answers before you embark on the journey. Our future needs each of us to begin the Regenerative Leadership Journey, not next year, but now, as you hold this book in your hands. This journey can be deeply satisfying and wildly exciting – as it's the journey of living and leading from the heart in service of all life.

The only thing holding us back, really, is our own fears, insecurities and anxieties related to leaving the comfort of the old ways behind. We do not need to build Rome in a day. We need to embrace each day as a step on a journey, learning as we go, and becoming more conscious and authentic as we move forward.

> "Another world is not only possible, she is on her way.
> On a quiet day, I can hear her breathing."
>
> Arundhati Roy, author

It would be foolish to attempt to predict the future. And yet, we can be damn sure about a couple of things:

1.  The systemic challenges humanity now faces – such as climate change, biodiversity loss, soil degradation, ocean acidification, rising stress levels, widening social inequality, and more – are not going away. Instead they will rise in priority over the next decade.

2.  In 10 years' time, all the main components that make up Regenerative Business & Leadership – such as developmental cultures, circular economics, bio-inspired innovation, Ecosystemic Facilitation, and more – will become higher and higher up the priority stack for far more organizations.

So our advice is simply this: Step-in to the new way, before it's too late.

Responsible intelligent leaders now have a business and moral imperative to start working with the Logic of Life. This is a major shift for most of today's conventional leaders, but the shift is already happening as we write this book. In writing this book, we have gathered cases and spoken with numerous pioneering executives, and it's clear to us that this new norm is quietly going main-stream. Those organizations that fail to embrace the regenerative approach to leadership and organizational development will, in due time, render themselves ineffective, uncompetitive, and unfit for the future.

The future is ours to create. We are currently creating the future for our children and children's children to inherit. And they are demanding urgent action from us now – as Greta Thunberg, the mobilizer of the children's climate strikes, recently said addressing world leaders in Davos:

> "You say you love your children above all else and yet you are stealing their future in front of their very eyes."
>
> Greta Thunberg, climate activist

We have all the technological solutions needed. It's now the transformation of human consciousness that we so urgently need. Now is the time to start building windmills and flow with these winds of change. Yes, we may need to build some bunkers as well as windmills, but let's ensure we face into the future with all our human ingenuity and evolutionary potential.

How?

It *all* starts with *you*. Regenerative Leadership is an inside job above all else. *Your* inner state will cause either positive or negative ripples throughout your organization, family, and wider ecosystem. There exists no outer policy, technology, or mechanism that alone can fix the situation we're in right now. We need a root-and-branch approach to the seismic challenges we face as a species. We need to have the courage now to go to the root-cause of the mess we are in. Heal ourselves to heal our organizations and our societies – from the inside out.

> "The most important kind of freedom is to be what you really are. You trade in your reality for a role. You trade in your sense for an act. You give up your ability to feel, and in exchange, put on a mask. There can't be any large-scale revolution until there's a personal revolution, on an individual level. It's got to happen inside first."
>
> Jim Morrison, singer song-writer

You are here not just to be a better leader, but to be truer to yourself, truer in your relationships, and truer to life. Allow life to start showing you synchronicities and patterns, and coupled with your power of purpose, you will align with a force far greater that your ego-mind could ever imagine.

We wish you luck on the journey. Have fun and enjoy the process. And thank you for the part you play in this necessary revolution of human consciousness. We are here to help, so please do feel free to contact us on *www.regenerativeleadership.co*

But before you close this book, we want you to know our secret ... The Logic of Life is nothing more nor less than ... Love.

Nature's Wisdom *is* Love, pure and simple. Regenerative Leadership *is* living and leading with Love. Love creates conditions conducive for life. Love feeds on and grows from Love. Love breeds virtuous cycles.

Now, if we had started the book with *Love*, you'd probably have put it down and moved on to something that seemed a bit more serious or important or practical or tangible for leaders. And we wouldn't blame you! But the Regenerative DNA Model is truly a model that activates love and vitality throughout our ecosystems and enlivens organizations-as-living-systems. It brings Love in practical tangible ways right into the heart of today's business mindset, because Love is what enables tomorrow's companies to thrive.

Business is perhaps the most powerful organized force of human creativity on this planet today, and by transforming the business mindset we go a very long way to transforming our civilization.

With great love,

Laura and Giles

# Acknowledgements

We would like to thank everyone out there currently contributing to the emergence of the Age of Regeneration: The CEO's, entrepreneurs, activists, writers, practitioners, teachers, young and old. This regenerative movement is growing, more and more in number by the day.

This book is a testament to all the great pioneers and practitioners – past and present – who have had the courage to bring trailblazing paradigm shifting visions to life. Our work does its best to stand on the shoulders of these giants, to honour their work, while weaving in fresh ideas and connect the dots between fields. We already mention many of these pioneers in the book; yet, also acknowledge all the others not mentioned who have worked directly or indirectly with us, and within this global regenerative movement. There are simply too many for us to list here – you know who you are!

We would also like to thank the business leaders we interviewed for the cases and insights, and the specialists and executives who have kindly lent their support through book endorsements at the front and back of the book, and more found on our book site *www.regenerativeleadership.co*

And a BIG thank you to True Story (who kindly provided the graphics and look-and-feel for much of this book, out of the kindness of their heart) and to Peter Thompson, who kindly made a video trailer for the book, and has supported us on our journey from its early days of swimming in Swedish lakes.

**Above all:** We thank our families for their unwavering love, patience and support. Much love to our partners in life, Star and Ulrik and our wonderful children, Lilly-Belle, Hazel and Roxie. And to our parents, Phil, Diana, Leif and Nina. You are all the foundation for us to flourish and thrive.

# Glossary

*Overview of words key to the field of Regenerative Leadership used throughout this book*

**Age of Regeneration** – there are positive signs of a shift in business and beyond; the birthing pangs of an epochal shift from the Age of Separation into the Age of Regeneration, where humanity once again remembers its deep connection with self-other-world.

**Ecosystemic Awareness** – awareness and understanding of the material, information and relational energy flows through the organization and also the wider stakeholder ecosystem the organization operates within (including society and the environment). Being able to regularly tap into this awareness equates to Tier 2 Regenerative Leadership Consciousness.

**Ecosystemic Facilitation** – facilitating diverse stakeholders from across the ecosystem to enable systemic transformation toward life-affirming futures.

**Ecosystemic Facilitator** – the leadership ability to cultivate the health of the organizational system and its ecosystem relations.

**Journey of Separation** – From around 10,000 years ago humanity started to separate from a deep connection with self-other-world, and this separateness really heightened around 500 years ago til the present day.

**Living Systems Designer** – a product, service or place designer who draws upon the Regenerative DNA model.

**Living Systems Field** – a field that interconnects all life, also referred to by scientists as the the Quantum Field or Zero-Point Energy Field.

**Living Systems Partnership** – a partnership that creates systemic win-win-win synergies across multiple systems.

**Logic of Life** – there are 7 principles that describe how life on Earth operates. These 7 principles underpin the entire DNA model.

**Organization-as-living-system** – perceiving the organization as a complex living system that adapts and evolves to its changing environment.

**Organization-as-machine** – seeing the organization as a rigid, mechanistic entity to be controlled through power-based hierarchies and divided into silos.

**Regenerative** – creating the conditions conducive for life to continuously renew itself, to transcend in to new forms, and to flourish amid ever-changing life-conditions. This primary principle underpins life-affirming leadership and organizational development, where our organizations help rather than hinder the evolutionary dynamic of life.

**Regenerative Business** – businesses that thrive while contributing to life-affirming futures by applying Living Systems Design, Culture and Being.

**Regenerative Leadership** – a way of living and leading that contributes more to life (across all systems) than it takes.

**Regenerative Leadership Consciousness** – this equates to Tier 2 Consciousness as applied to today's leadership, where the leader applies ecosystemic awareness by drawing upon the Logic of Life in seeking life-affirming futures.

**Rhythm of Life** – the seasonal phase-cycles of nature follow a rhythmic figure-of-eight pattern of spring (innovation) summer (growth) autumn (harvest and release) winter (reconfiguration and renewal).

**Social Synergy** – where two or more people come together with different ideas and perspectives, and through the different inputs emerges something greater than the sum of the parts.

**Tier 1 Consciousness** – a term from Spiral Dynamics and Clare Graves' adult developmental research, referring to all the levels of consciousness up to Tier 2. Of relevance for this book is the Tier 1 levels of Orange (organization-as-machine) and Green (organization-as-family) where leadership perspectives are still largely rooted in separateness and mechanistic logic.

**Tier 2 Consciousness** – Clare Graves spoke of the shift from Tier 1 to Tier 2 as a momentous leap, from Green into Teal. This is a shift from separateness into interconnectedness, whereupon the leader understands the organization-as-living-system.

# Bibliography

*These are all books either directly referenced or indirectly drawn-upon.*

## Books

- Anderson, Ray & White, Robin (2009): Confessions of a Radical Industrialist, Random House Business Books
- Arvay, Clemens G. (2018): The Biophilia Effect, A Scientific and Spiritual Exploration of the Healing Bond Between Humans and Nature, Sounds True
- Bacon, Francis (1603): The Masculine Birth of Time
- Bacon, Francis (1620): Novum Organum, Book 1, Aphorism 3. Translated as The New Organon: Aphorisms Concerning the Interpretation of Nature and the Kingdom of Man)
- Bakke, Dennis (2005): Joy At Work, PVG
- Barfield, Owen (1988): Saving the Appearances, A Study in Idolatry, Wesleyan University Press
- Baring, Anne & Cashford, Jules (1993): The Myth of the Goddess, Evolution of an Image, Arkana Penguin Books
- Barret, Richard (2010): The New Leadership Paradigm, Lulu
- Barrett Richard (2014): Evolutionary Coaching, Lulu
- Bateson, Gregory (2000): Steps to an Ecology of Mind, The University of Chicago Press
- Beck, Edward et al. (2018): Spiral Dynamics in Action, Wiley

- Berman, Morris (1981): The Reenchantment of the World, Cornell University Press

- Bhat, Nilima and Sisodia, Raj (2016): Shakti Leadership, Embracing Feminine and Masculine Power in Business, Berrett-Koehler

- Bohm, David (1957): Causality and Chance in Modern Physics, Routledge

- Bortoft, Henri (1996): The Wholeness of Nature, Lindisfarne Books

- Bortoft, Henri (2012): Taking Appearance Seriously, The Dynamic Way of Seeing in Goethe and European Thought, Floris Books

- Boyatzis, Richard & Annie McKee Boston (2005): Resonant Leadership, Harvard Business School Press

- Bradgon, Jay (2016): Companies That Mimic Life, Greenleaf Publishing

- Branson, Richard (2011) Screw Business As Usual, Virgin Books

- Braungart, Michael & McDonough, William (2009): Cradle to Cradle, Re-making the way we make things, Vintage

- Brown, Stuart (2010): Play – How It Shapes the Brain, Opens the Imagination, and Invigorates the Soul, J P Tarcher/Penguin Putnam

- Buhner, Stephen Harrod (2004): The Secret Teachings of Plants, The Intelligence of the Heart in the Direct Perception of Nature, Bear & Company

- Campbell, Joseph (1988): The Power of Myth, Doubleday

- Capra, Fritjof (1997): The Web of Life: A New Synthesis of Mind & Matter, Anchor

- Capra, Fritjof (2003): The Hidden Connections: A Science for Sustainable Living, Flamingo

- Capra, Fritjof & Pier Luigi Luisi (2014): The Systems View of Life, Cambridge University Press

- Carson, Rachel (1962): Silent Spring, Penguin Books

- Choy, Peter Chin Kean (1998): T'ai Chi Chi Kung, fifteen ways to a happier you, Kyle Cathie Ltd

- Claxton, Guy (2015): Intelligence in the Flesh, Yale University Press

- Conner, Clifford (2015): A Peoples History of Science; Bold Type Books

- Corby, Rachel (2015): Rewild Yourself: Becoming Nature, CreateSpace Independent Publishing

- Currivan, Jude (2017): The Cosmic Hologram, Inner Traditions
- Darwin, Charles (1859): On the origin of the species by means of natural selection: Or, the preservation of favoured races in the struggle for life, J. Murray
- De Botton, Alain (2004): Status Anxiety, Hamish Hamilton
- De Saint-Exupéry, Antoine (2002): The Little Prince, Egmont
- Deluca, Denise (2016): Realigning with Nature, White Cloud Press
- Denning, Steve (2018): The Age of Agile, Amacom
- Doczi, György (1981): The Power of Limits, Shambhala Publications
- Eisler, Riane (1988): The Chalice & The Blade, Our History, Our Future, Harper & Row
- Elworthy, Scilla (2014): Pioneering the Possible, Berkeley, North Atlantic Books
- Field, Reshad (1990): The Alchemy of the Heart, Element, Shaftesbury
- Fisher, Andy (2013): Radical Ecopsychology, Psychology in the Service of Life, Suny Press
- Fisher, R.A. (1930): The Genetical Theory of Natural Selection, Clarendon Press
- Flannery, Tim (2010): Here on Earth, A Natural History of The Planet, Harper-Collins
- Flannery, Tim (2005): The Weather Makers, The Text Publishing Company
- Freud, Sigmund (1933): New Introductory Lectures on Psychoanalysis, W.W.Norton
- Freud, Sigmund (1991): The Future of An Illusion, In Civilization, Society and Religion, Penguin
- Frankl, Vicktor (2004): Man's Search for Meaning, Random House
- Gerzema, John and D'Antonio, Michael (2013): The Athena Doctrine, How Women (and the men who think like them) Will Rule The Future, Jossey-Bass
- Gorrisen, Leen & Meynaerts, Erika (2018): Change the World City by City: A Change Maker's Guide to Fast Forward Sustainability, Lannoo Publishers

- Gowing, Nik & Langdon, Chris (2018): Thinking the Unthinkable, John Catt Educational Ltd
- Gunderson, Lance H & C.S. Holling (2002): Panarchy, Island Press
- Harman, Jay (2013): The Shark's Paintbrush: Biomimicry and How Nature is Inspiring Innovation, White Cloud Press
- Hartmann, Thom (2004): The Last Hours of Ancient Sunlight, Harmony
- Hawken, Paul (1993): The Ecology of Commerce – A Declaration of Sustainability, HarperBusiness
- Haisch, Bernard (2006): The God Theory, universes, zero-point fields, and what's behind it all, Weiser
- Harding, Stephan (2006): Animate Earth, Science, Intuition and Gaia, Green Books
- Harner, Michael (1990): The Way of the Shaman, HarperCollins
- Hayden, Gina (2018): Becoming a Conscious Leader, TWF
- Heidegger, Martin (1977): Basic Writings: Martin Heidegger, edited by David Farrell Krell, Routledge
- Hemenway, Toby (2015): The Permaculture City, Regenerative Design for Urban, Suburban, and Town Resilience, Chelsea Green Publishing
- Hilton, Steve (2015): More Human, WH Allen
- Hobbes, Thomas (1949): The Citizen, Appleton Century Crofts
- Holliday, Michelle (2016): The Age of Thrivability, Cambrium
- Holmgren, David (2002): Permaculture: Principles and Pathways beyond Sustainability, Holmgren Design Services
- HRH The Prince of Wales et al (2010): Harmony, A New Way of Looking At Our World, Blue Door
- Hutchins, Giles (2012): The Nature of Business, Redesigning for Resilience, Green Books
- Hutchins, Giles (2014): The Illusion of Separation, Floris Books
- Hutchins, Giles (2016): Future Fit, CreateSpace Independent Publishing
- Jaworski, Joseph (2011): Synchronicity, The Inner Path of Leadership, Berrett-Koehler Publishers

- Jung, Carl (1973): The Collected Works of C.G. Jung, (ed. Gerhard Adler et al) Routledge
- Jung, Carl (1976): Letters 2, 1951–1961, (ed. Gerhard Adler), Princeton University Press
- Jung, Carl (1990): The Undiscovered Self, in Collected Works of Carl Gustav Jung, vol. 10, Princeton University Press
- Kahneman, Daniel (2013): Thinking, Fast; Farrar, Straus and Giroux, 1st edition
- Kegan, Robert & Lisa Lahey (2016): An Everyone Culture, Harvard Business School Publishing
- Kiuchi, Tachi & Shireman, Bill (2002): What we Learned in the Rainforest, Berrett-Koehler
- Kotter, John (2014): Accelerate, Harvard Business Review Press
- Kuhn, Thomas (1996): The Structure of Scientific Revolutions, Chicago, University of Chicago Press
- Laloux, Frederic (2014): Reinventing Organizations, Nelson Parker
- Laszlo, Chris and Judy Sorum Brown (2014): Flourishing Enterprise, Stanford Business Books
- Laszlo, Ervin (2016) et al: What is Reality, New Paradigm Books
- Leider, Richard (2015): The Power of Purpose, Berrett-Koehler
- Lerner, Jaime (2016): Urban Acupuncture, Celebrating Pinpricks of Change That Enrich City Life, Island Press
- Lipton, Bruce (2008): The Biology of Belief - Unleashing the Power of Consciousness, Hay House
- Lipton, Bruce & Steve Bhaerman (2009): Spontaneous Evolution, Hay House
- Lipton, Bruce (2016): The Biology of Belief (Anniversary edition), HayHouse
- Mackey, John & Raj Sisodia (2014): Conscious Capitalism, Harvard Business Review Press
- Mang, Pamela & Haggard, Ben (2016): Regenerative Development and Design – A Framework for Evolving Sustainability, Wiley

- May, Gerald (1991): The Awakened Heart, Opening Yourself To The Love You Need, Harper Collins, New York.
- McDonough, William and Braungart, Michael (2002): Cradle to cradle
- McGeeney, Andy (2016): With Nature in Mind, The Ecotherapy Manual for Mental Health Professionals, Jessica Kingsley Publishers
- McGilchrist, Iain (2009): The Master and His Emissary, The Divided Brain and the Making of the Western World, Yale University Press, New Haven.
- Merchant, Carolyn (1980): The Death of Nature, Women, Ecology and the Scientific Revolution, HarperOne
- Mies, Maria and Shiva, Vandana (1993): Ecofeminism, Zedbooks
- Milton, John (2006): Sky Above Earth Below, Sentient Publications
- Mitchell, Stephen (1999): Tao Te Ching, Lao Tzu, An Illustrated Journey (translated), Frances Lincoln, London.
- Overy, Richard (2006): The Times: Complete History of the World, Times Books
- Palmer, Parker J (2004): A Hidden Wholeness, Jossey-Bass
- Parsons, Tony (1995): The Open Secret, Open Secret Publishing
- Pawlyn, Michael (2016): Biomimicry in Architecture; 2nd edition; RIBA Publishing
- Pert, Candace (1998): Molecules of Emotion, Simon and Schuster Ltd
- Pinchbeck, Daniel (2017): How Soon is Now, From Personal Initiation to Global Transformation, Watkins, United Kingdom
- Puchner et al. (2012): The Norton Anthology of World Literature, Third edition, WW Norton & Company
- Sanford, Carol (2017): Regenerative Business, Nicholas Brealey Publishing
- Sardello, Robert (2006): Silence, The Mystery of Wholeness, North Atlantic Books
- Scharmer, Otto (2010): The Blind Spot of Institutional Leadership, MIT Presencing Institute paper for the World Economic Forum
- Scharmer, Otto (2016): Theory U, Berrett-Koehler (second edition)
- Scharmer, Otto and Kaufer, Katrin (2013): Leading From The Emerging Future, From Ego-System To Eco-System Economies, Berret-Koehler Publishers

- Semler, Ricardo (1993): Maverick! Arrow Books
- Senge, Peter et al (2004): Presence, Human Purpose and the Field of the Future, SoL
- Sheldrake, Rupert (1990): The Rebirth of Nature, The Greening of Science and God, Park Street Press
- Sherwood, Dennis (2002): Seeing the Forest for the Trees: A Manager's Guide to Applying Systems Thinking, Nicholas Brealey
- Smuts, Jan Christiann (1926): Holism and Evolution, Macmillian
- Speth, James Gustave (2008): The Bridge at the Edge of the World, Capitalism, the Environment, and Crossing from Crisis to Sustainability, Yale University Press
- Stacey, Ralph (2012): Tools & Techniques of Leadership and Management, Routledge
- Stamets, Paul (2005): Mycelium Running, How Mushrooms Can Help Save the World, Ten Speed Press
- Strozzi-Heckler, Richard (2014): The Art of Somatic Coaching, North Atlantic Books
- Tarnas, Richard (2010): The Passion of the Western Mind, Understanding the Ideas That Have Shaped Our World View, Pimlico
- Taylor, Steve (2005): The Fall, The Insanity of the Ego in Human History and The Dawning of A New Era, O Books
- Van Lysebeth, Andre (1995): Tantra, The Cult of the Feminine, Weiser Books
- Wahl, Daniel (2016): Designing Regenerative Cultures, Triarchy Press
- Watson, Lyall (1974): SuperNature, A natural history of the supernatural, Coronet
- Western, Simon (2013): Leadership: A Critical Text, Sage, Second Edition
- Wholleben, Peter (2015): The Hidden Life of Trees: What They Feel, How They Communicate, Discoveries from A Secret World, Greystone Books
- Wilber, Ken (2001): A Theory of Everything, An Integral Vision for Business, Politics, Science and Spirituality, Gateway
- Williams, Florence (2017): The Nature Fix, W. W. Norton & Company

- Wilson, Edward (1984): Biophilia, Harvard University Press
- Woolley-Barker, Tamsin (2017): Teeming, White Cloud Press
- Wulf, Andrea (2015): The Invention of Nature, The Adventures of Alexander Humboldt, the Lost Hero of Science, John Murray
- Zohar, Danah & Ian Marshall (2000): Spiritual Intelligence, Bloomsbury

## Articles & Blogs

- Associated Press (Sep 1, 2015): "Up to 90% of seabirds have plastic in their guts, study finds", Guardian
- Confino, Jo (May 15, 2014), How to lead with integrity, interview with Paul Polman, The Guardian, The Guardian Sustainable Business Awards
- Denning, Steve (Dec 2, 2018): Drucker Forum 2018: A Major Shift in Management Is Already Underway, Forbes
- Editorial in LA Times (2008), Volume 6
- Ellen McArthur Foundation (2017): The New Plastics Economy – Catalysing action
- Gray, Alex (June 8, 2018): "90% of plastic polluting our oceans comes from just 10 rivers" World Economic Forum
- Nielsen, Tinna (2016): Is this why we've not achieved gender equality at work?; WEF Agenda, World Economic Forum
- Robin McKie (Nov 6, 2016): "Nicholas Stern: cost of global warming 'is worse than I feared', Guardian
- Romm, Joe (September 2011): "NASA's Hansen: "If We Stay on With Business as Usual, the Southern U.S. Will Become Almost Uninhabitable"; Thinkprogress.org
- Schwab, Katharine (2018): 7 of the World's Greenest Offices (Litterally), FastCompany
- Seppälä, Emma (September 2013): "20 Scientific reasons to Start Meditating Today: New research shows meditation boost your health, happiness, and success; Psychology Today

- Stefon, Matt & Tikkanen, Amy (July 20, 1998): "Nature Worship"; Encyclopedia Britannica
- Tonn, Sarah (November 17, 2015): Termites Are Teaching Architects To Design Super-Efficient Skyscrapers, Wired Magazine
- Useem, Jerry (July/August 2017 Issue): Power Causes Brain Damage; The Atlantic
- Vidal, John (December 18, 2009): "Low targets, goals dropped: Copenhagen ends in failure", Guardian
- Vidal, John (March 16, 2019): "The Rapid Decline Of The Natural World Is A Crisis Even Bigger Than Climate Change", Huffington Post
- Vitello, Paul (2011): Ray Anderson, Businessman Turned Environmentalist, Dies at 77, New York Times, New York
- Watts, Jonathan (October 8, 2018): "We have 12 years to limit climate change catastrophe, warns UN"; Guardian
- Wearden, Graeme (Jan 19, 2016): "More plastic than fish in the sea by 2050, says Ellen MacArthur", The Guardian
- Yang, Sarah (May 7, 2015): "Human security at risk as depletion of soil accelerates, scientists warn"; Berkeley News

## Reports & Scientific Papers

- Adobe (2012): State of Create: Global Benchmark Study on attitudes and beliefs around creativity at work, school and at home; Adobe
- Appleby, Andrew B (1980): Journal of interdisciplinary history, (643-663)
- Bohn, Roger & Short, James (2012): Measuring Consumer Information; University of California, San Diego
- Davis, DR (December 2004): Changes in USDA food composition data for 43 garden crops, 1950 to 1999; Journal of the American College of Nutrition (669-82)
- Gallup (2018): Global Emotions Report 2018
- Gimbutas, Marija (1973): The Beginning of the Bronze Age in Europe and the Indo-Europeans: 3,000–2,500 BC, Journal of Indo-European Studies 1

- Glover, Vivette (October 7, 2014): Prenatal Stress and Its Effects on the Fetus and the Child: Possible Underlying Biological Mechanisms; Institute of Reproductive and Developmental Biology, Imperial College London, Hammersmith Campus London UK

- Hallmann, Caspar et al., (October 18, 2017): More than 75 percent decline over 27 years in total flying insect biomass in protected areas; PLoS ONE 12(10)

- Hawkins, Peter (2016): Tomorrow's Leaders, The Necessary Revolution In Today's Leadership Development, Henley Business School, University of Reading

- Hunt, Vivian et al. (2015): Why Diversity Matters, McKinsey

- Kaku, Michio (2005): Unifying The Universe, New Scientist, Issue 16, April 2005

- Key, David & Kerr, Margaret (2013): Transpersonal Patterns in the Natural Change Project, Journal of Transpersonal Psychology

- Klepeis, N.E., et al. (2001): The National Human Activity Pattern Survey (NHAPS): A Resource for Assessing Exposure to Environmental Pollutants. Journal of Exposure Analysis and Environmental Epidemiology, 11, 231-252

- Kuo, F.E., & Sullivan, W.C. (2001). "Environment and crime in the inner city: Does vegetation reduce crime?" Environment and Behavior, 33(3), 343-367, Sage Journals

- Lewer, Dan et. Al. (2015): Antidepressant use in 27 European countries: associations with sociodemographic, cultural and economic factors; The British Journal of Psychiatry (221-226)

- Mang, Pamela & Reed, Bill (2012) Designing from place, a regenerative framework and methodology, Building Research & Information, 40:1, p.23–38

- Margulis, Lynn and Sagan, Dorion (2001) Marvellous microbes, Resurgence Issue 206

- McKinsey (2015): Diversity Matters

- Nielsen & Kepinski, Inclusion Nudges, 2019

- Osborne, Richter-Menge & Jeffries (2018): The Arctic report Card; NOAA

- Pratt, Laura et. Al. (August 2017): Antidepressant Use Among Persons Aged 12 and Over: United States, 2011–2014, NCHS Data Brief No. 283
- PwC (2018): Workforce of the Future, PriceWaterhouseCoopers, report
- Rensselaer Polytechnic Institute (July 2011): Minority rules: Scientists discover tipping point for the spread of ideas
- Simon, Blockley (March 26, 2018): "The resilience of postglacial hunter-gatherers to abrupt climate change", The University of York
- Wilcox, Chris et. Al. (2015): "Threat of plastic pollution to seabirds is global, pervasive, and increasing", PNAS; onas.org
- Wilson, David Sloan et al (2014): Evolving the future: Toward a science of intentional change; US National Library of medicine, National Institutes of health, May 15, 2014
- World Economic Forum (2016): The New Plastics Economy – Rethinking the future of plastics
- WWF (2018): Living Planet Report 2018: Aiming higher, World Wildlife Fund
- Yaraghi, Niam & Ravi, Shamika (2017): The Current and Future State of the Sharing Economy, Brookings Institute
- Zimmerman, Mary Jane (2004): Being Nature's Mind: Indigenous Ways of Knowing and Planetary Consciousness *http://www.delvingdeeper.org/pdfs/being.pdf*.

## Podcasts

- Taylor, Jill (2018), Sounds True Podcast, Insights at the Edgew

# Praise for
# *Regenerative Leadership*

"Hutchins' and Storm's *Regenerative Leadership* **shines a bright light on one of the most critical, and least understood capacities required of anyone and any institution seeking to work regeneratively—understanding and living into the three-fold dynamics of what the book calls the DNA of regenerative leadership.** By growing the consciousness required to simultaneously work on developing ourselves, the wholes we are a part of, and the unique contributions we and they are called to make to the larger life world we depend on, we just might be able to achieve the regenerative capacity the Earth is asking for."

**PAMELA MANG,**
CO-FOUNDER OF REGENESIS AND CO-AUTHOR OF *REGENERATIVE DEVELOPMENT AND DESIGN.*

**"The clarity, inspiration, synergy and wisdom** of Giles Hutchins latest book, co-authored with Laura Storm, is breath-taking. It offers a rich delicious mixture of theory, case studies, invaluable tools and leading edge practices and insights. For leaders genuinely seeking to be effective, sustainable and successful while contributing to making the world, and their organizations far better places. This is **the must read book of 2019. I couldn't put it down."**

DR **LYNNE SEDGMORE** CBE, FORMER CHIEF EXECUTIVE OF 157 GROUP, CENTRE FOR EXCELLENCE IN LEADERSHIP

"The world is changing fast and organizations are not keeping up with the pace of transformation. **This book invites leaders to catalyse the necessary regeneration to not just catch up, but to lead the world into the 21st century."**

**CHRISTIANA FIGUERES,** EXECUTIVE SECRETARY UNFCCC 2010-2016

"*Regenerative Leadership* starts with an unavoidable conclusion: the world's most pressing challenges are interconnected, and only through a systems view could we hope to solve them. **Hope is what Giles and Laura offer, exploring the wisdom, rules, and models for thinking, being, and doing that the natural world offers us. Business leaders will enjoy this mind-expanding journey.**"

**ANDREW WINSTON**, SUSTAINABILTY STRATEGIST,
AUTHOR OF THE BIG PIVOT AND CO-AUTHOR OF GREEN TO GOLD

"**Hutchins and Storm demonstrate that they are clearly at the forefront of a new leadership paradigm that maps an emerging model for sustainable organization in any institution that wishes to thrive.** *Regenerative Leadership* is built upon developing awareness of self and system that embraces the wisdom of Nature alongside creative human consciousness. It is an ideal model that recognizes the potential of living systems to revive organizations and leadership to be effective drivers for the next step in our human story. Hutchins and Storm know what they are talking about – and we should start listening."

**KINGSLEY L. DENNIS**, *THE SACRED REVIVAL – MAGIC, MIND & MEANING IN A TECHNOLOGICAL AGE*

"**Leaders of today and tomorrow must be equipped with the right knowledge and skills about regenerative design, culture and lifestyle to build organizations geared for transitions towards sustainable systems that the world needs.** They have to be systems-thinkers, ecosystem-facilitators and brave enough to address both inner & outer sustainability. This book is an excellent read for all leaders and change makers."

**GUNHILD STORDALEN**, FOUNDER & PRESIDENT, EAT FOUNDATION

"Giles and Laura bring their vast experience and deep wisdom of natural design and development to create an evolutionary blueprint for a sustainable future for business, people and the planet. **An evolutionary blueprint for a sustainable future for business, people and the planet.**"

**RICHARD BARRETT**, PRESIDENT OF THE BARRETT ACADEMY FOR THE ADVANCEMENT OF HUMAN VALUES

"Earth is in the thick of a mass extinction event. We are justifiably scared of the ecological tipping points that threaten us. But there's one tipping point that should give us hope: **Laura Storm and Giles Hutchins delineate how an economic and social transformation is brewing, with a new regenerative paradigm at its heart. If this is our future, we could avert the worst of the ecological crisis, and live happier more connected lives as well.**"

**TRISTRAM STUART**, FOUNDER FEEDBACK.ORG & TOAST ALE

**"Storm and Hutchins confront the challenge of redesigning the world to deliver a sustainable future with vision, energy, and creativity.** Their concept of "regenerative leadership" recognizes the importance of systems thinking, integrated approaches to business and the environment, innovation, and renewal — all critical foundations for a society in which we all can thrive."

DAN ESTY, ENVIRONMENTAL LAWYER & POLICYMAKER, AUTHOR OF BEST-SELLING GREEN TO GOLD

"This book is full of wisdom and determination! A book that will inspire leaders to pave the way towards practices in harmony with our inner nature and the ecosystems we depend on. **Just what we need to succeed in the 21st Century."**

TIM FLANNERY, SCIENTISTS & AUTHOR OF WEATHER MAKERS, HERE ON EARTH

"Seeking inspiration in the natural world, the principles in *Regenerative Leadership* provide a framework for **a more inspired path forward in business and life."**

RYAN GELLERT, CEO EMEA PATAGONIA

"This book is a **brilliant and succinct** synthesis of leading-edge scientific, philosophical and ecological ideas with practical examples of how readers can apply regenerative leadership to their own working lives. It is written with admirable clarity and articulates exactly the regenerative vision we now require to work with the principles of nature. Sustainability is no longer enough – we need to co-create a regenerative future and **this highly informative book lays out an implementable road map ahead."**

DAVID LORIMER, PROGRAMME DIRECTOR, SCIENTIFIC AND MEDICAL NETWORK

"This book succinctly brings together the importance business leaders have in redefining and supporting their organisations and communities to do more good. **Both Giles and Laura have captured the vision and practical skills regenerative business leaders need today, to create a climate fit for life, tomorrow."**

NIGEL STANSFIELD, PRESIDENT OF INTERFACE EAAA

"**A must read** for anyone who wants to shape a regenerative organization, the only one type which will survive. **This practical book elegantly brings together different theories helping leaders grow to the level of consciousness needed to build the regenerative solutions the world absolutely needs."**

JEAN-CLAUDE PIERRE, CEO SCOTT BADER

"In this important, timely and deeply insightful book, the authors fully understand that as our beliefs drive our behaviours, to heal ourselves, our organizations and our relationship with our planetary home, we need to heal our fragmented worldview from the inside out. **Not only does this offer the vital potential for us to survive and thrive as a species - it may be our only hope to do so.**"

DR **JUDE CURRIVAN** COSMOLOGIST, EX BUSINESS LEADER AND AUTHOR *OF THE COSMIC HOLOGRAM*

"The only thing we know for certain is that radical upheaval is coming - and it threatens not just our organizations and industries, but our democracies, societies, economies, and the very planet we depend on. Will change happen to you, or will you lead the change? **Storm and Hutchins share their deep passion and expertise to show you how to ignite shared purpose and break down the silos of information and trust that are stopping you and your people from making their greatest impact on the world.** *Regenerative Leadership* is a critical resource for anyone who wants to be a part of the growing movement to lead for greater richness and resilience. Future generations will thank you!"

DR. **TAMSIN WOOLLEY-BARKER**, PRINCIPAL AND FOUNDER,
TEEM INNOVATION GROUP AND AUTHOR OF *TEEMING*

"With *Regenerative Leadership* Giles Hutchins and Laura Storm **offer a valuable resource to leaders ready to reinvent themselves** so that their personal transformation might enable them to better serve in the transformation of the businesses and organizations they are responsible for."

**DANIEL WAHL**, AUTHOR OF DESIGNING REGENERATIVE CULTURES

"Leadership today is trying to navigate a rapidly transforming world with an old map. **Hutchins and Storm propose a new operating mental and organization model leaders can draw from to adapt to and thrive in sync with today's environment.**"

**PIA MANCINI**, CO-FOUNDER DEMOCRACY EARTH & OPEN COLLECTIVE

# The Authors of this Book

The authors – Giles Hutchins and Laura Storm – decided to join efforts on bringing this book into the world as they share a common passion and purpose for transforming how we lead and operate in ways that are truly regenerative.

They have both worked with corporate executives, city leaders, public bodies, entrepreneurs, charity and political leaders for decades and have used these insights to bring forth a leadership framework that addresses the challenges leaders now face.

The authors advise leaders about next-stage leadership and facilitate retreats, seminars and workshops on the new regenerative leadership paradigm. It is their hope that this Regenerative DNA Model helps catalyze the shift toward the emerging Age of Regeneration.

See more and get in touch with the authors here:
*www.regenerativeleadership.co*

## Laura Storm

Laura is an international thought leader and expert on sustainability and leadership. She has spent her entire career advising global leaders on sustainability and building impact- and purpose-driven organizations, and movements. All have they focused on the global transformation to sustainability and they includes the Copenhagen Climate Council, the World Business Summit on Climate Change, Project Green Light and Sustainia. Under Laura's leadership, Sustainia became a global mega-brand within sustainability with an outreach to more than 150 million people, a database of 4000 sustainable solutions, multiple state-of-the art publications and a unique partner network.

In 2018, she founded Regenerators - a collective focused on teaching leaders from all walks of life about regenerative design, regenerative organizations and leadership and regenerative living. For her work, she has been awarded the title 'Worldchanger' by Greenbiz and is selected by the World Economic Forum as a 'Young Global Leader'. She serves on multiple Boards and on the World Economic Forum's Expert Network as an expert in sustainable development and climate change. Her academic background is a Master in Political Communication and Leadership from Copenhagen Business School.

*www.laura-storm.com + www.regenerators.co*

# Giles Hutchins

Giles is a pioneering practitioner and senior adviser at the fore-front of the [r] evolution in organizational and leadership consciousness and developmental approaches that enhance personal, organizational and systemic agility and vitality. He is author of several leadership and organizational development papers, and the books *The Nature of Business* (2012), *The Illusion of Separation* (2014) and *Future Fit* (2016). Over the last 25 years he has been an international Management Consultant and Head of Practice with KPMG, and Global Sustainability Director for Atos, a technology multinational with over 100,000 employees worldwide. He has helped transform organizations across the world, and across all sectors, has been interviewed by the BBC and advises a number of forward-thinking leadership academies. He contributes to international business school research, runs deep-dive transformation Learning Journeys, is Chair of *The Future Fit Leadership Academy*, is co-founder of *Regenerators*, co-founder of *Biomimicry for Creative Innovation* and an executive coach to senior leaders. He runs a 60-acre ancient woodland Leadership Immersion center near London, UK.

*www.gileshutchins.com  + www.ffla.co + www.leadershipimmersions.com*

Lightning Source UK Ltd.
Milton Keynes UK
UKHW050630161219
355459UK00007B/75/P